Vol. VI

No. 2

Bible Expositor and Illuminator
Large-Print Edition

SPRING QUARTER   March, April, May 2015

The Spirit Comes

UNIT I: The Pledge of God's Presence

Mar.	1—The Lamb of God—John 1:29-34	2
Mar.	8—The Promise of a Comforter—John 14:15-26	16
Mar.	15—The Spirit of Truth—John 16:4-15	30
Mar.	22—Receive the Holy Spirit—John 20:19-23	43
Mar.	29—Coming in the Name of the Lord—Mark 11:1-11	57

UNIT II: The Community of Beloved Disciples

Apr.	5—Resurrection Guaranteed (Easter)—I Cor. 15:1-11, 20-22	70
Apr.	12—Love One Another—I John 3:11-24	84
Apr.	19—Believe God's Love—I John 4:13—5:5	97
Apr.	26—Watch Out for Deceivers!—II John 1:1-13	110
May	3—Coworkers with the Truth—III John 1:1-14	123

UNIT III: Woven Together in Love

May	10—Gifts of the Spirit—I Cor. 12:1-11	136
May	17—Members of One Body—I Cor. 12:14-31	149
May	24—Gift of Languages—Acts 2:1-7, 12; I Cor. 14:13-19	162
May	31—The Greatest Gift Is Love—I Cor. 13:1-13	175
	Topics for Next Quarter	188
	Paragraphs on Places and People	189
	Daily Bible Readings	190
	Review	191

Editor in Chief: Grace M. Todd

Edited and published quarterly by
**THE INCORPORATED TRUSTEES OF THE GOSPEL WORKER SOCIETY
UNION GOSPEL PRESS DIVISION**

Rev. W. B. Musselman, Founder

Price: $5.45 per quarter*
$21.00 per year*

shipping and handling extra

ISBN 978-1-59843-330-2

Lessons based on International Sunday School Lessons; the International Bible Lessons for Christian Teaching, copyright © 2011 by the Committee on the Uniform Series and used with permission. Edited and published quarterly by The Incorporated Trustees of the Gospel Worker Society, Union Gospel Press Division, 2000 Brookpark Road, Cleveland, Ohio 44109-5812. Mailing address: P.O. Box 6059, Cleveland, Ohio 44101-1059. www.union gospelpress.com

LESSON 1   MARCH 1, 2015

Scripture Lesson Text

JOHN 1:29 The next day John seeth Je'sus coming unto him, and saith, Behold the Lamb of God, which taketh away the sin of the world.

30 This is he of whom I said, After me cometh a man which is preferred before me: for he was before me.

31 And I knew him not: but that he should be made manifest to Is'ra-el, therefore am I come baptizing with water.

32 And John bare record, saying, I saw the Spir'it descending from heaven like a dove, and it abode upon him.

33 And I knew him not: but he that sent me to baptize with water, the same said unto me, Upon whom thou shalt see the Spir'it descending, and remaining on him, the same is he which baptizeth with the Ho'ly Ghost.

34 And I saw, and bare record that this is the Son of God.

NOTES

The Lamb of God

Lesson: John 1:29-34

Read: John 1:29-37

TIME: A.D. 26   PLACE: east of Jordan

GOLDEN TEXT—"The next day John seeth Jesus coming unto him, and saith, Behold the Lamb of God, which taketh away the sin of the world" (John 1:29).

Introduction

Our lesson series this quarter deals with the Holy Spirit and His ministry to and through the church. The Holy Spirit is a divine Person, equal to the Father and the Son in the Godhead. But He never undertakes His works independently of the other two. It is the Father who has sent the Spirit into the world for His ministry in this age, and He comes in the name of the Son (John 14:26). The truth He reveals comes from Jesus, and He thus calls attention to Him, not Himself (16:12-14). He is completing what Jesus began to do.

Most people judge the high points of their careers by the power they wield, the reputation they achieve, or the wealth they accumulate. But John saw his career fulfilled when he could introduce One greater than himself. He had gained a wide hearing among the Jews and achieved considerable influence. He had even gathered a core of disciples around him. But the apex of his ministry came when he could introduce his followers to Jesus Christ. Our passage this week focuses on that moment.

LESSON OUTLINE

I. JOHN'S PROCLAMATION CONCERNING JESUS—John 1:29-31

II. THE SPIRIT'S WITNESS CONCERNING JESUS—John 1:32-34

Exposition: Verse by Verse

JOHN'S PROCLAMATION CONCERNING JESUS

JOHN 1:29 The next day John seeth Jesus coming unto him, and saith, Behold the Lamb of God, which taketh away the sin of the world.

30 This is he of whom I said, After me cometh a man which is preferred before me: for he was before me.

31 And I knew him not: but that he should be made manifest to Israel, therefore am I come baptizing with water.

The Lamb of God (John 1:29). John the Baptist's ministry had attracted such widespread attention that the Jewish religious authorities sent a delegation from Jerusalem to ask him who he was. They wanted to know how he fit in with Jewish history and religion (vs. 19). He told them he was a voice crying in the wilderness, calling people to prepare the way for the Lord (vss. 20-23). He baptized only to prepare them for One greater than himself—One already standing among them (vss. 25-27).

The day after this inquiry, Jesus Himself arrived at the place east of the Jordan where John was baptizing (John 1:28). Seeing Him coming, John announced, "Behold the Lamb of God, which taketh away the sin of the world" (vs. 29). Our passage makes it clear that this was not the first time John had seen Jesus. He had already been baptized (cf. vss. 32-33), so this may have occurred just after Jesus was tempted by Satan.

John's identification of Jesus as the sin-bearing Lamb of God shows his intimate understanding of Old Testament history, law, and prophecy. The Passover lamb set the pattern, substituting for the firstborn sons of Israel when those of Egypt were struck dead (Exod. 12:3-13). Lambs were offered as guilt and sin offerings in the cleansing ritual for leprosy (Lev. 14:10-12, 19). And Isaiah foretold the Suffering Servant as a lamb led to the slaughter as He died for sin (Isa. 53:1-8).

Unlike Old Testament sacrifices, which only postponed judgment for sin, Jesus died to take them away. Levitical priests offered sacrifices daily, year after year, because they could not remove sin. But Jesus' sacrifice of Himself was singular and final because He bore it away (cf. Heb. 10:10-12). The Greek word translated "taketh away" in John 1:29 carries the dual implication of picking up and removing. John saw clearly this finished work of Jesus.

Although Jesus died to remove individual sins, John used the singular term to emphasize the collective weight of guilt that rests on mankind. Only the divine Lamb could lift this burden from human shoulders. Furthermore, He has done this for the whole world, not just for Israel, as the previous sin offerings were. As Paul later stated it, "God was in Christ, reconciling the world unto himself" (II Cor. 5:19). This does not mean that every person is reconciled but that reconciliation is provided for all.

The One greater than John (John 1:30-31). In introducing Jesus, John also said that although He appeared on the scene after him, He was "preferred before [him]: for he was before [him]." Jesus' appearance was the anticipated climax of John's ministry, as he had repeatedly stated (cf. vss. 15, 27). And now, said John, He had finally come.

John's witness included the fact that Jesus existed before him. From a purely earthly standpoint, this was not true. John was about six months older than Jesus, and he also preceded Jesus in ministry. So it is clear that John recognized Jesus as a divine Person who existed eternally. He was introducing the Eternal Word, who was the Life and Light of men.

Because of Jesus' divine and eternal nature, John recognized that He had surpassed him in position, rank, and honor. Although John had enjoyed widespread acclaim and had even accumulated some disciples, he recognized his proper place. He saw it as presumptuous even to take on the role of Jesus' servant, the one who stooped down and loosened the thongs of His sandals (Matt. 3:11; Mark

1:7; Luke 3:16-17). John was the mere friend of the Bridegroom, rejoicing in His presence (John 3:28-29).

John leaves a powerful example for us. It is easy for a Christian entrusted with a successful ministry to bask in the recognition it brings. It is easy to take credit for ourselves instead of passing it on to God, who deserves it. When we do, it is the beginning of spiritual failure and ruined service. It is better to take a humble place with John, who declared, "He must increase, but I must decrease" (John 3:30).

John revealed that as he began his preparatory ministry, "I knew him not" (John 1:31). This seems like a strange statement, since John and Jesus were related (cf. Luke 1:36). As he grew up, John was probably aware that he had a relative named "Jesus" from Nazareth. Whether they ever met, however, is another question. From an early age (since his parents were elderly and did not live long into his lifetime), John lived in desert areas (vs. 80). So it is possible that he had never met Jesus before Jesus came to be baptized.

In addition, the Greek word for "knew" in John 1:31 does not mean knowing by observation or experience. It generally refers to knowing by mental reflection on information received. Thus, though John knew of one called Jesus, he did not understand beforehand that He was the Messiah. That revelation had to wait until he was engaged in his baptizing ministry.

John knew that it was his responsibility to make the Messiah known to Israel. This revelation was essential because Christ came, first and foremost, to fulfill the covenants God had made that nation (Rom. 15:8). It was through Him that God's promise to bless the world through Abraham's seed was fulfilled (Gal. 3:13-14, 27-29). He was the promised Heir to David's throne (Luke 1:32-33) and the Mediator of the new covenant promised to Jeremiah (Matt. 26:28; cf. Jer. 31:31-34).

"Therefore am I come baptizing with water" (John 1:31) shows that John saw a connection between baptism and Messiah's manifestation. Baptism was an outward sign of repentance for those who wished to be prepared for His coming. The kingdom of heaven Jesus was about to inaugurate was more than a political entity. It required the Jews to "prepare . . . the way of the Lord" and "make his paths straight" (Matt. 3:3).

There was no room in Messiah's kingdom for unrepentant hypocrites. He would separate the true from the false, just as threshers separated grain from chaff. He would gather the grain to Himself and consign the chaff to the fire of judgment (Matt. 3:12). John therefore minced no words with the Pharisees and Sadducees, the religious "pretenders" of his day. Their descent from Abraham would prove worthless in the Day of Judgment (vss. 7-10).

Thus, John the Baptist recognized Jesus as the sin-bearing Lamb of God. But he also saw Him as the divine Messiah who demanded repentance of those who would enter His kingdom.

THE SPIRIT'S WITNESS CONCERNING JESUS

32 And John bare record, saying, I saw the Spirit descending from heaven like a dove, and it abode upon him.

33 And I knew him not: but he that sent me to baptize with water, the same said unto me, Upon whom thou shalt see the Spirit descending, and remaining on him, the same is he which baptizeth with the Holy Ghost.

34 And I saw, and bare record that this is the Son of God.

His descent upon Jesus (John 1:32). John knew who Jesus was because of the Holy Spirit's witness concerning Him. He may not have known Him ahead of time, but he had been given a sign of identification. To this John now referred: "I saw the Spirit descending from heaven like a dove, and it abode upon him." Although John made no reference to Jesus' baptism as such, the other Gospel writers all identified the descent of the Spirit with His baptism (Matt. 3:16; Mark 1:10; Luke 3:22).

As John recounted this, he spoke from vivid memory. The tense of "I saw" (John 1:32) is better expressed as "I have seen," implying that the image of what he had seen still remained with him. On the other hand, "It abode" uses a Greek tense in keeping with a single, decisive act—"it came to rest" on Him. "Abode" (or "remained"), of course, means that the endowment of the Spirit for Jesus was permanent. Though He had been filled with the Spirit since conception, this was a special anointing for His messianic ministry.

The Holy Spirit normally does not have a bodily form. But on this unique occasion, He appeared as a dove descending from the open heavens and alighting on Jesus. From the wording of Matthew 3:16 and Mark 1:10, it appears that this was visible only to Jesus and John the Baptist. To Jesus, it was the confirmation of divine approval and empowerment for His ministry. For John, it was the confirmation that Jesus was indeed the One for whom he had prepared the people.

The significance of the event (John 1:33-34). For John the Baptist, the descent of the Holy Spirit upon Jesus had immense meaning. This sign had been given him by the One who had sent him to baptize with water, that is, the Heavenly Father. John was keenly aware of the divinely prescribed limits of his ministry, which would reach its climax in this event. It was important that the Spirit not only come upon Jesus but also *remain* on Him, signifying a permanent endowment of power.

We know from other Scriptures that the Holy Spirit directed everything in the life and ministry of Jesus. The Spirit led Him to the place of temptation and sustained Him in it (Luke 4:1, 14). He endowed Him for His preaching (Matt. 12:18-21; Luke 4:18-21) and empowered Him to perform miracles (Matt. 12:28; Luke 4:18). The accusation that Jesus cast out demons by satanic power was thus blasphemy against the Holy Spirit (Matt. 12:28-32). The Spirit also was involved in His death and resurrection (Rom. 8:11; Heb. 9:14; I Pet. 3:18).

But to John, the descent of the Spirit upon Jesus meant more than this. Not only was He the *recipient* of the Spirit's power; He was also the *dispenser* of it to others. He was the one who "baptizeth with the Holy Ghost" (John 1:33). John's water baptism was limited in its purpose: it could signify only repentance, cleansing, and readiness for the Messiah. Jesus' baptism with the Spirit would impart the divine power for a new life.

The baptism of the Spirit first occurred when the church was born on the Day of Pentecost, and it has been repeated for all believers who became part of that body afterward (Acts 1:5; 2:1-4; 11:15-16). According to Paul, every person, without exception, who is part of the church through faith in Christ is baptized in the Spirit (I Cor. 12:12-13). It occurs at the moment of conversion.

Spirit baptism, though real, is not experienced with our senses. It is an act of God by which He identifies us with Christ and fellow believers. It is part of our position in Christ in heavenly places (Eph. 2:5-6)—a position we take by faith and rejoice in as we come to understand its spiritual implications. Through Spirit baptism, we gain access to all the other wonderful ministries of the Spirit.

When John the Baptist saw the Spirit descend upon Jesus, he knew that "this is the Son of God" (John 1:34). It was one thing to be filled with the Spirit from conception, as John was (Luke 1:15); it was quite another to oversee the ministries of the Spirit, as Jesus did. This could be none other than the Son of God.

Though John did not specifically mention it here, he must also have heard the Father's voice from heaven, which accompanied the descent of the Spirit. God declared, "Thou art my beloved Son, in whom I am well pleased" (Mark 1:11). All Persons of the Triune God were thus involved in this momentous testimony. The Son was identifying with His upcoming task through baptism, the Spirit was endowing Him with power, and the Father was confirming His divine identity.

To call Jesus "the Son of God" (John 1:34) does not make Him a lesser being than His Father. Indeed, the title speaks of His full deity. He is the eternal, living Word who created all things and the source of life and light (vss. 1-4). He is the final revelation of what God is like (vs. 18), for He alone has direct knowledge of the Father (6:46; 10:15). It is the Father's will that all honor the Son with the same honor they give the Father (5:23).

In that inscrutable relationship we call the Trinity, all three Members are equal in essence; but each assumes certain roles in relationship to the other two. Just as the Holy Spirit calls attention to Christ and glorifies Him (John 14:26; 15:26; 16:13-14), so Christ obeys and glorifies His Father (5:30; 6:38; 17:4). The enemies of Jesus understood perfectly that "Son of God" was a claim to deity, and they thus accused Him of blasphemy (10:33-36).

John the Baptist's portrayal of Jesus is a marvelous testimony of His Person and work. As the Lamb of God, He provided redemption for mankind. As the One who baptizes with the Spirit, He provides the foundation for the Christian church. And as the Son of God, He deserves all faith, worship, and obedience. That is the challenge of this portrait for us.

—Robert E. Wenger.

QUESTIONS

1. When did the incident in this week's lesson occur?
2. What precedents from Israel's history, law, and prophecy gave rise to the term "Lamb of God"?
3. How did Jesus' self-sacrifice differ from other sacrifices?
4. On what basis did John say that Jesus was preferred before him?
5. In what sense did John not know Jesus until His baptism?
6. Why was John's baptism necessary to prepare for Jesus' manifestation as Messiah of Israel?
7. For whose benefit did the Holy Spirit descend upon Jesus bodily?
8. How has Jesus' ministry of baptizing with the Holy Spirit been fulfilled historically?
9. Who gave witness of Jesus' deity at the time of His baptism?
10. Does being the Son of God make Jesus less than deity? Explain.

—Robert E. Wenger.

Preparing to Teach the Lesson

Jesus' birth is recorded in detail in both Matthew and Luke. Luke also provides information about Jesus' trip to the temple at age twelve. Other than that, the Bible is silent about Christ's early life.

In the Gospel of John, Jesus is the revealed and eternal Word, the Creator of everything, who became flesh that we might become God's children in Him. John then turns attention immediately to why we should acknowledge Christ for who He is.

TODAY'S AIM

Facts: to learn when John the Baptist recognized Christ and how he knew Him.

Principle: to place believing faith in the Christ whom God has revealed.

Application: to understand that trusting in Christ as Saviour is grounded in the reality of His identity as the Lamb of God.

INTRODUCING THE LESSON

In the Old Testament Mosaic system, various animals were sacrificed: oxen, cattle, goats, turtledoves, pigeons, sheep, and lambs. Of all these animals, the lamb appears the most docile and helpless. Lambs willingly followed their shepherd and, when sacrificed, never offered any cry of objection or act of resistance.

Jesus did not come as the "ox of God" or the "goat of God" or like any other sacrificial animal. Jesus was the Lamb of God. This week's lesson helps us see the importance of Jesus as the Lamb of God.

DEVELOPING THE LESSON

1. The moment of recognition (John 1:29-31). John the Baptist had been questioned by the religious leaders on the previous day about who he was (vss. 19-28). He assured them he was not "the Christ," or Elijah, or "that prophet." Who was he, then? He was only the "voice" announcing the coming of the Messiah. Why did he baptize? He did it because the One who was more worthy was in their midst.

On the next day, John saw Jesus coming toward him. As Christ approached, John said the words that are so well-known today: "Behold the Lamb of God, which taketh away the sin of the world" (John 1:29). Interpreters debate exactly what John meant, since the phrase "Lamb of God" occurs only in this verse and verse 36. John doubtless had several ideas that all found fulfillment in Jesus Christ.

The Passover lamb (Exod. 12:4-5; cf. I Cor. 5:7) was critical in the deliverance of Israel from Egypt's bondage, and Christ would deliver from sin's bondage. The twice-daily sacrifice of a lamb (Exod. 29:38-39) reminded Israel of their continuing need for blood atonement; Christ's sacrifice, by contrast, was once for all (Heb. 10:10). Christ, as a Lamb, willingly gave Himself (Isa. 53:7).

John's expression distinguished Jesus from all Old Testament sacrifices. Every sacrificial lamb was brought to the altar by a sinful person. In contrast, Jesus was the Lamb of God, sent by God Himself. In addition, each sacrificial lamb was given specifically for Israel. Jesus gave His life to take away the sin of the world. Only through having sins taken away can any person have the assurance of access to the Heavenly Father.

John removed any doubt concerning his identification of Christ by amplifying what he had said the previous day (John 1:30; cf. vs. 27). This clear

March 1, 2015

understanding of who Jesus really was, however, had only recently come to John (vs. 31). He was looking for the Messiah and baptized so that Christ would become evident to Israel. John had expected that God would reveal the Messiah through His baptism. John may have met Jesus during their childhood or early adult years, but he did not know that Jesus was the Messiah of Israel until he baptized Him.

2. The means of recognition (John 1:32-34). The Apostle John, who wrote this Gospel, probably assumed that his readers were familiar with the account of Jesus' baptism given in the Synoptic Gospels (Matt. 3:13-17; Mark 1:9-11; Luke 3:21-22). His purpose was not to detail that event but to show its messianic emphasis.

John the Baptist testified that at Christ's baptism, he saw the Holy Spirit descend (John 1:32). The Greek verb for "saw" emphasizes a completed event that has continuing results. What John saw, he continued to remember vividly. John saw that the Holy Spirit "abode" on Christ. That fact is not mentioned in the Synoptic Gospels. The verb translated "abode" indicates that the Spirit stayed permanently on Jesus.

John repeated his assertion that until Christ's baptism, he did not know that Jesus was the promised Messiah. God had told John, however, that when he saw the Spirit descend and remain, it would be the identifying sign for the Messiah. John clearly knew that Jesus was the Promised One and that He would be baptizing with the Holy Spirit.

The statements in John 1:34 are forcefully worded. The verbs "I saw" and "bare record" both stress continuing results. The statement continues with the full effect: Jesus is without doubt "the Son of God." The Davidic King is God's Son (II Sam. 7:14), and the Messianic King is God's Son (Ps. 2:7). Jesus is this Son. Significantly, the Gospel of John never uses the phrase "son of God" for a believer in Christ, but only for Jesus Himself.

ILLUSTRATING THE LESSON

A lamb holding a cross is a picture of the Lamb of God, who gave His life for us.

CONCLUDING THE LESSON

John the Baptist identified Jesus Christ as God's Messiah and Son. His entire life and ministry centered around that truth. From that time on, his life could be summarized by his own words: "He must increase, but I must decrease" (John 3:30).

Jesus had the closest possible relationship with the Father—He was the Son. He came to this earth as God's Lamb, to give His life for our sins so that we could become children in God's family by faith in Him and enjoy His presence forever.

ANTICIPATING THE NEXT LESSON

Next week we continue our study on God's presence in our lives by learning about the promise of the Comforter, the Holy Spirit.

—*R. Larry Overstreet.*

PRACTICAL POINTS

1. Forgiveness of sin is ours only through faith in Christ, the Lamb of God (John 1:29).
2. Believers serve God freely because Jesus' perfect sacrifice has released us from the power and penalty of sin.
3. As Christians humble ourselves before God, He accomplishes His work through us (vss. 30-31).
4. Through the Holy Spirit, believers live for God and share His message of salvation with the world (vss. 32-33).
5. All people are seeking something, and the believer's job is to point them to Christ (vs. 34).

—*Cheryl Y. Powell.*

RESEARCH AND DISCUSSION

1. What are similarities and differences between the Lamb of God in John 1:29 and the sacrificial lamb of the Old Testament (cf. Exod. 29:38-42; Lev. 16:5-28; Heb. 10)?
2. What is the difference between atonement and remission of sin (cf. Exod. 30:10; Matt. 26:28; Acts 10:43)?
3. What names and titles of Jesus Christ have been most meaningful in your life?
4. How does Jesus Christ reveal Himself to believers? How has He revealed Himself to you?
5. How does the act of water baptism compare and contrast with the baptism of the Holy Spirit (cf. Acts 2:38-39; Rom. 6:3-4; I Cor. 12:13)?
6. What does it mean to modern-day believers that Jesus is the Lamb of God (cf. Heb. 9:11-15)?

—*Cheryl Y. Powell.*

ILLUSTRATED HIGH POINTS

Behold

When I was in college, I was part of the Army ROTC military program. When one of the leaders wanted a squad or company to listen to him, he would call out "Attention!" All of us would fall into line immediately. That may reflect what John the Baptist was after when he used the word "Behold" in John 1:29. The Greek term is *Ide* (EE-day), an imperative particle.

John was commanding his listeners to stop what they were doing and pay attention to who Jesus was—the Lamb of God who takes away the sin of the world. Actually, John was saying, "Take a lasting look at Jesus Christ. He is your Saviour! Believe in *Him*!"

Lamb

I remember visiting my grandmother's farm, where they raised sheep. Sometimes when a lamb was born, it needed special care. So they would put the small lamb in a box, bring it into the house, and put it by the kitchen stove, where it could keep warm. They would also feed it. A lamb is so innocent and vulnerable. What a picture this is of Jesus Christ, who came to the world to bear our sin! He was harmless, without blemish or spot.

And I saw

In our first pastorate, we were told that there was a beautiful waterfall some distance from our place of residence.

We decided to travel to see the falls. Seeing the falls, we believed the commendations. In fact, we took some of our visitors there. When John saw God's Lamb, he believed He was the Son of God. Blessed are those who have not seen the Lord physically but still believe in Him as their Saviour.

—*Paul R. Bawden.*

Golden Text Illuminated

"The next day John seeth Jesus coming unto him, and saith, Behold the Lamb of God, which taketh away the sin of the world" (John 1:29).

There was great messianic expectation in Israel when John the Baptist appeared on the scene. Knowledgeable Jewish people understood from Daniel's prophecy (Dan. 9:24-27) that the Messiah would appear soon. In fact, John himself had been asked whether he was the Messiah (John 1:19-20; cf. Luke 3:15-17).

By the time John spoke the words in our golden text, he had already baptized Jesus. That baptism confirmed to John that Jesus was the Messiah, the Son of God (John 1:31-34). It was the God-ordained role of John as the Messiah's forerunner to introduce Him to Israel. However, the introduction given to him in verse 29 must have been shocking to John's audience. They were primarily looking for a messiah who would deliver the nation from oppression. They were not looking for someone who would die for them.

The expression "Lamb of God" presents a familiar and precious picture to us, but it was extremely hard for the Jews of John's day to grasp it. The expression does not appear in the Old Testament; only here and in John 1:36 does this specific term appear in the New Testament. "Lamb" clearly is used symbolically of Christ, as it is in the book of Revelation.

Some suggest that a particular lamb is in view here, whether the Passover lamb, the lamb led to slaughter in Isaiah 53, or one of the daily sacrificial lambs offered in the temple. It is probably best to take it as a general reference to a lamb of sacrifice, for all of these references point to atonement by means of a substitute. That is, the offering of a lamb indicated a substitute offered in sacrifice for sin.

The imagery, therefore, pointed ultimately to the cross of Christ. Just as a lamb was something valuable and precious, so Jesus, the valuable and precious Lamb of God, would be sacrificed for mankind's sin.

This lamb, however, would be "of God," that is, provided by or belonging to God. John was saying that God Himself would supply this sacrifice. In Judaism, the people themselves provided the sacrifice. Now God had provided the perfect, final, and sufficient sacrifice, who would take away "the sin of the world."

Hebrews 10:4 tells us that "it is not possible that the blood of bulls and of goats should take away sins." The blood of an animal could never "lift up" and remove sin. But this "Lamb" would suffer the penalty for human sin and remove its guilt. Here "sin" is singular, speaking of the totality of human sin.

So it was at the very beginning of Jesus' public ministry that God gave clear testimony to the purpose of the Messiah's coming. He came to "seek and to save that which was lost" (Luke 19:10), and He did so by offering Himself as the atoning sacrifice for sin (cf. I Pet. 1:18-19).

While John's disciples may not have understood all that was meant by the image of the Lamb of God, they understood this much: the Lamb of God was the One they had to follow (John 1:35-37). If we recognize Him as the true Lamb of God, we too must follow Him.

—Jarl K. Waggoner.

Heart of the Lesson

It is interesting to see how history unfolds before us. There are those among us who remember a world that was different from the world we now inhabit. If there is any lesson for us from history, it is that there is always something to look forward to. There is a sense of excitement. The promises of excitement that some secular prophets of doom trumpet as certain prove to be false. God's history, however, gives us sure and certain promises.

Jewish believers in the time of Jesus looked forward to the coming of the Messiah. Every Jew was raised with this in mind. Jews were to look toward the day of redemption, when the promised Messiah would come to earth. He would be their final redemption. After all, the Jewish people had gone through so much suffering over the centuries. It was time they got their reprieve. The Messiah gave them hope. He would one day be here.

1. The identification (John 1:29-31). Jesus was the answer the people of God had been waiting for. He was the embodiment of their hope and their dreams of salvation and redemption. He existed long before the world began, and now He was in their midst. They could now touch Him and feel Him. It was truly a dream come true. Their hope had finally come to fruition.

The Jews also knew that the Messiah would take away their sins. They knew the Old Testament Scriptures that promised that He was coming to do just that. Their system of sacrifices demanded that blood be shed and that the demands of the law be fulfilled. No one could fulfill those demands except the Messiah, for He was greater than John. John called Him the "Lamb of God" (John 1:29). Jesus would be that perfect sacrifice. There was now an answer for man's sin problem.

2. The declaration (John 1:32-33). It began as just another ordinary day. John was baptizing in the Jordan River. When John baptized Jesus, he remembered what had been told to him about this public and historic moment. The people around them also saw what was happening. When the dove descended upon Jesus, John knew in his heart that Jesus was indeed the promised Messiah. God was now among men. He would empower and baptize people with the Holy Spirit.

This was in contrast to what John was doing—baptizing by water. What Jesus had come to do was for all of us for all time.

3. The affirmation (John 1:34). When Jesus came to the Jordan River to be baptized by John, there was something about that meeting that told John that this was the one the people of God had been waiting for. This was the promised Messiah, God Himself walking among them. When the Holy Spirit descended like a dove upon Jesus, it was sufficient public confirmation that He was indeed the promised Messiah. On this testimony, we are to recognize Him and receive Him as our sacrifice for our own sins.

When we recognize God's presence in our midst—for the Messiah is now with us—we will see the Lamb as He who takes away all our sins. He is the Redeemer.

—A. Koshy Muthalaly.

World Missions

There are so many tragedies that come from the brokenness of the human condition. When heartache comes, everyone responds differently, even among Christians. And when faced with profound loss, everything we know about God and His tender love for us can seem cold. What is a follower of Jesus to do?

The Waodani (formerly known as Auca) of Ecuador were a vicious tribe. They were known for their brutal killings—not just of foreigners but even of their fellow tribesmen. Their history and culture were steeped in violence. The concept of forgiveness was completely unknown to them.

Perhaps what happened in January 1956 was not much of a surprise. The new year, for many, is a time of starting new goals. It carries a sense of hope for the future. But for the families of five missionaries, the news they received that new year seemed anything but hopeful.

Nate Saint, Jim Elliot, Ed McCully, Pete Fleming, and Robert Youderian all had a heart for the stone-age Indian tribes of the Ecuadorian jungle. Their goal was to make contact with them and bring the gospel to the hostile Waodanis.

Their plan, "Operation Auca," was to send down gifts to the tribe using a basket that descended from a jungle plane. Initially, they had success, and their plan worked. They could not have known that trouble was brewing.

The men were attacked at their campsite along the bank of a river. None of them survived the unprovoked killing raid.

The news of the missionaries' deaths shocked the world. Instead of demanding government action and seeking justice, Nate Saint's family reacted by seeking the killers in order to love them and share the gospel with them.

Before his death, Nate's sister, Rachel, had befriended a Waodani woman who trusted in Jesus. Through this friendship, Rachel was invited to live in a Waodani village. She worked very hard forging relationships and translating the Bible into their language.

The Spirit of God was at work, and many Waodani became followers of Jesus—even those who had killed Nate and his friends. The following is a portion of the testimony given by one of the warriors—Mincaye. "My ancestors lived angry and hating each other . . . It was a bad way to live, but they didn't know any other trail. . . . My heart was black and sick in sin, but then I heard that God sent His own Son. His blood dripping and dripping, He washed my heart clean. Now I live well. Now you—God followers from all over the dirt—now I see you well because you are truly my brothers, God's having washed your hearts clean too" (Saint, *End of the Spear*, Tyndale).

Some might ask, "Did those men really have to die? Why did God turn His back on those who loved Him?" Little do we understand the ways and trails of God. Even Peter, when Jesus spoke of His death, refused to believe what Jesus was saying, telling Him that surely they would not let that happen!

Through the death of Jesus, many were reconciled to God. Out of love, Nate Saint and his friends were not afraid to die so that many might know and live in Christ. They died, not knowing what the future would bring but believing that God can and will bring good things even out of tragedies.

I love how I Corinthians 13:12 puts it: "For now we see through a glass, darkly; but then face to face: now I know in part; but then shall I know even as also I am known."

—Christina Futrell.

The Jewish Aspect

This is the Jewish year 5775. The Passover will begin the evening of April third, two days before Easter. By now, most Jewish homemakers have begun making their Passover Seder plans for the religious celebration and dinner. Originally a home feast, today it is observed in synagogues as well.

"Seder" means "order" and refers to the sequence of the meal and the related readings. It begins with the recitation of the historic Exodus of the Jews from Egyptian slavery under God's man, Moses. The story unfolds in the readings from the Haggadah, a beautiful book, sometimes having a silver metal cover.

The Bible book of Exodus relates that Moses directed all Israelite families to choose a lamb from the flock on the tenth day of the month Nisan. It had to be a healthy animal, without spot or blemish. It was placed in a separate pen in order to ensure its pristine appearance. The animal was to be sacrificed in the evening of the fourteenth day of the month (12:3-6).

Next, the Israelites were to collect the blood of the lamb and paint the outside of their doorframe with it (Exod. 12:7). That strange-sounding requirement was the sign under which God spared His people, for that night God slew the firstborn of man and beast at every home in Egypt where the covering of blood was missing (vss. 29-30). In Israelite homes, the lamb was roasted and eaten (vss. 8-10).

In the Seder ceremony, you will hear the dreadful story of Egyptian oppression, the call of Moses to lead God's people, and the grace of God in leading Israel out of slavery. You may listen carefully, but something important is missing! Where is the lamb? The leader of the service does mention that there is the shank bone of a lamb on the Seder plate, but the bone has no significance in the service.

The lamb is missing, and the purpose of slaying the lamb and eating it is not explained. A full dinner concludes the Jewish Seder, but it ordinarily involves some meat other than lamb.

John the Baptist pointed to Jesus and told his followers, "Behold the Lamb of God, which taketh away the sin of the world" (John 1:29). Paul said it this way: "Christ our passover is sacrificed for us" (I Cor. 5:7).

We note that Paul's words were addressed to Gentiles. It says that every person in the world needs the blood of Christ on the doorposts of his heart in order to have God pass over him in the Day of Judgment. This is God's plan of salvation, pure and simple.

Why would the Jews of today omit the very heart of the Exodus story, the story of the lamb? Surely Satan has worked hard to keep Jews from hearing of the Lamb of God who takes away the sin of the world.

A lamb is a very important image in Scripture. "Lambs are associated with gentleness, innocence, and dependence. Thus God as shepherd gathers lambs in his arms because they are helpless" (Ryken, Wilhoit, and Longman, eds., *Dictionary of Biblical Imagery,* InterVarsity).

The most important image of the lamb is as a sacrifice. The historic Passover points clearly to the Lamb John identified: Jesus. His perfect sacrifice was offered once for sin, for all, forever (Heb. 9:28).

—Lyle P. Murphy.

Guiding the Superintendent

It is reasonable to believe that John the Baptist experienced a feeling of great comfort when he saw the fulfillment of a long-awaited promise begin to take shape. When John saw Jesus, he saw God's promise of the coming Messiah unfolding just as God had said it would and just as John had declared it repeatedly among the people. When John saw Jesus, he told his companions to behold—to look or take notice of—their salvation.

DEVOTIONAL OUTLINE

1. Jesus, the sin-bearing Lamb (John 1:29). There is so much that one whose eye is fixed on Jesus can see. How is it that when John saw Jesus, he called Him the Lamb of God? How is it that he added that as the prophetic Lamb, Jesus would take away the sin of the entire world? The explanation is in part in the fact that John was chosen by God to be the forerunner of Jesus. His task was to proclaim Christ's coming and urge the nation to prepare their hearts and minds to receive Christ as Saviour and Lord. Whom God calls, He also equips.

John's charge was comparable to what modern pastors, teachers, and evangelists are called to do—to inform humanity of the assurance of Christ's return and to exhort men, women, boys, and girls to open their hearts in order to receive God's free gift of grace.

2. Jesus, the revealed Messiah (John 1:30-33). John had no personal vision of grandeur. He knew all too well that the Jews were still waiting for the fulfillment of the promised Messiah. He clarified that he was neither the Messiah nor even worthy to be His servant. The truth is that John truly did not know Jesus as the Christ, any more than anyone else at that time. Yet John was content to cry aloud and urge his hearers to clear a path for Christ's arrival and to baptize all who accepted Christ by faith.

John was confident of his message because God had given him a sign. When he saw the dove come down from heaven as God had said, John's testimony that Jesus was indeed the revelation of prophecy was strengthened and confirmed.

God genuinely desires that men come to fully know Him, and all that had transpired in the life of John the Baptist was to that end. God chose John and gave him his unique wilderness ministry. At the appointed time, Christ would manifest the words of John's message of repentance and faith and transform the life of every believer through the baptism of the Holy Spirit.

3. Jesus, the Son of God (John 1:34). John the Baptist was born into his role as forerunner of Christ and given the sign by which he should recognize Christ. Through His Word, God informs believers today of who Christ is. Now we, like John, have indisputable evidence that Jesus is the Christ, the Son of the Living God.

AGE-GROUP EMPHASES

Children: Most children are familiar with lambs. Teach them that Jesus is gentle like a lamb and that they do not have to be afraid to love and trust Him.

Youths: Help the youths understand that while Jesus continually takes away our sins, we must commit to lives of obedience to God.

Adults: When John beheld Jesus, he saw the Lamb of God. Ask the adults what God sees when He looks at them.

—Jane E. Campbell.

LESSON 2   MARCH 8, 2015

Scripture Lesson Text

JOHN 14:15 If ye love me, keep my commandments.

16 And I will pray the Father, and he shall give you another Comforter, that he may abide with you for ever;

17 *Even* the Spir′it of truth; whom the world cannot receive, because it seeth him not, neither knoweth him: but ye know him; for he dwelleth with you, and shall be in you.

18 I will not leave you comfortless: I will come to you.

19 Yet a little while, and the world seeth me no more; but ye see me: because I live, ye shall live also.

20 At that day ye shall know that I *am* in my Father, and ye in me, and I in you.

21 He that hath my commandments, and keepeth them, he it is that loveth me: and he that loveth me shall be loved of my Father, and I will love him, and will manifest myself to him.

22 Ju′das saith unto him, not Is-car′i-ot, Lord, how is it that thou wilt manifest thyself unto us, and not unto the world?

23 Je′sus answered and said unto him, If a man love me, he will keep my words: and my Father will love him, and we will come unto him, and make our abode with him.

24 He that loveth me not keepeth not my sayings: and the word which ye hear is not mine, but the Father's which sent me.

25 These things have I spoken unto you, being *yet* present with you.

26 But the Comforter, *which is* the Ho′ly Ghost, whom the Father will send in my name, he shall teach you all things, and bring all things to your remembrance, whatsoever I have said unto you.

NOTES

The Promise of a Comforter

Lesson: John 14:15-26

Read: John 14:15-26

TIME: A.D. 30   PLACE: Jerusalem

GOLDEN TEXT—"The Comforter, which is the Holy Ghost, whom the Father will send in my name, he shall teach you all things, and bring all things to your remembrance, whatsoever I have said unto you" (John 14:26).

Introduction

Crucial questions always arise when a competent individual resigns or retires from a position in which he or she was considered indispensable. An innovative entrepreneur has started a small company and carefully guided it into prominence as a nationally recognized corporation. Now he is retiring. Will the business continue to thrive as it has? What changes in direction might occur under new leadership?

A high school basketball coach has taken a struggling team and built it into a winner. Now he is retiring.

A faithful and beloved pastor of many years decides to move on to another ministry. Who now can fill his shoes?

Jesus' disciples faced a similar uncertain future as He neared the time of His crucifixion and final departure from them. Who could possibly take His place? Anticipating their questions, He sought to set their minds at ease.

LESSON OUTLINE

I. EXHORTATION AND ENCOURAGEMENT—John 14:15-21

II. INSTRUCTION AND ILLUMINATION—John 14:22-26

Exposition: Verse by Verse

EXHORTATION AND ENCOURAGEMENT

JOHN 14:15 **If ye love me, keep my commandments.**

16 **And I will pray the Father, and he shall give you another Comforter, that he may abide with you for ever;**

17 **Even the Spirit of truth; whom the world cannot receive, because it seeth him not, neither knoweth him: but ye know him; for he dwelleth with you, and shall be in you.**

18 **I will not leave you comfortless: I will come to you.**

19 **Yet a little while, and the world seeth me no more; but ye see me:**

because I live, ye shall live also.

20 At that day ye shall know that I am in my Father, and ye in me, and I in you.

21 He that hath my commandments, and keepeth them, he it is that loveth me: and he that loveth me shall be loved of my Father, and I will love him, and will manifest myself to him.

The obedience of love (John 14:15). Jesus had gathered with the Twelve for their last Passover meal. He had washed their feet and taught spiritual lessons from the act (13:1-17). He had announced the betrayal, and Judas had left (vss. 18-30). He had announced His departure and Peter's denial (vss. 31-38). Then He began to teach the disciples to prepare them for challenging days ahead (chaps. 14—16). Our lesson is taken from this Upper Room Discourse.

Jesus encouraged His bewildered followers by promising them an eternal home—a home to which He Himself was the way (John 14:1-11). He also assured them that they would have a ministry even more productive than His if they depended on Him in prayer (vss. 12-14). Then He exhorted them, "If ye love me, keep my commandments" (vs. 15). This serves to place His promise of answered prayer in a proper light. One who expects answers must be an obedient servant who loves his Master.

Jesus has set the example in this. His love for His Father led to unconditional obedience (John 5:30; 12:49; 14:31). Now He asked the disciples to follow His pattern (14:15). The "commandments" consisted of all the teachings He had given them verbally and by example. Love, not slavish fear, provides the incentive for obedience. While "keep my commandments" is a command in the Authorized Version, it can be rendered as a simple future: "will keep." This states the logical outcome of love, which is obedience.

The Spirit's enabling (John 14:16-17). Disciples will be able to keep Jesus' commands because, as He said, "I will pray the Father, and he shall give you another Comforter." "Pray" here is the Greek word for "ask" and does not imply any inferiority of Jesus, as if He were entreating the Father as His superior. He would simply ask Him to send the Holy Spirit to replace Him in the world to aid His disciples.

The Spirit here is called "another Comforter" (John 14:16). The word for "Comforter" means "one called to one's aid." In I John 2:1, it refers to Christ as our "advocate," or a legal counselor who intercedes for us. But in John's Gospel it refers exclusively to the Holy Spirit and is used in the general sense of "helper." The word for "another" indicates another of the same kind. He would be another like Jesus, helping His own as Jesus did. Thus, there would be no spiritual loss when Jesus departed.

The prospect of abiding forever contrasts the Spirit with Jesus. Jesus was about to complete His earthly work and leave; the Spirit's work in Christian believers would last forever. He was not yet present in this manner; that would commence on the Day of Pentecost, when He came upon the church (Acts 2:1-4, 33).

Jesus identified the coming Helper as "the Spirit of truth" (John 14:17), a title He also used in 15:26 and 16:13. He is so called because He bears witness to God's truth. He has produced the truth of His written Word (cf. Acts 28:25; II Pet. 1:20-21), but—more important in our context—He testifies of Jesus Christ, the Truth (John 14:6; 15:26). During Jesus' earthly ministry, He substantiated His claims through miraculous deeds (cf. Matt. 12:28); now that Jesus was going away, He would do so through an internal witness.

Jesus stated that the Spirit is God's gift exclusively to His own. He is One "whom the world cannot receive, because it seeth him not, neither knoweth him" (John 14:17). Though He is real and active, the unbelieving world has no perception of Him or His work. Just as radio broadcasts go undetected unless we are tuned in to the proper frequency, so the Spirit's presence goes undetected by unbelievers (cf. I Cor. 2:9, 11, 14).

But disciples of Jesus know the Spirit (John 14:17) not just as an abstract concept but by personal experience, as the Greek verb emphasizes. "He dwelleth with you" is, literally, "He remains with you." The Holy Spirit has always worked among God's people, and Jesus' disciples had seen Him work in remarkable ways through Jesus. Jesus assured them that this presence would continue.

But now, in addition, He would be *in* them. Although Old Testament saints might have been selectively and temporarily indwelled by the Holy Spirit, His universal, permanent indwelling is reserved for Christians in this age. Jesus had previously announced that this would happen (John 7:37-39), and it came about first on the Day of Pentecost (Acts 2:4, 16-18). Every believer, without exception, is now indwelled by the Spirit (cf. Rom. 8:9; I Cor. 6:19).

Jesus' continuing ministry (John 14:18-20). When Jesus said, "I will not leave you comfortless: I will come to you," He may have been referring, as some believe, to His continuing presence through the Holy Spirit. But it is more likely that He was speaking of His appearances to the disciples after His resurrection. "Comfortless" is, literally, "orphans." They felt bereaved, alone, and helpless when He died, but His appearances changed their sorrow to joy (cf. 20:17-22).

After a short time, the world would see Jesus no more. The suffering figure hanging on a cross would be their last memory of Him. He would not appear to them again after His resurrection (cf. Acts 1:2-3; 10:40-41). But the disciples would see Him again—and what a glorious transformation they would behold! His resurrection body, though recognizable, would no longer be subject to earthly limitations.

The present tense of "but ye see me" and "because I live" (John 14:19) is striking. It strongly suggests that His death was but a minor shadow passing over His divine life (cf. Luke 24:5; Acts 2:24; Rev. 1:17-18). By contrast, the future tense of "ye shall live also" (John 14:19) reveals the coming impact of His resurrection on His followers. His life would become theirs (John 10:10; I Cor. 15:20-22).

"At that day," said Jesus, "ye shall know that I am in my Father, and ye in me, and I in you" (John 14:20). Here He could have been reverting to His teaching on the Holy Spirit; if so, "that day" would refer to Pentecost. And it is surely true that the coming of the Spirit helped the disciples understand their unity with Christ and the Father more completely (cf. Acts 5:29-32).

However, it seems more natural to see the phrase as referring to the day of Jesus' resurrection. That is when the disciples would first understand that He and His Father were one in life and purpose and that they had been graciously included in this unity (cf. John 17:21-23). It is a privilege that His resurrection life brings to all who are united with Him by faith (Eph. 2:4-6).

The call to obedience repeated (John 14:21). Jesus now expanded on the principle that He had stated earlier—that love and obedience go hand in hand: "He that hath my commandments, and keepeth them, he it is that loveth me." This obedience would then bring a loving response from His Father and Himself.

In this He was not teaching that we earn His favor through good deeds. Our obedience to His commands is the outgrowth of our love for Him; this love, in turn, is engendered by a life transformed by faith. Saving faith is the basis for our union with God and the loving deeds we do for Him (cf. Gal. 5:6; I John 5:3-4). Efforts to gain His favor through good works will be rejected (Rom. 4:4-5; Phil. 3:4-9).

The one whose love overflows in obedience "shall be loved of my Father, and I will love him, and will manifest myself to him" (John 14:21). Both Father and Son are free to display love to the obedient child, and Christ is free to manifest Himself in spiritual blessings. Though He would not show Himself physically, as He did after His resurrection, He would always remain with His own (Matt. 28:20).

INSTRUCTION AND ILLUMINATION

22 Judas saith unto him, not Iscariot, Lord, how is it that thou wilt manifest thyself unto us, and not unto the world?

23 Jesus answered and said unto him, If a man love me, he will keep my words: and my Father will love him, and we will come unto him, and make our abode with him.

24 He that loveth me not keepeth not my sayings: and the word which ye hear is not mine, but the Father's which sent me.

25 These things have I spoken unto you, being yet present with you.

26 But the Comforter, which is the Holy Ghost, whom the Father will send in my name, he shall teach you all things, and bring all things to your remembrance, whatsoever I have said unto you.

A disciple's question (John 14:22). At this point, a disciple named Judas had a question. Although Judas Iscariot had already left the room at this point, the Apostle John found it wise to add "not Iscariot." The traitor's name had become so infamous in the church by the time he was writing (about A.D. 90) that he wanted no misunderstanding.

Luke is the only other Gospel that includes a disciple of this name besides Judas Iscariot. There he is called "Judas the brother of James" (Luke 6:16; cf. Acts 1:13). Matthew and Mark call him "Thaddaeus" instead (Matt. 10:3; Mark 3:18). Nothing further is known concerning him.

Judas asked, "Lord, how is it that thou wilt manifest thyself unto us, and not unto the world?" (John 14:22). This arose out of Jesus' previous statement (vss. 18-19) that He would come to them again but that the world would not see Him. Perhaps he thought this would be impossible over a period of time. But he may also have thought it would be inconsistent with Jesus' messianic claims. How could He enter His glory if He restricted His appearance to a few?

The importance of Jesus' words (John 14:23-24). In answering Judas, Jesus did not have in mind His postresurrection appearances. Instead, He focused on His continuing spiritual presence after returning to heaven. In essence, He said He could abide only with those who loved and obeyed Him. He identified them in this way: "If a man love me, he will keep my words." Earlier He spoke of keeping His commandments (vss. 15, 21); here He identified them with His words (teachings).

Of such a person He declared, "My Father will love him, and we will come unto him, and make our abode with him" (John 14:23). The word "abode" is the singular of the same word translated "mansions" in verse 2. These are its only occurrences in the New Testament. It signifies a dwelling place or room. Jesus had promised future dwellings in His Father's house, but that hope was distant. Now He promised that His people themselves would become the present dwellings of Him and His Father.

This, of course, can never be true of the world, which neither loves nor obeys Christ. Anyone who does not love Him will not adhere to His precepts. Love and obedience are so inseparable that a claim to one without the other is false. One who claims to walk with God in love, yet walks in the darkness of sin, is a liar (I John 1:6; 3:9-10). Just as surely, one who slavishly follows biblical commands out of pride or fear instead of love for Him cannot please Him (Rom. 10:1-4; I John 4:8).

This is all the more serious because the words that the disciples heard were not Jesus' own; they were from the Father, who had sent Him. Jesus and His Father are always in harmony; so when He came into the world, He spoke only what was consonant with His Father's will (cf. John 12:49; 14:10). He always took the role of the obedient Son. Thus, there is never a rift in Scripture between Jesus' words and God's larger revelation (cf. Heb. 1:1-2).

There have always been cults that claim to be worshipping the true God while rejecting the claims and teachings of Jesus. But this is impossible, for Jesus is God's supreme revelation of Himself (John 8:19). Those who reject Jesus' authority are rejecting His Father's as well (I John 2:22-23; II John 1:9).

The Spirit's continuing enlightenment (John 14:25-26). Referring again to His teaching of the Twelve, Jesus said, "These things have I spoken unto you, being yet present with you." They were responsible to obey and preserve these words (cf. vss. 23-24). But, as He would tell them later, He had much more to teach them that they could not handle yet (16:12). Even what He had already taught them was imperfectly grasped.

But the Holy Spirit would take up this teaching ministry. He was the one whom the Father would send in Jesus' name. Just as He had come in the Father's name, so the Spirit would be sent in Jesus' name.

In saying that the Spirit would teach the disciples all things, Jesus was not promising unlimited knowledge to His people. The promise is limited by what follows, namely, the assurance that the Spirit would bring to their remembrance everything that Jesus had said to them during His earthly ministry. What the apostles now understood so imperfectly, the Holy Spirit would bring to their minds with new clarity and fullness. They could then teach and write Christ's truth with authority.

At the beginning of Acts, Luke referred to "all that Jesus began both to do and teach" (1:1). He then described in detail what the Holy Spirit continued to do through the apostles (cf. vs. 8). This fulfilled Jesus' promise at the Last Supper.

—Robert E. Wenger.

QUESTIONS

1. What was the setting for Jesus' teaching in this week's lesson?
2. What is the logical outcome of one's love for Jesus?
3. What is the idea behind the word "Comforter" (John 14:16)?
4. Why is the Holy Spirit referred to as the Spirit of truth?
5. How does the Spirit's indwelling in Christians differ from His ministry in Old Testament times?
6. What new insight would Jesus' resurrection give the disciples?
7. What was the question Judas had for Jesus?
8. What blessing did Jesus promise to those who keep His words?
9. Why is it impossible for a person to worship the true God without believing Jesus' teachings?
10. Why was it necessary for the Spirit to continue Jesus' teaching?

—Robert E. Wenger.

Preparing to Teach the Lesson

Christians rejoice in the salvation we have in Christ, the Lamb of God. We think of His earthly life and ministry, His sacrificial death, burial, resurrection, and His ascension to heaven. We await His return.

In that process, we may overlook the current ministry of the Holy Spirit, whom Jesus Himself promised would come to indwell us and minister to and through us.

TODAY'S AIM

Facts: to discover why Jesus sent the Holy Spirit as our Comforter.

Principle: to gain assurance of the Lord's plan for our spiritual growth.

Application: to live obediently to Christ through the Spirit's continual ministry.

INTRODUCING THE LESSON

The Gospel of John has several references to the Holy Spirit. The Spirit came upon Christ at His baptism (1:32-33). Jesus said that the Spirit is the Agent of the new birth (3:5-8, 34) and that God is Spirit (4:24). Jesus promised the Spirit would come (7:39).

Jesus' disciples—and future readers of this Gospel—would have questions. When will the Spirit come? Why will He come? What will be the differences when He comes? Answers to such questions begin to emerge in this week's text.

DEVELOPING THE LESSON

1. The pledge of the Comforter (John 14:15-17). Jesus had assured His disciples of the privilege of prayer (vss. 13-14). He asserted that whatever they asked in His name would be granted. The promise is that when we pray in the same character as Jesus—that is, just as He would pray—that prayer will be answered. Answered prayer is not merely for our benefit, but just as much (or more) for the Father to be glorified.

The promise of answered prayer is then balanced with a call to obedience. Our obedience to the Lord's commandments should be based on our love for Him.

Not only were the disciples to pray; Jesus would also pray. His prayer was for the Father to give "another Comforter" (John 14:16). One of the definitions of the Greek word for "Comforter" (*parakletos*) refers to a "defense attorney" in the full sense of one who helps, encourages, aids, and comforts while pleading one's cause.

This Comforter is identified as the Spirit of truth. The world cannot receive Him, or know Him, because the world does not see Him. We cannot see radio waves or television signals, but we know they are real. For the disciples, the comforting Spirit had a present ministry in His dwelling with them and a more intimate future ministry as He would be in them. The Holy Spirit continues to indwell all believers today.

2. The guarantee of the Comforter (John 14:18-21). Jesus promised He would not leave His disciples "comfortless." Instead, He would come to them; this was His guarantee that His words concerning the Holy Spirit would also come to pass. Jesus here referred to His coming resurrection appearances. The disciples did see Him come back to them after His resurrection, as indicated by verse 19. The words "a little while" point to an imminent event. The world did not see Him in His postresurrection appearances, but His disciples did. Even more than that, His resurrection and victory over death provide the guarantee that they will also have victory over death: "ye shall live also."

The words "at that day" in John 14:20 refer to the time after Christ's resurrection. The disciples would fully realize that He is exactly who He says (cf. 20:28).

The idea that a disciple can *have* Jesus' commandments emphasizes that the commands become a vital, integrated part of his life and understanding. As a result, he keeps them in obedience. The benefits gained from loving Jesus this way are that the Father loves us, the Son loves us, and we have the confidence of the Son's abiding presence in our lives. We enjoy that presence through the comforting Spirit.

3. The teaching of the Comforter (John 14:22-26). The preceding words of Christ prompted a question from Judas, also called Thaddaeus (Matt. 10:3; Mark 3:18). Exactly how would Jesus do what He said? In John 14:23, Jesus expanded on what He had said in verse 21. The disciple who truly loves Christ will obey Him. As that occurs, the Father will love that disciple, and both the Father and the Son will indwell that person. The word "abode" (vs. 23) is the same Greek word translated "mansions" in verse 2 and refers to a place where someone dwells. Believers, not an earthly tabernacle or temple, have become the place where our Lord dwells during this current time.

Jesus continued teaching that anyone who does not love Christ does not keep His commands. When a person rejects the teachings of Christ, he simultaneously rejects the word of the Father who sent Him. Jesus gave this teaching while He was still present with the disciples, but they did not grasp its depth. They needed more teaching, but Christ was leaving. How would they learn His truths?

Jesus answered by assuring them of the comforting Spirit's teaching. After Jesus' death, resurrection, and ascension, the Father would send the Holy Spirit. The Father did that on the Day of Pentecost. When the Spirit came, He taught the disciples all things. The comforting Spirit taught all the deep truths of God so that the disciples would fully understand.

This explains how the Apostle John could write with such depth in this Gospel. The Spirit was present to bring to his remembrance all that was important to record. It explains how John could write such a detailed account some sixty years after the event. The Spirit's ministry gives us full confidence in Scripture's accuracy and integrity.

ILLUSTRATING THE LESSON

Our responsibility as Christ's followers is to submit to Scripture, which was inspired by the Holy Spirit.

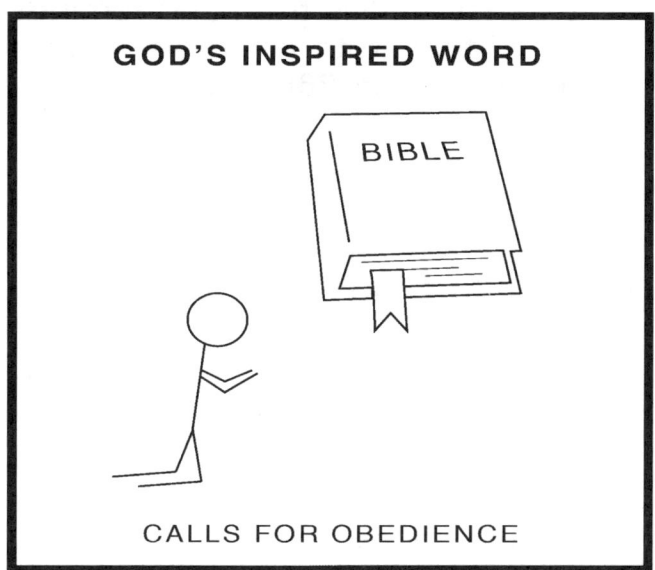

CONCLUDING THE LESSON

Jesus taught that obedience gains His disciples true freedom. As we love the Lord who gave the commands, we experience the liberty to serve Him. As we love, He provides His comforting Holy Spirit so that we may know His Word and have His power.

ANTICIPATING THE NEXT LESSON

In our next lesson we explore the implications of the reality that the Holy Spirit is the Spirit of truth.

—*R. Larry Overstreet.*

PRACTICAL POINTS

1. If we love God, we will obey Him (John 14:15).
2. The Holy Spirit is always at work within the believer (vss. 16-18).
3. Believers can live confident lives knowing that Jesus will never leave us.
4. The Holy Spirit gives believers a new perspective on life and God's love (vss. 19-21).
5. When we love and obey God, He reveals more of Himself and His truth (vss. 22-24).
6. As we study God's Word, He teaches us His truth and reminds us of that truth when we need it most (vss. 25-26).

—Cheryl Y. Powell.

RESEARCH AND DISCUSSION

1. What does John 14:15-26 tell us about the relationship between the Father, the Son, and the Holy Spirit?
2. How does the Holy Spirit help the believer obey God's will?
3. What does it mean in your everyday life that the Holy Spirit is your Comforter?
4. How does the Holy Spirit lead the believer (cf. Rom. 8:14)?
5. What judgment for the unbeliever is found in John 14:15-26?
6. How does our faith in God help us live confidently?
7. Does the Holy Spirit's presence mean a believer will never be afraid (cf. Pss. 27:1; 56:3-4)? Explain.
8. What promises did Jesus make to believers in John 14:15-26?

—Cheryl Y. Powell.

ILLUSTRATED HIGH POINTS

Keep my commandments

The story is told of the little boy who loved to play with a friend who lived next door. When it was time for supper, the boy's mother would call for him to come home. From the back door of the house, she called out, "Johnny, it's time to come home." Little Johnny kept playing with his friend. His mother called a second time. Johnny still kept playing with his friend. Soon he heard his mother yell at the top of her lungs, "Johnny, come home!" Johnny finally told his friend, "I have to go now."

When God speaks to the believer in His Word, the one who loves Him obeys immediately.

That he may abide with you

There is no place like home. It is the place where we can sit in an easy chair, take off our shoes, and relax by reading the Bible or a good book. Jesus taught that the Holy Spirit would no longer just be *with* the disciples; He would actually live in them spiritually. He would come to make His home in believers in Jesus Christ.

He shall teach you

One of the challenges of growing up is learning to be teachable. I remember having to learn that as a boy. Sometimes I thought that I knew better than my father. In one instance, I disobeyed him by going where I was told not to go—and I almost drowned in the river near our home. For my disobedience, I was sent to bed early that night. I learned the hard way to listen to my father and to follow his directions—to be teachable and accept instruction that could save my life. May our lives be open to the Holy Spirit's teaching, and may we do what He says in the Word of God!

—Paul R. Bawden.

Golden Text Illuminated

"The Comforter, which is the Holy Ghost, whom the Father will send in my name, he shall teach you all things, and bring all things to your remembrance, whatsoever I have said unto you" (John 14:26).

In the upper room, just prior to His arrest and eventual crucifixion, Jesus told His disciples that He was going away (John 14:1-3). However, He promised that in His absence, they would be given "another Comforter" (vs. 16). Jesus identified the Comforter as the "Spirit of truth" (vs. 17) and in our golden text as the "Holy Ghost," or Holy Spirit.

A "comforter" (*parakletos*) is literally one who comes alongside to help. It "conveys the ideas of strengthener, encourager, advocate, or helper" (Kent, *Light in the Darkness,* BMH). The Spirit would take Jesus' place in His followers' lives, remaining with them forever (John 14:16) and thus not leaving them "comfortless" (vs. 18).

The Spirit who would come, like God the Father and God the Son, would be "Holy." This identifies Him closely with the other two Members of the Trinity and is perhaps the central characteristic of God. The Spirit would come in Jesus' name, that is, with His authority. There is never any conflict among the Spirit, the Father, and the Son; nor is there any conflict between the Spirit and the Word of God He inspired.

The Holy Spirit came in power on the Day of Pentecost, as recorded in Acts 2. From that point on, He has indwelled permanently all who have placed their faith in Christ (cf. Rom. 8:9). The ministries of the Holy Spirit are many and varied. One particular ministry of the Spirit, however, related specifically to the disciples of Jesus. Jesus said the Spirit would "teach" the disciples "all things." Morris noted that "'all things' is comprehensive and probably means 'all that you will need to know'" (*The Gospel According to John,* Eerdmans).

The disciples, or apostles, would serve a unique function in the church. As the continuing witnesses of Christ in the world, they would have to convey the gospel message accurately. Thus, it was necessary for the Spirit to "bring all things to [their] remembrance." Like us, the apostles were human and prone to forgetting or confusing things they had heard Jesus say. They would need the supernatural work of the Holy Spirit to ensure that all they were to convey was passed on with complete accuracy. The very words of Jesus would be brought to their memories by the Spirit.

Thus, the apostles were assured that the Spirit would be supplying the "remembrance and true interpretation of Christ's words. Many things the disciples did not presently understand would be made clear. Implicit in this statement was the authorization of the apostles as the witnesses who would be qualified to give the New Testament record to the church" (Kent).

What a wonderful assurance it is to us that God Himself in the Person of the Holy Spirit directed the memories and understanding of the apostles so that all they recorded in Scripture can be trusted as "given by inspiration" (II Tim. 3:16)! As the Spirit taught the apostles, He continues to teach us through the Bible He inspired.

—Jarl K. Waggoner.

Heart of the Lesson

When Joni Eareckson Tada was seventeen, a diving accident caused her to be paralyzed from the neck down. She is in her sixties now and has developed breast cancer on top of the chronic pain that she bears daily. When people ask her how she can endure all of this, she tells them, "The greater thing is . . . the advancement of the gospel, it's the giving of the kingdom, reclaiming what is rightfully Christ's" (*Christianity Today*, October 8, 2010). Joni has acknowledged that this is only because of the power of the Holy Spirit.

In our lesson this week, we have the promise of the Comforter, the Holy Spirit, for us today.

1. Jesus promised the Holy Spirit (John 14:15-21). How close do you want to be to God? Many who read a lesson like this wish that they could be closer to God. When Jesus left this earth, He said that we were never going to be left alone but that we would have divine help in the form of the Holy Spirit, who would dwell within each of us. There is no closer comfort than that. When we go through trouble, He is there to let us know that He cares enough to stay by us. His presence will stay with us always.

This fulfillment of the promise of the Comforter could only take place after the resurrection of Jesus from the dead. The physical presence of the incarnate Jesus would be replaced by the intangible but omnipresent (everywhere-present) Holy Spirit. So while we cannot see Him, He will appear more real to us because of His comforting presence so close to us. He will show Himself to us through His nearness to us, and we will surely know that He is there.

2. The Holy Spirit showed Himself (John 14:22-25). This lesson shows us clearly that we must receive the Lord Jesus in order to experience the comforting presence of the Holy Spirit. Jesus came so that we may experience that closeness with God through His indwelling presence. He is, indeed, our Helper. The prerequisite for experiencing the comfort of God through His Spirit is that we must love our Lord Jesus. The Spirit is given to those who are His children. This comes through trusting in Jesus.

3. The Holy Spirit teaches us (John 14:26). The promise of God's comforting presence through the gift of His Holy Spirit to His children comes with an added bonus of a perpetual Guide and Teacher who is always with us. If the Holy Spirit, the very embodiment of God, is with us all the time, then we have the wisdom of God with us all the time. Jesus promised the disciples that the presence of God Himself would stay with them, guiding them every step of the way and showing them what they were to do and say. He would remind them of everything He had ever taught them.

For us as His children, Jesus promises the same benefit. Every step of the way, He will guide us and show us what we need for that next step. Divine guidance comes through the promise of His Spirit. He is our Teacher, and He reminds us of what we need to know. When the Holy Spirit indwells us as Christian believers, we cannot go astray. He Himself is with us.

God keeps His Word; and though we sometimes doubt His presence because of His seeming silence in our lives, He is always there. He never leaves us, especially in our darkest times. We can count on His ever-present comfort and His divine wisdom.

—A. Koshy Muthalaly.

World Missions

> The omnipotent is Y'wa; . . .
> He has a perfect knowledge
> of all things! Y'wa created
> men at the beginning;
> He knows all things to the
> present time! . . . The earth is the
> treading place of the feet of Y'wa.
> And heaven is the place where He
> sits. He sees all things, and we
> are manifest to Him.
> (A Karen hymn)

An elder related the history of the Karen people: "O Children and grandchildren, formerly Y'wa loved the Karen nation above all others. But they transgressed His commands. . . . Because Y'wa cursed us, we are in our present afflicted state and have no books.

"But Y'wa will again have mercy on us, and again He will love us. Y'wa will save us again. It is [because we listened] to the language of Mu-kaw-lee (Satan) that we suffer" (Richardson, *Eternity in Their Hearts,* Regal).

The Karen are a minority, indigenous tribe living among the Burmese. Long have they been afflicted and harassed by their neighbors; so they chose to live in the jungles and the hills, away from others.

The Karen have very interesting beliefs and customs that have been passed down from generation to generation by means of oral tradition.

They believe in a supreme god and creator, whom they call "Y'wa" (note the similarity to the Hebrew "Yahweh").

They have a creation story that mirrors that of Adam and Eve in the Garden of Eden, who were deceived by an evil being. And many of their hymns have an uncanny resemblance to those in the book of Psalms.

At one point they had "the Book of Y'wa," but they lost it. They have been walking in darkness ever since. However, their sages tell them that one day Y'wa's book will return to them, and they eagerly anticipate its coming. Moreover, they believe that white foreigners, "the children of Y'wa," will bring it to them.

In 1813, an American missionary named Adoniram Judson settled in Rangoon, Burma. He learned the Burmese language and preached the gospel among the Buddhist Burmese—with little success. After seven years of preaching, he had only one convert to the Christian faith. Discouraged, he decided to focus on translating the Bible into Burmese.

One day, a Karen man named Ko Thah-byu came to him, looking for work. Judson began sharing the gospel with Ko. At first, Ko did not seem very interested. However, a short time later, Ko started asking specific questions about the origin of the gospel and about the foreigner's book. Suddenly, things clicked for Ko, as he realized that Judson's gospel message from the Bible was the returning of Y'wa's teachings!

Jesus said His Father would give another Comforter so "that he may abide with you for ever" (John 14:16). Surely, these words of Jesus electrified the Karen, who had waited so long for their reconciliation to Y'wa.

This aha moment did not end with one man. Ko learned to read so that he could study Y'wa's book. He and his missionary friends traveled all over Burma, from village to village, preaching God's truth. Hundreds of thousands of new Karen believers dotted the hills and jungles. These ecstatic new believers carried their joyful message all over Burma, even to other ethnic groups.

The testimonies of the Karen believers astounded their neighbors, who also had beliefs about the one true God. They too chose to return to Him through the redemptive work of Jesus.

—*Christina Futrell.*

The Jewish Aspect

The high holy season for the Jews concludes with the scrolls of the Law being carried around the synagogue. The scrolls contain the five books of Moses, called the Torah. Congregants eagerly reach out to touch the ornately covered scrolls and then bring the touch back to their lips.

Sad to say, this parading of the Torah scrolls is the best Judaism can offer with regard to honoring Scripture. If religious Jews actually read the simple truths of Scripture and let God's Spirit guide them, they would experience something much more meaningful.

Jesus promised a Comforter. Comfort of any kind is most welcome. When I am on the streets, going door-to-door with the gospel, I need a deeper understanding of the Comforter. I find it in the Latin word *Confortare*. The prefix *con-* (*com-*) means "with," and the root word, *fortis*, means "strong." Believers need the Spirit with them to fortify them and strengthen them for the battle for the souls of men.

God promised that the Jews would have a full ministry of the Holy Spirit. Distinct from the Father, the Spirit is the *Ruach* (roo-akh; spirit) *Elohim* (el-o-heem; God). "It is the activity, not the nature of the Spirit, that is emphasized in the Old Testament; and it is the Spirit's activity in man that is stressed" (Harrison, ed., *Baker's Dictionary of Theology*, Baker).

God's plan for the Jews is found in the new covenant revealed by the Prophet Jeremiah (Jer. 31:31-34). Jeremiah taught the indwelling of the Holy Spirit, the teaching of the Holy Spirit, regeneration, and forgiveness of sins. These verses convey the blessing in the new covenant that we in the body of Christ hold dear. Paul urged us to speak of these blessings in order for the Jews to be provoked to jealousy (Rom. 11:11) and to emulation (vs. 14).

The blessing of the Spirit's presence was not hidden in Old Testament days; it was just not widespread. Pharaoh's dream was able to be unlocked because the Spirit was in Joseph (Gen. 41:38). When Joshua was called to replace Moses, the great leader laid his hands upon him, and Joshua was filled with the Spirit (Deut. 34:9). David had the Spirit for definite ministry, but after his sin with Bathsheba, he feared it might be taken from him (Ps. 51:11). Ceremonial anointing of prophets, priests, and kings was emblematic of the promise to give these key, important leaders the information needed to carry out their ministries.

There was a highly significant ministry of the Spirit in the Old Testament. Both the New and Old Testaments bear clear evidence of holy men of God being moved by the Holy Spirit, who protected them from error. The indwelling Holy Spirit is definitely an experience of all the righteous in Christ's kingdom and the new covenant (Heb. 8:6-13).

Old testament prophets were able to say, "Truly I am full of power by the spirit of the Lord, and of judgment, and of might, to declare unto Jacob his transgression, and to Israel his sin" (Mic. 3:8). And after the Spirit was poured out at Pentecost, Peter said, "In the last days, saith God, I will pour out of my Spirit upon all flesh: . . . and on my servants and on my handmaidens I will pour out in those days of my Spirit; and they shall prophesy" (Acts 2:16-18; cf. Joel 2:28-29).

—Lyle P. Murphy.

Guiding the Superintendent

The Bible is full of promises to the saints. There are far too many to number, although some Bible researchers have tried. According to II Peter 1:4, God has given us "exceeding great and precious promises," each of which will be fulfilled according to the Lord's timetable. This week's lesson inspires hope in the faithfulness of God, the great Promise-Keeper, and the assurance of His love and continuous presence.

DEVOTIONAL OUTLINE

1. Love invokes God's presence (John 14:15-18). In verse 14 of this chapter, Jesus affirmed that He would honor any request the disciples made in His name. All He asked of them was the same thing that He asks of every believer—that is, to love Him with all our hearts. Because we love Him, we walk in His Word. Our obedience is undergirded by the indwelling of the Holy Spirit, our Helper who knows the truth because He is truth. He leads faithful believers into righteousness and truth.

Man has neither the strength nor the will to submit to God. The Holy Spirit convicts the sinner's heart; otherwise, deliverance cannot take place. But the Spirit abides in the heart that is completely surrendered to God, mind, body, and soul. Man is God's precious possession, the apple of His eye. He would never abandon His creation or leave us defenseless targets for the evil one.

2. Love promotes obedience (John 14:19-21). Jesus' time on earth was quickly diminishing, but His determination to prepare His disciples for the Great Commission did not wane. To that end, Jesus taught them on numerous occasions that although He would be crucified, He would be raised alive on the third day. All who believed in Him would be given life everlasting (cf. John 6:47). Scripture teaches that God's ways are far above our ways (cf. Isa. 55:9), so it is understandable that these men needed clarity and comfort. Christ assured His followers that their love and loyalty to His commandments connected them to Him and to God the Father. This bond gave them full revelation of the Person of Jesus Christ, God's Son.

3. Love reveals the Father and the Son (John 14:22-26). The world is the enemy of all godliness. The darkness of this world is in utter contrast with Jesus, the True Light. God's Word calls believers into intimacy with the Father and the Son. Christ promises to reveal Himself to those who love God and commit to His will. The world cannot experience God in this manner, as light has no communion with darkness (cf. Eph. 5:11). Unbelievers do not recognize Christ as Saviour and Lord or the teachings of God's Word. Therefore the rich blessing of the promise of the Holy Spirit as Teacher and Advocate is not available to them.

AGE-GROUP EMPHASES

Children: Children cannot easily grasp the work and Person of the Holy Spirit, but they can understand what it means to have a loving, constant friend.

Youths: Teach them that in times of difficulty, they are never alone. The Holy Spirit advocates for them on earth, and Jesus advocates for them in heaven.

Adults: Love for God is not necessarily demonstrated in the daily doing of religion. Encourage your adults to allow the Holy Spirit to lead them to works that are in keeping with God's Word.

—Jane E. Campbell.

LESSON 3   MARCH 15, 2015

Scripture Lesson Text

JOHN 16:4 But these things have I told you, that when the time shall come, ye may remember that I told you of them. And these things I said not unto you at the beginning, because I was with you.

5 But now I go my way to him that sent me; and none of you asketh me, Whither goest thou?

6 But because I have said these things unto you, sorrow hath filled your heart.

7 Nevertheless I tell you the truth; It is expedient for you that I go away: for if I go not away, the Comforter will not come unto you; but if I depart, I will send him unto you.

8 And when he is come, he will reprove the world of sin, and of righteousness, and of judgment:

9 Of sin, because they believe not on me;

10 Of righteousness, because I go to my Father, and ye see me no more;

11 Of judgment, because the prince of this world is judged.

12 I have yet many things to say unto you, but ye cannot bear them now.

13 Howbeit when he, the Spir′it of truth, is come, he will guide you into all truth: for he shall not speak of himself; but whatsoever he shall hear, *that* shall he speak: and he will shew you things to come.

14 He shall glorify me: for he shall receive of mine, and shall shew *it* unto you.

15 All things that the Father hath are mine: therefore said I, that he shall take of mine, and shall shew *it* unto you.

NOTES

The Spirit of Truth

Lesson: John 16:4-15

Read: John 16:4-15

TIME: A.D. 30　　　　　　　　　　　　　　　　　　　　　PLACE: Jerusalem

GOLDEN TEXT—"When he, the Spirit of truth, is come, he will guide you into all truth: for he shall not speak of himself; but whatsoever he shall hear, that shall he speak" (John 16:13).

Introduction

Sheep are by nature gentle and defenseless. They are known for their flocking and following instinct. In the absence of wise guidance, they have been known to wander into disastrous situations. They have to be led to food and water, and if one gets lost, it has no instinct for finding its way home.

Thus, when biblical writers describe people as "sheep without a shepherd," they are depicting a pathetic situation.

Jesus declared Himself the Good Shepherd who would give His life for His sheep (John 10:11). But His death would temporarily leave His disciples without direction (Matt. 26:31)—scattered, aimless, and vulnerable. So He spoke to them frankly about their plight. He also gave them assurance that the Holy Spirit would replace Him and provide the leadership they needed in a hostile world.

LESSON OUTLINE

I. **MATTERS RELATED TO JESUS' DEPARTURE**—John 16:4-7

II. **MATTERS RELATED TO THE SPIRIT'S COMING**—John 16:8-15

Exposition: Verse by Verse

MATTERS RELATED TO JESUS' DEPARTURE

JOHN 16:4 But these things have I told you, that when the time shall come, ye may remember that I told you of them. And these things I said not unto you at the beginning, because I was with you.

5 But now I go my way to him that sent me; and none of you asketh me, Whither goest thou?

6 But because I have said these things unto you, sorrow hath filled your heart.

7 Nevertheless I tell you the truth; It is expedient for you that I go away: for if I go not away, the Comforter

will not come unto you; but if I depart, I will send him unto you.

The prospect of persecution (John 16:4). Our lesson begins at the end of an extended passage (15:18-27; 16:1-3) in which Jesus forewarned His disciples of coming persecution. It was something they should expect, for the world already hated Him. He had exposed sin, and people resented it (cf. 3:19-20; 7:7). And if they hated Jesus, His disciples could expect no better, for their lives and message would condemn the world (Matt. 10:24-25; II Tim. 3:12).

Jesus was telling the disciples this in advance to keep them from illusions that would later cause them to stumble (John 16:1). They would be expelled from synagogues, which meant ostracism from Jewish society. In fact, some would be killed in the name of religion (vs. 2). Saul of Tarsus later testified that he persecuted Christians because of misguided zeal for God (Acts 26:9-11; Gal. 1:13-14; Phil. 3:6; I Tim. 1:13). Persecutors invoked God's name, but they did not know Him (John 16:3).

Jesus was telling the disciples this so that when the hard times came, they would remember His warnings. They could face opposition with faith, not dismay. He had earlier foretold persecution for the disciples in general terms (Matt. 5:11; 10:17; Luke 6:22), but now He provided more specifics on what they could expect.

Jesus' reason for waiting was "because I was with you" (John 16:4). This is a striking statement because, technically speaking, He was *still* with them. But in this discourse, He was projecting Himself to the time when He would have returned to His Father (cf. 17:4, 11-12). He looked to the day when His personal presence would no longer shield the apostles from His enemies' venom.

The sorrow of separation (John 16:5-6). Jesus now had to deal with the heaviness of heart that had fallen upon the disciples. His statement that none of them had asked Him where He was going at first seems at odds with the facts. Had Simon Peter not asked this very question a short time earlier (13:36)? Had Thomas not asked something similar (14:5)? They had, indeed, but only with the narrow focus of His immediate separation from them. They had no curiosity about the divine plan of which His departure was a part.

But now Jesus clarified that plan: He was going back to the One who had sent Him, a reference to His Heavenly Father. Throughout His earthly ministry, Jesus repeatedly expressed a consciousness that He was here on His Father's mission (cf. Luke 4:18, 43; John 8:42). That mission was, first, to reveal what the Father was like and thus glorify Him before mankind (John 1:18; 5:36; 11:42; 17:4). Second, it was to bring salvation to men (3:17; 17:3). All that He did was designed to draw attention to the Father.

Once that mission was accomplished, His role on the earth was finished. It was time for the apostles to carry forward His work (cf. John 17:18-21; 20:21). Yet, ironically, they did not yet understand their role, and they were emotionally unprepared for it. Jesus knew this, for He added, "But because I have said these things unto you, sorrow hath filled your heart" (16:6). What was included in "these things"?

Jesus had said several things that evening that had unsettled them. He had announced that a betrayer was in their midst. He had told them He would be leaving them. He had prophesied Peter's threefold denial. And now He revealed that persecution lay ahead. He had also taught many encouraging things, but it is unlikely that these made much of an impression. The disciples were preoccupied with personal grief and could see nothing beyond it.

Surely there is a lesson in this for us. When bad news, uncertainty, disappointment, and tragedy crowd in upon us, we can see only disaster ahead. We become so absorbed in our own problems that we genuinely believe God has forsaken us. The promises of Scripture ring hollow, and our prayers seem unheard. We have lost our vision of His larger plan for our life or for the world.

The necessity of departure (John 16:7). Jesus attempted to unveil this larger plan: "Nevertheless I tell you the truth; It is expedient for you that I go away." Far from being a tragedy for His disciples, Jesus' departure would be to their advantage. As we now know, without His death, resurrection, and ascension, there would be no gospel of salvation. There would be no High Priest to intercede for His own. And there would be no glorified Saviour to send forth the Holy Spirit.

It was this last point that the Lord emphasized. The Comforter (Helper) would not come if Jesus remained with them. And why would this be a disadvantage? Would the exchange of one divine Person for another make any difference? Yes, indeed, for if Jesus remained here in His body, He would be confined to one place at a time, and His deeds would also be limited in time and space. But divine power could be multiplied if distributed among all His disciples (cf. John 14:12; Acts 1:8).

MATTERS RELATED TO THE SPIRIT'S COMING

8 And when he is come, he will reprove the world of sin, and of righteousness, and of judgment:

9 Of sin, because they believe not on me;

10 Of righteousness, because I go to my Father, and ye see me no more;

11 Of judgment, because the prince of this world is judged.

12 I have yet many things to say unto you, but ye cannot bear them now.

13 Howbeit when he, the Spirit of truth, is come, he will guide you into all truth: for he shall not speak of himself; but whatsoever he shall hear, that shall he speak: and he will shew you things to come.

14 He shall glorify me: for he shall receive of mine, and shall shew it unto you.

15 All things that the Father hath are mine: therefore said I, that he shall take of mine, and shall shew it unto you.

His convicting work in the world (John 16:8). One of the Spirit's prominent ministries would be to "reprove the world of sin, and of righteousness, and of judgment." "Reprove" refers to exposing all the facts so as to pronounce a guilty verdict before God. Often it is translated "convince" (cf. I Cor. 14:24; Titus 1:9; Jas. 2:9; Jude 1:15). Conviction does not always result in conversion, but conversion is not possible without it.

The conviction brought by the Spirit would apply to three areas—sin, righteousness, and judgment. He would bring sinners to realize that their misdeeds were offenses against a holy God, not just human standards. They would be confronted with the divine righteousness that made their behavior sinful. And He would reveal to them the awful judgment to which their sin exposed them.

The reasons for His convicting work (John 16:9-11). The Spirit will convict of sin, said Jesus, because of their refusal to believe in Him. Unbelief has ever lain at the heart of sin, for it rejects whatever revelation God has given (cf. Gen. 2:17; 3:4-6) and acts contrary to it. This unbelief reached its climax when men rejected His final revelation—His Son (Heb. 1:1-2; 2:2-4).

Jesus gave indisputable proof, in word and deed, that He is the divine Messiah. Yet His enemies rejected every shred of evidence He gave and labeled Him a blasphemer (cf. Mark 2:6-7; 3:22; 14:63-64). As in Jesus' parable of the wicked tenant farmers, they killed the Son they should have embraced (12:6-8). Now they had no cloak to cover the nakedness of their unbelief. And neither do those today who brazenly reject the Spirit's witness of Christ.

Second, Jesus said the Spirit will convict the world "of righteousness, because I go to my Father, and ye see me no more" (John 16:10). Jesus' generation judged Him to be unrighteous because of the disgraceful death He died (Luke 22:37; Gal. 3:13). But He was vindicated by His resurrection, ascension, and glorification. The Father's reception of Jesus at His right hand proved Him to be His own righteous Son (Acts 2:36; 3:14-15; 5:30-32; cf. Isa. 53:11-12).

Through this message the Spirit convicts sinners of their incorrect views of Jesus. Not only did He suffer innocently for others' sins; He is also the standard of righteousness by which all must be judged. None can afford to ignore Him.

Third, the Spirit convicts "of judgment, because the prince of this world is judged" (John 16:11). In this respect, again, a massive misconception accompanied Jesus' death. Some who witnessed it may have assumed He was being judged by God and condemned to an untimely death. Others may have lamented the triumph of evil in the death of an innocent victim. But neither of these conclusions would have been correct.

Instead, it was the powers of evil that were defeated by the Cross. Satan, here referred to as "the prince of this world" (John 16:11; cf. 12:31; 14:30), is said to be "judged." The Greek tense indicates a settled condition—"stands judged." Through Jesus' death and resurrection, the power of sin and death has been broken, and Satan's kingdom stands condemned (Col. 2:14-15; Heb. 2:14; I John 3:8). Though he is still feverishly active (I Pet. 5:8), Satan's doom is fixed, and he will be punished at God's chosen time (Rev. 20:10).

Satan's defeat is a key element in God's message to sinners, for it reminds them that their own sin is under His judgment as well. The Holy Spirit uses it to convict them and prepare them to receive salvation (cf. Acts 17:30-31).

His revelation of the truth (John 16:12-13). "I have yet many things to say unto you" reminded the disciples that Jesus' revelation to them was still incomplete. It would do no good to pursue these things at present, for "ye cannot bear them now," Jesus said. Their immaturity made it impossible for them to appreciate His fuller revelation. They still had no understanding of the necessity of His death and resurrection. They were overwhelmed by grief at the loss of their hopes for an immediate earthly kingdom.

His fuller revelation had to await the coming of the Spirit of truth. Here, then, is a second ministry of the Holy Spirit: besides convicting the world, He would guide the disciples into the full truth. The apostles would come to know in-depth the things Jesus could teach them only in elementary form now. In ordinary terms, to guide a person is to lead him to a literal destination (cf. Luke 6:39; Rev. 7:17). But one can also figuratively give guidance in understanding (cf. Acts 8:31).

Here the Spirit is said to guide the apostles into "all truth" (John 16:13). This reads, more accurately, "all the truth." It is not a promise to give understanding in every realm of human knowledge. It relates to a specific realm of truth we commonly call the "spiritual"—truth related to God's redemptive work in Christ. He would not speak "of (from) himself"—not independently or on His own authority. He would speak only "whatsoever he shall hear" from the Heavenly Father concerning His Son.

He also would show them things that were to come. These included, most immediately, things that lay ahead after Jesus' death, resurrection, and ascension—the very things they presently did not understand. But it also related to truths concerning His return.

For the apostles, this promise was fulfilled in their post-Pentecost ability to teach the church and to write the books that would nourish God's people. Thus, our New Testament is the product of the Spirit's teaching ministry to the apostles. In addition, He continues to teach us by enlightening our minds to understand and apply scriptural truth (I Cor. 2:9-15; I John 2:27).

His relationship to Jesus (John 16:14-15). Lest the disciples think the Holy Spirit's teaching would compete with His own, Jesus added, "He shall glorify me: for he shall receive of mine, and shall shew it unto you." "Receive of mine" means to take the truth possessed by and related to Jesus. The Spirit would not seek to magnify His own Person.

The Holy Spirit is not visible as Jesus once was, but His presence in the world is no less real. He is active in both convicting sinners and teaching saints the truths of Christ.

—Robert E. Wenger.

QUESTIONS

1. What conditions would Jesus' disciples face after His departure?
2. What mission did Jesus have to accomplish while on earth?
3. What was the disciples' outlook at the Last Supper? Why?
4. Why was Jesus' departure an advantage to His disciples instead of a tragedy?
5. Why could God accomplish more in the world in Jesus' absence?
6. What ministry does the Holy Spirit have to the unbelieving world?
7. What was the major sin of Jesus' generation in their relationship with Him?
8. What is Satan's present status before God? What should this tell sinners?
9. Why was the Spirit's enlightenment essential for the apostles?
10. What should be the purpose of any Spirit-directed ministry?

—Robert E. Wenger.

Preparing to Teach the Lesson

This week's lesson expands on last week's concerning the coming ministry of the Holy Spirit. We saw how Jesus promised that the comforting Spirit would come to be our Teacher. Our hearts are next assured by Christ's words foretelling that God's Spirit will effectively meet particular needs we face today.

TODAY'S AIM

Facts: to understand Jesus' fourfold prophecy concerning the Holy Spirit's ministry.

Principle: to see how Jesus' words directly affect our daily lives as we serve Him.

Application: to serve our Lord faithfully so that we glorify Him.

INTRODUCING THE LESSON

John 14:1 through 16:33 forms a unit in Jesus' instructions to His disciples. He began with words of comfort in chapter 14, including the promise of the Holy Spirit, which we saw in the previous lesson. Jesus then progressed to words of admonition in chapter 15 as He exhorted His disciples to abide in Him. In chapter 16, Jesus advanced to words of prophecy concerning why His followers needed the Holy Spirit.

DEVELOPING THE LESSON

1. The Spirit's ministry to the persecuted (John 16:4). In verses 1-3, Jesus informed His followers that they should expect persecution and that it might come from people who actually thought they were doing God's will. Verse 4 explains why Jesus told His followers they needed to know this. It was so that their faith in His words would be firmly established. He had not said this earlier. He waited until He was ready to leave them because, up until then, He had been with them, His presence virtually shielding them from all animosity. In the coming persecution, they would need the Holy Spirit's strength.

2. The Spirit's ministry in Christ's absence (John 16:5-7). The words "But now" set forth a contrast to what Jesus had just said. He would return to the Father. That should have prompted the disciples to question where He was going. Their neglect to do so at this time showed they were more focused on themselves than on Christ. Earlier, Peter had inquired (13:36), and so had Thomas (14:5); but now they only saw and felt the sorrow that filled their hearts (16:6). They thought only of themselves, not of Christ.

In spite of the fact that Jesus was going away, He had vital information for them. What He told them was "the truth" (John 16:7). It was "expedient," that is, to their advantage, that He depart. It was better for them if they did not have to depend on a visibly present Lord. When Jesus left, He would send the "Comforter."

The Spirit comes to conduct His ministry in all believers as a result of Jesus' atoning work, which culminated with His ascension. While on earth, Jesus could only be in one physical place at a time, but the Spirit indwells all believers and multiplies Christ's ministry.

3. The Spirit's ministry in convicting the world (John 16:8-11). The Spirit also brings conviction upon the world. This passage is the only one in the New Testament that delineates that ministry of reproving "the world of sin, and of righteousness, and of judgment."

Jesus identified the particular area of sin of which the Spirit convicts. He convicts of the sin of not believing in Jesus Christ. As we witness to unbelievers, we must remember this and not try to bring conviction for their lifestyle or habits. We must focus on their need to believe in Christ. The Spirit also convicts concerning the need for righteousness. In order for anyone to reach the Father, that person must have Christ's righteousness, which comes only by faith. Finally, the Spirit convicts concerning the certainty of judgment.

4. The Spirit's ministry in individual lives (John 16:12-15). Jesus' teaching to His disciples was not complete; much more needed to be said. But the disciples were not able to bear that right then. This implies they were not spiritually ready to receive the additional teaching. The "Spirit of truth," therefore, would continue the teaching ministry that Christ began. He would guide them into "all truth"—that is, everything concerning Jesus, His work, and His continuing ministry through them.

The Spirit will not speak on His own; that is, He will not originate anything new. Rather, He will teach that which is consistent with what the Father and Son taught during Christ's earthly ministry. Beyond that, the Spirit will show what is to come. This has in mind the entire revealed truth of Christianity, not just prophecy.

The purpose of the Holy Spirit's ministry is not to honor Himself. His ministry is specifically stated to be Christ-centered. He will receive from Christ that which is Christ's and show it to Christ's followers.

Lest some disciples were to perceive a dichotomy between the Son and the Father, Christ added that the unity of the Father and the Son is fully maintained. Therefore, when the Spirit sets forth the things of Christ, He also sets forth those of the Father.

ILLUSTRATING THE LESSON

Christ sent the Holy Spirit to guide us into all the revealed truth found in His Word.

THE HOLY SPIRIT GUIDES US

IN GOD'S TRUTH

CONCLUDING THE LESSON

The Spirit convicts unbelievers, indwells each believer, helps us in any type of persecution, and guides us into all the revealed truth of Scripture. The ultimate purpose of the Holy Spirit is to glorify Christ; as we faithfully serve the Lord, we too will glorify Him. That is our task until Jesus comes again.

ANTICIPATING THE NEXT LESSON

Next week's lesson will enable us to better understand the concern Jesus had for His disciples and the Holy Spirit's ministry through them.

—R. Larry Overstreet.

PRACTICAL POINTS

1. In God's time, we will understand fully those things that now seem confusing (John 16:4-5).
2. Never allow any present circumstance to distract you from God's larger plan (vss. 6-7).
3. While Jesus was limited physically on earth, the Holy Spirit is available and present with every believer, anyplace, anytime.
4. The Holy Spirit convicts men of sin and leads believers to repentance and righteousness (vss. 8-10).
5. Satan has been judged and cannot condemn the believer (vs. 11).
6. God will reveal only as much of His truth as we are able to handle at the time (vss. 12-15).

—Cheryl Y. Powell.

RESEARCH AND DISCUSSION

1. What was keeping Jesus' disciples from understanding what He was telling them in John 16?
2. Why was Jesus teaching His disciples things that would grieve them at this point in His ministry?
3. When has Jesus taught you things that have been difficult to understand or accept?
4. What is the threefold ministry of the Holy Spirit (vss. 8-15)?
5. What is the sin of which the Holy Spirit convicts the world?
6. What would have happened if Jesus had never left His disciples (cf. 14:1-4; 16:5-7)?
7. What is the truth into which the Holy Spirit guides us?

—Cheryl Y. Powell.

ILLUSTRATED HIGH POINTS

I go away

A number of years ago, my wife and I drove our oldest daughter to college for registration and getting settled into her dorm room. Finally, it was time for us to say our good-byes and go back home. We all shed some tears in the process, but we knew it was best for her to transition into college. A whole new life was in the offing for her.

Jesus also knew that it was best for His disciples, even in their sorrow, that He go back to heaven after He finished His work on earth through His death on the cross, burial, and bodily resurrection. It was a necessary transition for them, for something even better for His disciples was about to happen. The Holy Spirit would come to be their Encourager and Teacher.

Reprove the world

There is a great emphasis today on physical health. We certainly need to take care of our physical bodies. But in doing so, have we put our spiritual health on the back burner of our lives? The Holy Spirit convicts of sin, righteousness, and judgment. Is that happening in our lives?

The Spirit of truth

As I look back on my years of formal education, I can easily remember the teachers who were my favorites. Their knowledge of the subject, their passion for teaching, and their interest in the students made them special. However, I now have only memories of their contributions to my life. On the other hand, the Holy Spirit is with me presently and eternally. He guides the believer into all truth. The Holy Spirit gives the believer insight from the Word of God.

—Paul R. Bawden.

Golden Text Illuminated

"When he, the Spirit of truth, is come, he will guide you into all truth: for he shall not speak of himself; but whatsoever he shall hear, that shall he speak" (John 16:13).

The Holy Spirit, who would come to indwell and empower the Lord's followers, was a central theme in Jesus' Upper Room Discourse (John 14—16).

Since at this point the disciples did not even fully grasp the concept of Jesus' leaving them, it is doubtful they understood a great deal about the Holy Spirit and the ministry He would have among them in the days ahead. Yet Jesus made it clear that the Holy Spirit, who would come to them, would guide them "into all truth."

Such would be expected from the One Jesus called the "Spirit of truth" (John 14:17). Jesus referred to Himself as "the truth" (vs. 6), and the One who was equally God and would be present with Jesus' followers in His absence would also be characterized by truth.

While the Spirit leads us to properly understand the revelation He Himself has inspired and had recorded in Scripture (cf. I Cor. 2:10-16; I John 2:27), this promise was more specifically for the disciples, or apostles, of Jesus. They could not at that time bear everything that Jesus wanted to teach them (John 16:12). However, the Spirit would see to it that they were directed into "all truth" (vs. 13).

This was a crucial ministry of the Holy Spirit. He would not only bring to the disciples' remembrance what Jesus had said and what these words meant (John 14:26), but He would also "reveal prophetic truths to them" (Kent, *Light in the Darkness,* BMH). This was new revelation that built upon Jesus' teaching and fully equips the church for ministry. "All of these truths are embodied in the New Testament, which was received by the church on the authority of the apostles."

To this, Jesus added that the Holy Spirit would not "speak of himself." Rather, He would be a mouthpiece who simply conveyed to the apostles what He heard.

"It is not said whether He hears them from the Father or the Son, but the point is probably not material. The emphasis . . . is on the Spirit rather than on either of the other Persons. This expression will indicate His harmony with Them. He is not originating something radically new, but leading men in accordance with the teaching already given from the Father and the Son" (Morris, *The Gospel According to John,* Eerdmans).

The Holy Spirit should neither be ignored on the one hand nor overemphasized on the other. He is the Third Person of the Godhead, but His ministry is to glorify God the Son (John 16:14). Any Spirit-led movement will place the focus properly on the One whom the Spirit glorifies: Jesus Christ.

—Jarl K. Waggoner.

Heart of the Lesson

We all wrestle with speaking the truth every day. We all know that lying is unethical. Even little children know that they have done wrong when they tell us lies in an effort to get out of immediate trouble. God wants Christian believers to speak the truth at all times. When we lie, it hurts Him deeply. It is as if we did not trust Him to take care of us. It is a slap in the face of Almighty God. The Bible tells us that His Word is truth, and we are called to follow His Word (cf. John 17:17).

1. Jesus' message (John 16:4). What would you want to tell the world if you were leaving the earth in a little while? That is something to think about seriously. Jesus stressed to His disciples that He had something important to tell them before He left the earth and that they were to listen intently. Because Jesus was leaving His disciples in a very short time, there was a sense of urgency about His message. It was good news about the Comforter.

Jesus had a message for the disciples that was good news for them. It was about the Person who would remain with them after Christ had left. The Holy Spirit would be with them always, for all time. Jesus' leaving would open the door for the power of the Holy Spirit to work in their lives. It was a dawning of a new age of following the Master. When we understand the power of the Christian message about the gift of the Spirit for us, it will transform our lives for the better.

2. The Holy Spirit's mission (John 16:5-11). It is important to see that the Holy Spirit was sent to us from the Father. He was sent with us in mind. When the Spirit came, it was to be the beginning of an age of righteousness for those who put their faith in Him and receive His ministry of help and healing. The Spirit would show the world how to put their trust in Jesus, for it is the Spirit's work to help the world look to Jesus. He points us to Him.

When we look to Jesus, we must realize that it is because the Holy Spirit works in our hearts that this trust in Him becomes possible. When we recognize the work of the Holy Spirit in our lives, we must heed His gentle nudging in our hearts. It is His way of pointing us to the Saviour. His presence in us is the holy presence of divine truth that plants itself in our hearts.

3. The Holy Spirit's guidance (John 16:12-15). One of the most important tasks of the Holy Spirit in the lives of those who believe in Jesus is to guide them into all truth. Jesus was essentially telling His disciples to listen to the voice of the Spirit, for He would always speak the words of God's truth to them. The Spirit is the Advocate of truth, for He speaks for God the Father Himself. He reflects for us who God is. We can never go wrong if we listen to the inner nudging of the Holy Spirit.

The work of the Holy Spirit can be exciting. For believers, this means that we ought to wait in eager excitement daily to see what the Spirit will reveal to us next about what He is going to do in our lives. He shows us the nature of God. He takes what belongs to God and opens up His treasures for His children. Too often the work of God's Spirit is either forgotten or misunderstood. He reveals the truth of God for us, for He is the very presence of the truth of God.

—A. Koshy Muthalaly.

World Missions

Younathan grew up in the Arabian Gulf and had a loving family. He studied the Koran in school and was taught all of Islam's teachings. He believed his religion was the true path to God, as all practicing Muslims do.

However, Younathan had many questions about God that could not be answered. Why was God so far away when he needed God's help most? Why did He create humans with a sinful nature and then condemn them to hell? Younathan became disillusioned, and a wall of anger went up between him and God.

One day, Younathan met a man from South Asia named David. At first he made fun of him, because that was the habit of his friends—to make fun of South Asians. In an attempt to stop the harassment, David befriended Younathan, and they eventually became best friends.

David was not a Christian; but his parents were, and they held Bible studies in their home. One evening Younathan attended their meeting and watched a film about Jesus. He made fun of Jesus and said insulting things.

When David became a Christian, Younathan got very upset. He was jealous that his friend had found something he did not have—peace and joy. So he thought to himself, *What is this Christianity thing, anyway?*

One night, Younathan had a dream. In the dream, Jesus said to him, "Come to Me, and I will show you the way, the truth, and the life."

In Islamic and Arab culture, dreams are very important. Dreams and their meanings are taken very seriously. God has used dreams to convey His message to people throughout biblical history. He still speaks through them today.

After his dream, Younathan was excited to know more. He began going to church with David and reading the Bible as one who is thirsty for truth. He gave his life to Jesus. When he took communion for the first time, the pastor said, "Younathan, this is the blood of Jesus, that was shed for you." Younathan was deeply touched and filled with God's presence. John 16:13 says, "When he, the Spirit of truth, is come, he will guide you into all truth."

Younathan now lives by the truth he received through the Holy Spirit. After being away for eight years, he is returning home to share this truth with his people.

—Christina Futrell.

The Jewish Aspect

Judaism has no teaching of a divine Son of God, and it no longer has a biblical understanding of the Holy Spirit. Some orthodox groups may, however, speak of the Spirit of God as an additional mode of the Father's ministry.

Evangelism by churches often involves inviting neighborhood residents to come to a service on Sunday. Hopefully, one may develop enough information from the resident to learn whether he has trusted Christ for salvation. This is God's Spirit in action.

I worked with Pastor Roy going door-to-door all afternoon. He suggested we close with a visit to an aged couple he had grown to love.

Joe and Josie were delighted to invite us in. They were of Italian extraction and were full of warmth and goodwill. We shared pleasantries, and when it seemed time to leave, we asked whether we might read some Scripture. They readily agreed.

For its clear salvation message, John 3 was chosen. I read aloud, but before I got to verse 3, we were amazed to hear Joe reciting the passage from memory! We paused to hear how that was possible. He related that as a boy, he had been placed in an orphanage in a midwestern city. Each Sunday, a local church sent a bus to the orphanage to pick up boys for Sunday school. Joe's family was of a different faith, but he got on the bus anyway. At the time, the Sunday school offered a new Bible to any boy who memorized the entire third chapter of John. "Josie, get my Bible, please," Joe requested. The Bible was well-worn.

When we finished reading the passage, we asked whether Joe had been given some instruction on what it meant. He said, "No. Just about that time, an uncle in Chicago agreed to take me into his home, so I never went back to Sunday school."

We talked to Joe and Josie about God's great plan of everlasting salvation in John 3 (especially verses 15-18). They seemed to grasp the facts of the new birth (vs. 3). They were clearly ready to trust Jesus for salvation and an eternity with God. Joe and Josie knelt with us and asked Jesus to forgive their sins.

This great couple became faithful in the pastor's church. Joe passed to his eternal reward a couple of years after that special decision. Until her death, Josie continued to witness to lost loved ones in the face of great persecution.

Our theme for today is the Spirit of truth. Joe and Josie represent a great ministry of the Holy Spirit, who planted the gospel seed deep in a small boy's heart. It bore fruit more than sixty years later! It was God's timing all the way.

A similar incident happened about

two years later. I accompanied a different pastor, who said, "Let's make one more call—next to the parsonage." "Choc," an American Indian, was at home. He had become as vile as the alcohol he drank. He gave me time to give a short testimony. I related the joy of sins forgiven in the blood of Christ. We did not feel welcome, but the next Sunday, Choc came to church, broken spiritually, and was saved.

—Lyle P. Murphy.

Guiding the Superintendent

DEVOTIONAL OUTLINE

1. Jesus prepared His disciples (John 16:4-6). There is a time and a purpose for all things (cf. Eccles. 3:1). The time when the disciples would endure great suffering had come. Jesus' presence had shielded them from the fiery darts of scorn, but it was time for His return to God. He loved His disciples and was compelled to remind them of His inevitable departure and to prepare them for the conflicts to come. This disheartened them.

They were worried about themselves at the prospect of losing their Leader. Their priorities may seem self-centered and shortsighted, but nevertheless entirely human. Christ offered specific knowledge of all that would come to pass; but being overwhelmed with sorrow, the disciples forgot that His stay on earth was temporary.

2. The truth comforts and convicts (John 16:7-11). One of God's attributes is His omnipresence. God as Spirit is everywhere present at the same time and at all times. This is profitable to believers who are at war against sin.

Jesus exemplified righteousness and true holiness, and believers should do likewise, thereby convicting the world of its unrighteousness. There is a way called the "way of holiness; the unclean shall not pass over it." (Isa. 35:8).

3. The truth builds faith and glorifies God (John 16:12-15). Roberta Martin of the Roberta Martin Singers wrote "He Knows Just How Much You Can Bear." The first verse says:

> We are our heavenly Father's children,
> And we all know that He loves us one and all;
> Yet there are times when we find we answer
> Another's voice and call;
> If we are willing, He will teach us,
> His voice only to obey no matter where,
> And He knows; yes, He knows,
> Just how much we can bear.

Christ recognized the strengths and weaknesses of His disciples. They needed the indwelling of the Holy Spirit to gradually teach all He wanted them to know. Believers accomplish more by yielding to His voice and not another. Our Heavenly Father proved His love. He will never send anyone into our lives to mislead us. The Spirit of truth will guide us through God's Word. Our response is to bring all glory to God our Father.

AGE-GROUP EMPHASES

Children: Explain the truth versus a lie. Teach that God honors the truth and hates lies.

Youths: Help them understand that the Holy Spirit has His own personality and specific work. Teach them not to hesitate to seek to be filled with the Holy Spirit.

Adults: Matters of personal health, economic pressures, and family issues often consume adults. Remind them that they are not alone. God loves us and knows just how much His children can bear.

—Jane E. Campbell.

LESSON 4   MARCH 22, 2015

Scripture Lesson Text

JOHN 20:19 Then the same day at evening, being the first *day* of the week, when the doors were shut where the disciples were assembled for fear of the Jews, came Je'sus and stood in the midst, and saith unto them, Peace *be* unto you.

20 And when he had so said, he shewed unto them *his* hands and his side. Then were the disciples glad, when they saw the Lord.

21 Then said Je'sus to them again, Peace *be* unto you: as *my* Father hath sent me, even so send I you.

22 And when he had said this, he breathed on *them,* and saith unto them, Receive ye the Ho'ly Ghost:

23 Whose soever sins ye remit, they are remitted unto them; *and* whose soever *sins* ye retain, they are retained.

NOTES

Receive the Holy Spirit

Lesson: John 20:19-23

Read: John 20:19-23; Acts 1:4-8; 2:1-4

TIME: A.D. 30   PLACE: Jerusalem

GOLDEN TEXT—"When he had said this, he breathed on them, and saith unto them, Receive ye the Holy Ghost" (John 20:22).

Introduction

An athletic team will perform to its maximum only under the direction of a competent coach. Such a person needs to have more than zeal for the sport. He or she should understand the rules of the game, the roles of various positions on the team, and the physical requirements the players must have. A good coach must have aptitude and background experience in dealing with players, subordinates, and officials. He should have learned to control his emotions.

Those who lead a college also need to prepare themselves for the challenges they will face. Board members and administrators should be thoroughly familiar with the acceptable goals of higher education, the financial burdens it will bring, and the best ways of attracting students.

Leadership in the Christian church requires preparation as well, though this includes a spiritual dimension that purely human enterprises do not. When Jesus was about to leave the earth, He sought to prepare His apostles for that leadership over His church. Though they seemed unlikely leaders, our lesson this week reveals how Jesus prepared them for that task.

LESSON OUTLINE

I. JESUS' APPEARANCE—John 20:19-20

II. JESUS' COMMISSION—John 20:21-23

Exposition: Verse by Verse

JESUS' APPEARANCE

JOHN 20:19 Then the same day at evening, being the first day of the week, when the doors were shut where the disciples were assembled for fear of the Jews, came Jesus and stood in the midst, and saith unto them, Peace be unto you.

20 And when he had so said, he shewed unto them his hands and his

March 22, 2015

side. Then were the disciples glad, when they saw the Lord.

The greeting (John 20:19). The events in this passage occurred on the day of Jesus' resurrection. It was a momentous day. Women bearing spices to the tomb found it empty and were told by angels that Jesus had risen. Jesus Himself then appeared to Mary Magdalene, the other women, Simon Peter, and the two disciples on the road to Emmaus.

The rest of Jesus' disciples had heard reports of these appearances, but at the beginning they considered them to be "idle tales" (Luke 24:11) and refused to believe them. Perhaps they were changing their minds somewhat by the time they heard from Simon Peter and the men from Emmaus (vss. 33-35), but they clearly were not expecting Jesus' resurrection.

This seems rather remarkable, for Jesus had foretold His resurrection several times (cf. Matt. 16:21; 17:9, 23; 20:19). The Jewish officials certainly had taken this claim seriously, for although they did not believe Jesus would actually rise, they took precautions against the disciples' possible theft of His body (27:62-64).

But they need not have feared. The disciples were not in a state of mind to believe Jesus would rise or to steal His body to make it appear that He had. Resurrection was the furthest thing from their minds (cf. Mark 16:14). To them Jesus was gone permanently, and so were their hopes for the kingdom. In fact, they now feared for their own lives and were hiding behind locked doors "for fear of the Jews" (John 20:19).

Their hopes had begun to unravel in the Garden of Gethsemane when Jesus refused the aid of Peter's sword and meekly yielded to His captors (John 18:10-12). At that point, all the disciples fled in fear (Mark 14:50). Although Peter later reappeared at the high priest's house, it was only to shamefully deny his Lord (vss. 66-72). Truly, the Shepherd had been smitten, and His sheep were scattered (Matt. 26:31). To them, Jesus' death was but the portent of their own. Their only hope now was to escape from Jerusalem.

Suddenly, even as the Emmaus disciples were relating their experience (cf. Luke 24:36), Jesus appeared in their midst. They were terrified initially, thinking they had seen a spirit (vs. 37). And well they might have, for Jesus' resurrection body was unimpeded by locked doors. He was more than a spirit, as He went on to demonstrate, but the limitations of the body of flesh and blood were now gone.

Jesus greeted the disciples with the words "Peace be unto you" (John 20:19). This carried the full import of the Jewish word "shalom," which indicates well-being in every respect. Jesus did not just speak this as a wish; He bestowed it on them in the power of resurrection life. If ever men needed peace, these disciples did at this point. Since Jesus' death, they had been filled with despair, anxiety, and sorrow. Their minds were in turmoil, and their future looked dark. Jesus brought them the soothing assurance of well-being.

When Jesus was born, the angels announced the advent of peace on earth (Luke 2:14), for the Prince of Peace had come (Isa. 9:6). Although He proclaimed peace (Acts 10:36), most of His generation rejected His message. He mourned over Jerusalem because it had not recognized the things that brought peace (Luke 19:41-42).

He did, however, promise peace to His own disciples (John 14:27)—a peace they could have even while suffering tribulation in a hostile world (16:33). And now that He had purchased this peace "through the blood of his cross" (Col. 1:20), He could proclaim it triumphantly to His own (John 20:19, 21, 26; cf. Luke 24:36).

The peace Jesus brings continues to work wonders in His church. It brings reconciliation with God for every believer (Rom. 5:1) and unites those once divided by cultural prejudice (Eph. 2:13-18). It is a fruit of the Spirit manifested by the committed Christian (Gal. 5:22), and it guards the mind in ways we cannot comprehend (Phil. 4:7). It should be a trait that characterizes every Christian (Rom. 12:18; Heb. 12:14).

The response (John 20:20). Eventually, the disciples were "glad, when they saw the Lord," but only after a period of doubt. Luke 24:37 tells us that initially they were terrified, thinking they had seen a spirit. Scripture teaches that at death, the immaterial aspect of man (the spirit) continues a separate existence from the body (cf. Eccles. 8:8; 12:7; Luke 8:55; Heb. 12:23). The disciples knew Jesus had died, and they could accept the possibility that His spirit could be revisiting them.

But the possibility of His bodily resurrection eluded them completely. Thus, they were stricken with terror at seeing, as they thought, a supernatural apparition. It took more than Jesus' proclamation of peace to reconcile them to reality.

According to John, He held out His hands and showed them His side. These bore the scars of His suffering, and whatever changes His glorified body entailed, He still carried the evidence of His finished redemptive work. According to Luke 24:37-43, it took even more than the sight of these marks to convince the disciples that His body was real.

Jesus actually invited them to touch Him to see that He was "flesh and bones" (Luke 24:39). Yet they were still skeptical. The expression "they yet believed not for joy" (vs. 41) tells us they desperately wanted to believe it was He but could not find it in themselves to do so. So He went even further and ate a piece of broiled fish in their presence (vss. 41-43). Thus were they finally convinced.

We sometimes single out Thomas as the one who demanded physical proof that Jesus was alive (John 20:24-29). But the other disciples were just as skeptical. For our sakes, it is probably good that they doubted, for it gave Jesus the opportunity to demonstrate, for all who have read this account, that He was victorious over death. His words "Blessed are they that have not seen, and yet have believed" (vs. 29) apply to all of us who believe the eyewitness accounts.

JESUS' COMMISSION

21 Then said Jesus to them again, Peace be unto you: as my Father hath sent me, even so send I you.

22 And when he had said this, he breathed on them, and saith unto them, Receive ye the Holy Ghost:

23 Whose soever sins ye remit, they are remitted unto them; and whose soever sins ye retain, they are retained.

The charge (John 20:21). Having calmed the disciples, Jesus repeated His salutation "Peace be unto you." This both reassured them and prepared them for the commission He would give. Jesus was about to continue what He had begun to teach in the Upper Room Discourse, and His proclamation of peace reassured them that His presence would always accompany them.

Though the charge Jesus was about to give continued a previous theme, the circumstances now had radically changed, for He had passed through death and resurrection. Only now did the apostles have a message of hope for the world. And only now was it possible for Jesus to send the Spirit to empower them for their mission.

Jesus gave them this charge: "As my Father hath sent me, even so send I you" (John 20:21). Jesus' Father sent Him to reveal the nature of God to man (1:14, 18), and especially His saving grace to sinners (Luke 19:10; John 3:16-17; 17:3). He accomplished this, first, through the words He spoke (John 3:34; 6:63; 7:16-18; 17:8). His message was clear, consistent, and authoritative. He amazed the crowds with His teaching (Matt. 7:28-29), and even His enemies had to admit, "Never man spake like this man" (John 7:46).

Jesus also revealed God's nature through His deeds (John 5:36). His miraculous works allayed the doubts of John the Baptist (Matt. 11:2-6), and the multitudes were stunned by them (Mark 1:27; 2:12). His works convinced many that He was the Messiah (Matt. 12:23), and His enemies had no alternative explanation except satanic influence (vs. 24). John's Gospel selects several of these signs of Jesus to incite faith and bring life (John 20:30-31).

Finally, Jesus revealed God's nature through His death for man's salvation. He spoke of this sacrifice as "a ransom for many" (Mark 10:45). When lifted up, He would draw all men to Himself (John 12:32-33). His cry on the cross, "It is finished!" (19:30), signaled the triumphant completion of this mission.

Jesus now passed on the mission to the disciples (John 20:21; cf. 17:4, 18). As He had borne witness concerning His Father, so they would bear witness concerning Him (John 15:26-27; cf. Luke 24:46-48). As He had performed works in His Father's name, so would they in His name (Mark 16:17-18; Acts 4:7-10). In fact, their works would be greater than His (John 14:12). And as He had laid down His life, so they would be expected to do the same (15:18-21; 16:1-3).

The endowment (John 20:22). Jesus' charge was weighty, but so was the power to carry it out. He "breathed on them, and saith unto them, Receive ye the Holy Ghost." This was a fitting bestowal, for both the Hebrew and Greek words for "spirit" mean "breath" or "wind." Wind is thus an apt symbol for the Holy Spirit (cf. John 3:8; Acts 2:1-2).

The word used for "breathed" in John 20:22 occurs only here in the New Testament. It also occurs once in the Septuagint (Greek) translation of the Old Testament—in Genesis 2:7, which says that God breathed into man's nostrils the breath of life. The two instances are parallel. Just as the breath of God vitalized mankind for earthly life and responsibility, so now it vitalized the apostles for their stewardship over the new creation, the church.

But how did this infusion of the Holy Spirit relate to the more spectacular outpouring on the Day of Pentecost, fifty days later (Acts 2)? It is possible that this was merely a symbolic act by which Jesus taught the apostles truths about the Spirit's ministry. Jesus had previously told them that the Spirit would replace Him on earth and continue His works. His act of breathing on them now would have reminded them how seamlessly this transition would take place. The Holy Spirit was the Spirit of Christ.

But this act may also have been a partial filling of the Spirit for the apostolic church leaders in preparation for the more general infusion on the Day of Pentecost. Interestingly, Jesus immediately followed it with a declaration of the power the Spirit would exercise through them. Thus, the breathing of the Spirit on the apostles was a preparation for their leadership.

The authority (John 20:23). Jesus' commission climaxed with the declaration that "whosoever sins ye remit, they are remitted unto them; and whosoever sins ye retain, they are retained." These words have often been misunderstood to mean that Jesus gave the apostles the power to forgive or withhold forgiveness of sins. The same misinterpretation is often seen in the earlier binding and loosing passages (Matt. 16:19; 18:18).

Part of the misunderstanding is caused by the Greek verb forms used in John 20:23. The first occurrence of "remit" and "retain" in this verse is simple enough; the verb tense refers to completed action. The second occurrence of each, however, is an unusual verb form that should be properly translated "will have been remitted," and "will have been retained." Thus, the sins the apostles declare forgiven or unforgiven have been previously declared so by God.

In simple terms, this means that the apostles (and, by extension, all believers) are empowered to declare forgiveness of sins for all who trust the atoning work of Christ for them. If they accept Jesus' sacrifice for them, we have the authority to declare, "Your sins are forgiven." But if they reject His sacrifice, we have the authority to declare, "Your sins are not forgiven." Sins can be declared forgiven only on the basis of God's previously stated terms.

This principle applies to church discipline as well as evangelism. This was the context of Jesus' teaching on binding and loosing authority in Matthew 18:18. If a sinning brother refused to repent, even when confronted by the church, the church had the authority to expel him (vss. 15-17). It also applied to the man in Corinth who was living in blatant immorality. Paul urged the church to gather, judge him, and expel him from membership (I Cor. 5:1-5). Such actions, of course, must never be undertaken lightly.

Jesus' appearance to His disciples was a momentous occasion. Through it, He proved the reality of His resurrection, gave the commission for them to bear witness of Him, bestowed the power they needed, and gave them the message of forgiveness of sins. And all this is provided for us as well.

—*Robert E. Wenger.*

QUESTIONS

1. What was the emotional condition of Jesus' disciples on the day of His resurrection?
2. How did Jesus greet the disciples? What did this mean?
3. What is the source of a Christian's peace?
4. How did Jesus convince the disciples that His body was real?
5. Why was Jesus' resurrection essential to the disciples' task?
6. How had Jesus fulfilled His mission? How was the disciples' mission similar?
7. How did Jesus impart the Holy Spirit to His disciples? Why?
8. How is Jesus' statement about remitting sins sometimes misunderstood?
9. What gives a Christian the authority to declare another person's sins forgiven?
10. Why was Jesus' appearance to the disciples a momentous occasion?

—*Robert E. Wenger.*

Preparing to Teach the Lesson

We go through numerous activities on a Sunday. We rise early, get the family ready, attend Sunday school and the morning service. In the afternoon we may have a church activity or a committee meeting, and then there is the evening service. At day's end, we are ready for some quiet time at home.

We are not the only ones to have a busy Sunday. On the day of His resurrection, the first day of the week, Jesus also was busy. He appeared on five occasions on that day, ministering to various people: Mary Magdalene (John 20:11-18), other women (Matt. 28:9-10), Peter (Luke 24:34; I Cor. 15:5), two disciples on the Emmaus road (Luke 24:13-32), and finally the disciples in the closed room (John 20:19-23). That last encounter is the subject of this week's lesson.

TODAY'S AIM

Facts: to understand the significance of Jesus' appearance and words.

Principle: to teach that Jesus' resurrected appearances culminated in instructions for serving Him.

Application: to see how Jesus' words encourage us to witness boldly for Him.

INTRODUCING THE LESSON

Imagine you feel an unexpected lump in your body. You visit your physician, and he wants to run tests because he fears that it might be a cancerous tumor. Two weeks later, you have the tests; then you must anxiously wait a week for the results. Now imagine your relief when the diagnosis is that the lump is a benign growth that requires no treatment. Your fears melt away.

Jesus' disciples had endured His crucifixion and were fearful that they would be persecuted as He was. What could possibly calm their fears? What could give them hope for the future? This week's lesson answers these critical questions.

DEVELOPING THE LESSON

1. Fearful disciples (John 20:19a). Jesus rose on the first day of the week, Sunday (Matt. 28:1). At early evening on that day, the disciples were together in a closed room. At least twelve were present. Ten of the Lord's apostles were there, excluding Judas Iscariot, who had hanged himself, and Thomas (John 20:24). In addition to these, Cleopas and his friend were present after their interaction with Christ on the road to Emmaus (Luke 24:33-35).

Even though they had been told of the Lord's resurrection by the women who saw the empty tomb and by Cleopas and his friend, these disciples continued in "fear of the Jews" (John 20:19). The term "the Jews" refers to the religious authorities responsible for Christ's death. The disciples had shut the doors, meaning they had locked them for their own safety.

2. Unexpected Lord (John 20:19b-20a). Jesus suddenly appeared and stood in their midst. This must have been a great shock to the disciples, and it was an indication of the abilities of Jesus' resurrection body. He immediately said, "Peace be unto you," no doubt to calm their troubled fears (cf. Luke 24:37-44) at His abrupt appearance.

Once He had spoken words of peace, Jesus showed them His hands and side. This enabled them to examine the wounds from His crucifixion and know that He really was the risen Lord. The New Testament thus makes clear that Jesus' resurrection was a bodily resurrection.

3. Joyful disciples (John 20:20b). Having seen the Lord's wounds and knowing that He was truly risen from the dead, the disciples were "glad." This translates the common Greek word for rejoicing. Seeing the living Lord in their midst must have filled them with such joy as we cannot imagine. John omitted the details included in Luke 24:37-44; his purpose was to focus on the Lord's commission.

4. Commissioning Lord (John 20:21-23). Jesus once again said "Peace be unto you" to introduce His coming commission. He began with sending them into ministry. The words "as my Father hath sent me" point to the completion of His work. In contrast, the words "so send I you" stress that their ministry would be a continuing one.

Jesus was sent as the Father's official representative. Now Jesus was sending His disciples as His official representatives, but they had been hiding in fear. Because of that, a special spiritual power was required (John 20:22). So Jesus "breathed" on them; the Greek word appears only here in the New Testament. The verb is used in two Old Testament texts in the Septuagint (the Greek translation of the Old Testament): Genesis 2:7, in the account of the creation of Adam, and Ezekiel 37:9, depicting the restoration of Israel to spiritual life.

Jesus thus anticipated the new creation in Him (cf. II Cor. 5:17; Eph. 2:8-10). To verify this, He gave His disciples preliminary power of the Holy Spirit on their lives until the Day of Pentecost, when the Spirit would permanently come upon all of them.

The words "they are remitted" and "they are retained" (John 20:23) are in the Greek perfect tense. These statements do not refer to any church or person having the power of absolution of sins. The verbs stress that the forgiveness and the retention are things that have already been done in heaven by God. Believers are merely proclaiming that act of God. The words "whosoever," furthermore, are in the plural. Jesus did not speak about forgiving any single person but about the concept of forgiveness in general. Jesus stressed that all believers have the right to proclaim that forgiveness of sins can be experienced in life.

ILLUSTRATING THE LESSON

God's power is communicated to us by the Holy Spirit.

THE POWER OF GOD

Bible

THE HOLY SPIRIT

CONCLUDING THE LESSON

Witnessing to others about Christ may give us butterflies in our stomachs. At times we are not much different from the disciples in the locked room. Christ's commission, however, remains unchanged. The message concerning forgiveness of sins must still be presented, and we can present it boldly because of the Spirit's abiding power and presence in our lives.

ANTICIPATING THE NEXT LESSON

Next week we turn our focus to how the pledge of God's presence centers in Christ the King, who came in the name of the Lord.

—R. Larry Overstreet.

PRACTICAL POINTS

1. In times of fear and uncertainty, believers find strength in fellowship (John 20:19).
2. Jesus brings peace and confidence when He enters our fearful situations.
3. Jesus reveals all we need to believe in His comfort (vs. 20).
4. Jesus has given every believer the privilege and responsibility of sharing the gospel (vs. 21).
5. God has given us the authority and power to do His work in the world (vss. 21-22).
6. As we share the gospel, people hear the message and receive forgiveness upon believing that message (vs. 23).

—Cheryl Y. Powell.

RESEARCH AND DISCUSSION

1. What was the mood like in the room where the disciples were gathered?
2. How was Jesus' statement "Peace be unto you" (John 20:19) significant in this setting?
3. What message does Scripture have for unbelievers seeking peace today?
4. How is God's peace different from the world's peace (cf. 14:27)?
5. How was this encounter critical to the work the disciples would do?
6. How does the work of the Spirit in the Old Testament contrast with His work in the New Testament?
7. Did Jesus give His disciples the power to forgive men their sins in 20:23? Explain.

—Cheryl Y. Powell.

ILLUSTRATED HIGH POINTS

Then were the disciples glad

My wife's sister lives in London, England. She went there from the United States to study art a number of years ago. While in London, she met her future husband. They now have three grown children and are grandparents. Since we live a great distance away, it is always a delightful time when we can get together as a family.

When the disciples saw Jesus, they too were glad. The situation was very different, to say the least, but seeing the risen Christ caused their faith in and friendship with the Lord to be renewed. May our friendships with each other bring us gladness, and may our friendship with Christ bring true, lasting joy to our lives as followers of Him!

The Holy Ghost

Some time ago, I had the privilege of going with a medical team to Romania. I was asked to speak (through an interpreter) at one of the churches, and at the end of my message, I gave an opportunity for people to trust Christ as Saviour. After the service, two men came up, wanting to do just that. The Holy Spirit gives the believer power to witness for Christ. May all believers be among that number!

They are remitted

A man went to pay his fine for a speeding violation. The clerk pulled up his file on the computer, turned to him, and said, "Sir, your fine has already been paid. You're free and clear."

The clerk had no authority to clear the man of his penalty. But she could declare him free based on the official record. So it is with believers. We can proclaim people free from sin's penalty based on their faith in Jesus.

—Paul R. Bawden.

Golden Text Illuminated

"When he had said this, he breathed on them, and saith unto them, Receive ye the Holy Ghost" (John 20:22).

Jesus had told His disciples beforehand of His approaching death and resurrection (cf. Matt. 16:21; 17:22-23); yet His words had not penetrated their understanding. His death brought them grief and hopelessness; and even when reliable witnesses told of His resurrection, they were slow to believe it was true.

Ten of Jesus' disciples were gathered in fear behind closed doors on the evening of His resurrection when the risen Lord suddenly appeared to them. He calmed their fears and showed them the scars in His hands and side (John 20:19-20). There could be no doubt that Christ had, indeed, risen from the dead.

Jesus' words to His disciples at that time might at first strike us as curious. He focused on two things: the future mission of the disciples and the divine power that would enable them to carry out that mission (John 20:21-23). While we might have expected some explanation for what His resurrection and victory over death meant, Jesus returned to two ideas He had previously taught His disciples.

Jesus reminded them that He was sending them into the world (John 20:21; cf. 17:18-21). He also reminded them of the empowering work of the Holy Spirit, whom He would send to them. Jesus had taught them about the future work of the Spirit in their lives during His Upper Room Discourse (chaps. 14—16). In mentioning the Spirit now, He was letting the disciples know that His time with them was soon coming to an end. His resurrection did not mean He would continue with them indefinitely.

Jesus' breathing on them perhaps recalls the breath of God in giving life to the first man (Gen. 2:7) and suggests the new life given by the Spirit. As He breathed, however, He said, "Receive ye the Holy Ghost."

Whatever Jesus meant by these words, this event does not mark the beginning of the indwelling ministry of the Holy Spirit. That event would come some seven weeks later on the Day of Pentecost. When Jesus ascended into heaven ten days prior to Pentecost, He told His disciples to wait in Jerusalem for the Holy Spirit to come upon them (Acts 1:4-8). When that day came, the Spirit came upon all the believers, indwelled them, and empowered them for ministry. And from that day forward, the Spirit has come to indwell every believer at the moment of salvation (I Cor. 12:13; cf. Rom. 8:9).

What is described in our golden text is probably a temporary empowering of the Spirit to sustain the disciples in the immediate future in carrying out their mission. Such empowerment would be much like the Spirit's work in the Old Testament era and would be consistent with the limited nature of such a work. Here the bestowal of the Spirit was limited to the circle of Jesus' closest disciples. The Spirit's coming on Pentecost was for *all* of Jesus' followers.

What is important for us to remember is that our Lord has not assigned us to be witnesses and then left us powerless. He has given us not only the Great Commission but also His Spirit. We have everything we need to do everything He asks.

—*Jarl K. Waggoner.*

Heart of the Lesson

Jesus came into this world so that we might experience the power of God in our lives. This happens because Jesus opened the way for us to receive the Holy Spirit into our lives and experience the power of God. Weak Christians fail to make an impact for God. Bold and powerful Christians know that it is God Himself, working through His Spirit, who gives them the power that they experience daily to witness to others about Jesus.

1. Jesus' peace (John 20:19). We live in a broken world of uncertainty and hopelessness. Even those who are financially stable often fear the future. This week we learn that the disciples were filled with fear because Jesus had been crucified and their hopes and dreams were dashed. They had forgotten all that Jesus had told them while He was with them. In the midst of this climate of uncertainty and fear, Jesus again showed Himself to them.

We must understand here that their fear turned to peace. We are reminded that where the presence of Jesus is, there is always peace. Fear has no place in our hearts because His presence drives out that fear and replaces it with the peace of His presence. Jesus is with us in the presence of the Holy Spirit, who has promised never to leave us. This means, then, that God's peace is here to stay. This is an encouragement to anyone who seeks to follow Jesus. The pathway is paved with His peace.

2. The disciples' joy (John 20:20-21). We see again how the presence of the risen Christ transformed a time of fear for the disciples during a tense situation into one of jubilant exhilaration. When the presence of God shows up, our fear is quickly changed, because Jesus cares for us especially when we are afraid. This is the work of the presence of God in our lives. It was the presence of the risen Christ, who had not abandoned them, that made all the difference.

Our Lord has a way of reaffirming His presence when we are discouraged and deflated by the pressures of life. He does not change, and He shows us that He can be counted on in such times of difficulty and pain. He offers us His help and the gift of His presence to reassure us that our fear can, indeed, be turned to joy in the most difficult circumstances. When life's difficult situations incapacitate us with fear, we still have Jesus, who has not left our side. He is worthy to be trusted.

3. The Holy Spirit received (John 20:22-23). In our lesson this week, we see something that is very special. Jesus reassured His disciples that He would never leave them alone because they were about to receive the life-giving Holy Spirit. In the Bible, breath is always symbolic of life. When the living, resurrected Jesus breathed on the disciples, they received the Holy Spirit. It was yet another reassurance that they were never alone and that they were recipients of His power.

God has ordained Christian believers to be people of divine power. The presence of the Holy Spirit is real. We have the promise that He will be with us for all time. He is the greatest resource that we can have as Christians. He sets us apart from others. We now can do what Jesus did because of the presence of the Spirit.

—A. Koshy Muthalaly.

World Missions

The disciples of Jesus were a peculiar bunch, and I have to laugh at their shortsightedness at times. They remind me that no matter how close a person is to the Lord, he still does not get it sometimes. Human nature has not changed much since the time of Jesus.

In the first chapter of Acts, Jesus told His disciples that they would soon be receiving the gift of the Holy Spirit. Instead of focusing on the work Jesus had given them beforehand—preaching His message to the whole world (Matt. 28:19-20)—they all pestered Him about when the kingdom would be restored to Israel (Acts 1:6)! This reveals the deep-seated misunderstanding of who the Israelites thought the Messiah would be and what they expected Him to accomplish when He came.

I mention all of this because we too can have a misunderstanding of what God's plan is really all about. When things do not turn out the way we expect or the end of a matter is hidden from us, it is easy to become discouraged. This is why the example of Philip is so encouraging.

We read about Philip in Acts 8. The believers were experiencing a great wave of persecution in Jerusalem and became scattered throughout Israel.

Philip made his way to Samaria, preaching the gospel along the way. Many people believed in Jesus after hearing his message. His usual way of serving the church was providing food to elderly widows; so it was probably a little surprising to him when an angel suddenly appeared with a message from God.

The angel told Philip to go south, to the desert road that ran from Jerusalem to Gaza. Many of us might have been unhappy with so little information. *Why go there? What am I supposed to do? What is going to happen when I get there?* But Philip did not question—he simply obeyed.

When he came to the road, he saw a chariot. In the chariot was an Ethiopian of great importance. He had come to Jerusalem to worship and was now on his way home to the royal court of the Ethiopian queen.

The Holy Spirit instructed Philip to walk alongside the chariot. As he did so, he heard the Ethiopian official reading aloud from the book of Isaiah.

Philip asked the man whether he understood what he was reading. The man replied that he did not because there was no one to instruct him.

The Scripture in question was Isaiah 53, which speaks of the Messiah. The official asked Philip to whom this passage was referring.

Philip was surely very excited to tell the man that this very passage of Scripture speaks of Jesus, the Messiah, who had come to Israel, been killed for the remission of our sins, and was raised again by God's power.

The Ethiopian official was so excited about the news of Jesus and the redemption of his soul that when the chariot passed by some water, he begged for Philip to baptize him then and there, which he did.

Immediately after the baptism, Philip was whisked away by God's Spirit. Truly, the official must have been mystified by this! But it did not matter. He continued on his way with much rejoicing.

Neither man knew what the outcome of their meeting would be; but they did not demand answers. They chose to rely on the Spirit's provision and their faith in God, knowing that all things would be made perfect in God's time.

—Christina Futrell.

The Jewish Aspect

Our text for this week begins with the Lord's resurrection day appearance to the disciples. The Lord greeted them with the usual Jewish expression, "Shalom," meaning "peace." Today, it is common to say, "Shalom, Shalom," indicating a double measure of peace.

The Lord's words of commission to His closest servants (John 20:21) indicate that the work He had been doing would now be theirs. Jesus seems to also have been placing these chosen ones on notice that the work was about to begin. The filling of the Holy Spirit (vs. 22) is essential to the role of the local church and will be until the Lord returns. In a matter of days, the Lord's disciples would experience rivers of living water welling up in their souls. It was the filling and indwelling of the Holy Spirit foretold at the Feast of Tabernacles (7:37-39). This is the basis of the world evangelistic outreach and a guarantee of its success.

One might ask, Were the Jews meant to be a missions-oriented people before Jesus came? After reviewing God's law for the people, Moses declared that they were to carefully obey it, "for this is your wisdom and your understanding in the sight of the nations" (Deut. 4:6). If Israel were faithful, the Gentile peoples would say, "Surely this great nation is a wise and understanding people. For what nation is there so great, who hath God so nigh unto them?" (vss. 6-7).

Jesus commented wryly about the pseudomissionary work of Jewish religious leaders in the first century. He said, "Woe unto you, scribes and Pharisees, hypocrites! for ye compass sea and land to make one proselyte, and when he is made, ye make him twofold more the child of hell than yourselves" (Matt. 23:15).

In spite of widespread apostasy, the common Jewish experience today has been to defend the Mosaic Law in the Bible we treasure so highly. A man I knew lived as a pious Jew the adult portion of his long life. He could recite from memory any passage in the first five books, with only a one- or two-word reminder.

Jewish religious authorities do not have to work as hard today at attracting followers as the leaders Jesus described. The more liberal forms of Judaism have attracted some surprising converts. Various famous personalities have converted to Judaism. Orthodox conversions are also on the rise.

One local rabbi is a missionary-statesman. Based on the fact that many Jews in Spain before the days of Christopher Columbus were forced into Catholicism, this rabbi feels their descendants should be found and brought back to the faith of their fathers. It is true that in Spain and in former Spanish colonies of Central and South America, many have no idea that their forefathers were Jews. This zealous rabbi employs history, tradition, and modern technology in this search for those lost to Judaism.

The difficulty in converting people into Jews is that Judaism needs a core group of faithful Jews who congregate because of viable Jewish homes, tradition, and even language. (The Jewish newspaper in my hometown has to spend a good deal of print translating Hebrew, explaining elementary Jewish articles of faith, and describing the background of the feasts of Israel to converts to the Jewish faith.)

Thankfully for Christians, the Holy Spirit has been given to guide us into all truth. Conversion to Christianity is not merely cultural; it is a spiritual new birth.

—Lyle P. Murphy.

Guiding the Superintendent

Receive the Holy Spirit. Open up your heart to be filled with His holy presence. He wants to fill us, to be our Teacher and our Guide. He knows the way we should take. He is the way to fulfilling the purpose for which Christ has called us into ministry. In this week's lesson, Christ offered peace and dispensed His power as He commissioned the disciples to go, teach, and baptize the nations.

DEVOTIONAL OUTLINE

1. Christ's appearance and assurance (John 20:19-21). A day like the day of Jesus' crucifixion understandably produced concern mixed with uncertainty. News of His resurrection heightened the disciples' anxiety. In the face of fear from any source, the appearance of a beloved friend bringing comforting words is welcomed and embraced. Whatever afflictions God's people may face, we can rest in the peace of God that is present to help us lay all doubts aside. There is no obstacle too high, too broad, or so deep that it can prevent Christ's loving hand from reaching His dear children.

When the dust of life settles, allowing us to see our God at work, surely joy from heaven fills our souls. Surely the disciples were soothed by each other's presence; but nothing can calm our troubled hearts like the presence of Almighty God, our Father.

2. Christ empowers for ministry (John 20:22-23). One thing prominent in John's writing is the promise of everlasting life to all who believe in Christ Jesus. He repeatedly pointed out that the mission of Christ was to do the will of God, who sent Him (cf. 9:4). His mission was to seek and to save those who were lost (cf. Luke 19:10); now He passed the mantle on to the men He had trained, taught, and prayed for so that they might carry out their portion of kingdom building. The redemption of mankind is sure. Christ fulfilled that need through His death, burial, and resurrection.

Perhaps the last phase of their preparation was to recognize that they were no longer bound by deep-rooted traditions and laws; Christ fulfilled the law. They were now a new creation as Christ blew a fresh breath of Himself upon them, empowering them with authority to work great exploits in His name. The judges of the Old Testament settled matters under the direction of the Spirit of God. So the apostles were sanctioned and approved under Christ to expose sin.

Those who acknowledged their sin and sought forgiveness were granted it. Those blatant in their wrongdoing did not receive forgiveness. The sinners brought judgment upon themselves. Apostles, having received the spirit of discernment, meted out God's punishment for sinners' transgressions.

AGE-GROUP EMPHASES

Children: They will find it curious that Jesus came into the room while the door was closed. Assure them that Jesus was not a ghost but a spiritual body with supernatural power.

Youths: Teach that a life in Christ assures them of the presence of God when facing difficult situations.

Adults: Christ is still sending workers into His vineyard. Remind the adults to faithfully attend Sunday school to gain knowledge to be fruitful teachers of others.

—Jane E. Campbell.

LESSON 5 MARCH 29, 2015

Scripture Lesson Text

MARK 11:1 And when they came nigh to Je-ru′sa-lem, unto Beth′pha-ge and Beth′a-ny, at the mount of Ol′ives, he sendeth forth two of his disciples,

2 And saith unto them, Go your way into the village over against you: and as soon as ye be entered into it, ye shall find a colt tied, whereon never man sat; loose him, and bring *him*.

3 And if any man say unto you, Why do ye this? say ye that the Lord hath need of him; and straightway he will send him hither.

4 And they went their way, and found the colt tied by the door without in a place where two ways met; and they loose him.

5 And certain of them that stood there said unto them, What do ye, loosing the colt?

6 And they said unto them even as Je′sus had commanded: and they let them go.

7 And they brought the colt to Je′sus, and cast their garments on him; and he sat upon him.

8 And many spread their garments in the way: and others cut down branches off the trees, and strawed *them* in the way.

9 And they that went before, and they that followed, cried, saying, Ho-san′na; Blessed *is* he that cometh in the name of the Lord:

10 Blessed *be* the kingdom of our father Da′vid, that cometh in the name of the Lord: Ho-san′na in the highest.

11 And Je′sus entered into Je-ru′sa-lem, and into the temple: and when he had looked round about upon all things, and now the eventide was come, he went out unto Beth′a-ny with the twelve.

NOTES

Bible Expositor and Illuminator

Coming in the Name of the Lord

Lesson: Mark 11:1-11

Read: Mark 11:1-11

TIME: A.D. 30   PLACE: Bethany

GOLDEN TEXT—"They that went before, and they that followed, cried, saying, Hosanna; Blessed is he that cometh in the name of the Lord" (Mark 11:9).

Introduction

Every society seems to have a special place for parades and processions of celebration. In America, athletic champions parade through the main streets of their cities and towns. Victorious armies and generals receive heroes' welcomes at the end of a war. Historic events are remembered perennially through parades. Presidential inaugurations are always accompanied by spectacular, lengthy parades.

Ancient societies were no different. Kings of ancient empires celebrated military victories through elaborate processions, displaying their plunder and captives.

So the triumphal entry of Jesus into Jerusalem was not unique. But it was highly significant. It marked the recognition of His remarkable ministry over the past three years. But, more important, it fulfilled the prophecy foretelling the presentation of the Messiah.

LESSON OUTLINE

I. THE PREPARATION—Mark 11:1-6

II. THE PROCESSION—Mark 11:7-11

Exposition: Verse by Verse

THE PREPARATION

MARK 11:1 And when they came nigh to Jerusalem, unto Bethphage and Bethany, at the mount of Olives, he sendeth forth two of his disciples,

2 And saith unto them, Go your way into the village over against you: and as soon as ye be entered into it, ye shall find a colt tied, whereon never man sat; loose him, and bring him.

3 And if any man say unto you, Why do ye this? say ye that the Lord hath need of him; and straightway he will send him hither.

March 29, 2015

4 And they went their way, and found the colt tied by the door without in a place where two ways met; and they loose him.

5 And certain of them that stood there said unto them, What do ye, loosing the colt?

6 And they said unto them even as Jesus had commanded: and they let them go.

The setting (Mark 11:1a). The events of this momentous day took place "when they came nigh to Jerusalem, unto Bethphage and Bethany, at the mount of Olives." Jesus and His disciples had come into this area from Jericho, where He had healed blind Bartimaeus and called Zacchaeus (Luke 18:35—19:10). They climbed the steep ascent to the Mount of Olives, east of Jerusalem, during the week prior to the Passover festival.

"Bethany," the name which probably means "house of dates," was on the eastern slope of the Mount of Olives, about two miles southeast of Jerusalem. It was the home of Mary, Martha, and Lazarus, Jesus' friends. It was here that, shortly before, He had raised Lazarus from death (John 11:1, 43-44). Bethany, also the home of Simon the leper, was where on this last visit Mary anointed Jesus with her perfume (12:1-8).

The location of "Bethphage," the name which means "house of unripe figs," is not certain. It is believed by some to have been a little to the northwest of Bethany, closer to the summit of the Mount of Olives. Both towns were no doubt on the main road leading into Jerusalem, a road sure to be frequented by pilgrims coming to the Passover Feast.

The instructions given (Mark 11:1b-3). Jesus instructed two unnamed disciples, "Go . . . into the village over against you." Assuming that they were setting out from Bethany, this was a reference to Bethphage. There, at the entrance, they would "find a colt tied, whereon never man sat." They were to untie it and bring it to Jesus.

The colt could have been the young of any animal, including a horse. But parallel accounts in other Gospels make it clear that the animal was a donkey (Matt. 21:2; John 12:14). The term implies an animal old enough to be used, but this particular one had never been ridden. This may have been the reason why, according to Matthew, its mother also was taken, to keep it calm.

The choice of an unbroken colt agrees with the Old Testament practice of giving the Lord only animals and other items that were previously unused or untampered with (cf. Exod. 20:25; Num. 19:2; I Sam. 6:7). During Jesus' time on earth, God used the same principle for His conception in the virgin womb of Mary and His burial in the new tomb of Joseph of Arimathea (Luke 1:34-35; 23:50-53).

In giving His instructions, Jesus anticipated a possible question: "Why do ye this?" (Mark 11:3). If it were asked, the disciples were to answer, "The Lord hath need of him." Because the word for "Lord" can also mean "master," some feel that this was a reference to the colt's owner, who may have been with Jesus at the time. It is alleged that Jesus was not called "Lord" until after His resurrection (however, see 5:19). But this meaning is unlikely, since Luke 19:33 says it was the colt's owners who questioned them.

We could attribute Jesus' knowledge of the donkey's location to His omniscience, but it is more likely that He had made prior arrangements with its owners, as He later did with the owner of the upper room (cf. Mark 14:12-15). But, lest His claim on the colt seem arbitrary, He also added this promise: "and straightway he will send him hither" (11:3). He committed Himself to return it promptly.

It is noteworthy that Jesus, the Lord and Owner of all things, was in such a position that He had to borrow a mount to ride into Jerusalem. It is equally remarkable that He promised to return what He had borrowed after He was finished with it. Truly the Lord of glory humbled Himself to accomplish His mission to the earth!

His choice of a donkey, however, was not a sign of humiliation. Donkeys were highly prized by the ancient Jews—not only as beasts of burden but also as status symbols. Persons of distinction rode on donkeys (cf. Judg. 5:10; 10:4; 12:14; I Sam. 25:20), and Isaiah pictures them pulling a chariot (21:7). When David was fleeing from Absalom, Ziba brought donkeys for his household to ride on (II Sam. 16:1-2). David and his sons also rode mules, which are hybrids between horses and donkeys (II Sam. 13:29; I Kings 1:33, 38).

The donkey, however, was a symbol of peaceful pursuits, unlike the horse, which military conquerors were likely to ride. Jesus came to fulfill the messianic prophecy of Zechariah 9:9-10 (cf. Matt. 21:4-5), which foretold His reign of peace. So a donkey was ideally suited to His purpose on this day.

The instructions followed (Mark 11:4-6). The two designated disciples did as Jesus told them "and found the colt tied by the door without in a place where two ways met." The detail given in this description leads one to think it came from an eyewitness who related it to Mark. Early church tradition held that Simon Peter was Mark's chief source of information. If this is true, he may have been one of the disciples Jesus sent for the donkey.

In any event, they found the animal where Jesus had indicated and untied it. As Jesus had forewarned them, someone asked why they were taking it. Mark describes these merely as some who were standing around there, but Luke identifies them as the colt's owners (19:33). When the disciples explained that the Lord needed it, the men readily granted them permission to take it.

As indicated before, this event has some unanswered questions. Was it divine intervention that inclined the owners to lend their animal to men they had never seen? Or were the words "the Lord hath need of him" (Mark 11:3) a prearranged password Jesus had given them? The latter explanation is likely, since Jesus had become well-known around Bethany, especially since He had raised Lazarus. After that event, many people of the area had believed in Him (cf. John 11:45). Perhaps these men were among them.

For the two disciples, the experience confirmed their growing reliance on the words of Jesus, which had repeatedly proved to be both accurate and authoritative. Whether Jesus' instructions were to go fishing at an unseemly time, to feed crowds from a few morsels, or to get a shekel from a fish's mouth, the disciples had learned to obey. They knew He could be trusted even if they did not always understand. We will find it the same in our spiritual experience.

THE PROCESSION

7 And they brought the colt to Jesus, and cast their garments on him; and he sat upon him.

8 And many spread their garments in the way: and others cut down branches off the trees, and strawed them in the way.

9 And they that went before, and they that followed, cried, saying, Hosanna; Blessed is he that cometh in the name of the Lord:

10 Blessed be the kingdom of our father David, that cometh in the name of the Lord: Hosanna in the highest.

11 And Jesus entered into Jerusalem, and into the temple: and when he had looked round about upon all things, and now the eventide was come, he went out unto Bethany with the twelve.

Jesus' demeanor (Mark 11:7). Having brought the colt to Jesus, the disciples threw their outer garments over it, making a kind of saddle for Him to sit on. He then mounted in preparation for the entrance into Jerusalem. Although Luke states that the disciples "set Jesus thereon" (19:35), it is clear that they merely assisted.

For Jesus, this was the day for messianic self-revelation. He did it in deliberate fulfillment of Zechariah 9:9-10, which portrays Israel's King coming peaceably yet openly. For some three years He had refrained from an open assertion of His messiahship, letting His words and works speak for Him. In fact, He had often counseled silence and discouraged attempts to make Him a king.

But now the time for silence was past. This was a special day when Jesus would openly present Himself as the Messiah. Even as He wept over Jerusalem's unbelief, He referred to the peace that the city could have had on "this thy day" (Luke 19:42). It was the day when, had He silenced His disciples, the rocks would have cried out (vss. 39-40). The issue had to be raised: Would Israel receive or reject their King? Only an open presentation would answer this.

The crowd's recognition (Mark 11:8-10). The crowds now joined the disciples in honoring Jesus. These people included pilgrims coming to Jerusalem for the Passover as well as people coming out of the city (cf. John 12:13). Many paid homage by spreading their garments on the road as a carpet for Him. This was an act of royal respect, as seen earlier in the loyalty of Jehu's officers to him (II Kings 9:13).

Others in the crowd "cut down branches off the trees, and strawed them in the way" (Mark 11:8). This agrees with Matthew's statement (21:8), but some manuscripts at Mark 11:8 read that they spread leafy branches that they had cut in the fields. The term for "branches" refers to a mat of leaves, rushes, or stalks. It would appear, then, that the people used whatever they found handy—branches, stalks, or leaves—to make a welcome mat for Jesus. Only John mentions palm branches (12:13).

The crowds surrounded Jesus, some preceding and some following. In keeping with the festive atmosphere, they joyfully chanted the words of Psalm 118:25-26. This was one of the Hallel Psalms (113—118) used liturgically at Passover and the Feast of Tabernacles. Psalm 118 has a number of messianic allusions. Because of the diversity of the crowd, many probably did not comprehend their significance. But many did, and their cries were especially appropriate on this unique day.

"Hosanna" (Mark 11:9) is a Hebrew word that means "save now." In Psalm 118:25, it occurs as "save now" with "I beseech thee, O Lord." But over the centuries it had come to be used as an exclamation of praise, like "Hallelujah!" Its use in Jewish liturgy was always accompanied, interestingly, by the waving of palm, myrtle, and willow branches. In addition to its liturgical use, "Hosanna" was often a welcome shout for pilgrims and noted dignitaries. On this occasion, its original meaning had deep significance, for only Jesus could save.

They also shouted, "Blessed is he that cometh in the name of the Lord" (Mark 11:9), a verbatim quotation from Psalm 118:26. It is not in itself a messianic reference but a blessing pronounced on any pilgrim coming to worship at the festival. But on this day, these words had a deeper significance. John states it clearly: "Blessed is the King of Israel that cometh in the name of the Lord" (12:13).

Mark's words that follow also bear this out: "Blessed be the kingdom of our father David, that cometh in the name of the Lord" (11:10). The crowd clearly identified Jesus with the kingdom of David's Son. Matthew's words (21:9) are similar and carry the same messianic message. Surely this was the way the Pharisees understood them; it was for this reason they told Jesus to rebuke His disciples (Luke 19:39).

The cry "Hosanna in the highest" (Mark 11:10) should be taken as a plea to God Himself: "Save us now, You who live in the highest heaven." It was the hopeful cry of a long-subjugated people who glimpsed in Jesus a hope for deliverance. Though their hope was not misplaced, the nature of the deliverance they sought was wrong. Defining their basic problem as Roman rule, they expected someone who could lead them to freedom. But they failed to see the need for deliverance from sin (cf. John 8:31-36).

The procession's aftermath (Mark 11:11). Our passage concludes with a calm ending to an exciting day. It seems anticlimactic that the crowds should disperse so quickly and Jesus should spend the rest of the day surveying the temple. He quietly returned to Bethany at evening, accompanied by none but the Twelve.

—Robert E. Wenger.

QUESTIONS

1. Where was Bethany? Why was it important in Jesus' ministry?
2. What errand did Jesus assign to two disciples He sent ahead?
3. Why was it important that the colt Jesus used be previously unbroken?
4. How can we explain Jesus' prior knowledge of the colt's location?
5. Why was it significant that Jesus rode a donkey, not a horse?
6. What truth about Jesus did the two disciples' experience confirm?
7. Why was Jesus' triumphal entry a crucial event for Israel?
8. What signs of royal homage did the crowds show to Jesus?
9. How do we know the people identified Jesus with David's kingdom? What did they not understand?
10. What did Jesus do upon entering Jerusalem?

—Robert E. Wenger.

Preparing to Teach the Lesson

In our lessons thus far, we have seen how the pledge of God's presence centers in His Son. God's presence came in the Person of Christ, the Lamb of God. Christ promised the continued presence of God in the Comforter to come—the Holy Spirit. That Spirit is also the Spirit of truth, who guides the Lord's followers into all truth while convicting the world of their need for Christ as Saviour. This week we see that Christ had the authority to assure His followers of God's presence because He is the promised King who came in the Lord's name.

TODAY'S AIM

Facts: to learn the significance of Christ's triumphal entry as the promised King.

Principle: to realize that the humble Jesus who entered Jerusalem on a donkey is truly the Lord of heaven and earth.

Application: to accept the King of kings as Saviour and the Ruler of life.

INTRODUCING THE LESSON

What is more fun than a parade? Many years ago, my family sat in the grandstand in Pasadena, California, and watched the Rose Parade. We have witnessed other parades over the years. There was something special, though, about watching the "granddaddy" of all American parades—the Rose Parade.

Parades are usually composed of floats, marching bands, and important people. The most significant "parade" in history, however, had no floats, no TV coverage, and only one central figure. That parade is found in our text this week, and we commonly call it "The Triumphal Entry."

DEVELOPING THE LESSON

1. The promised King (Mark 11:1-7). Jesus had been in Jericho, where He healed blind Bartimaeus (10:46-52). Leaving Jericho, Jesus and His disciples took about eight hours to walk the fifteen miles to Jerusalem. It is an uphill walk from Jericho (about 820 feet below sea level) to Jerusalem (about 2,500 feet above sea level). As they arrived at the eastern slope of the Mount of Olives, they came to Bethany. Crossing over the Mount of Olives (about 2,680 feet above sea level) and walking a mile, they came to Bethphage on its western slope, less than a mile from Jerusalem. From Bethphage they walked downhill through the Kidron Valley (about 170 feet below the temple) and then uphill to reach Jerusalem.

Jesus arrived at Passover time, when thousands of Jews made the pilgrimage to this reverent event. He sent two disciples to get a donkey's colt that had never been ridden (Mark 11:3). He told the disciples that if anyone questioned them, they were to answer, "the Lord hath need of him," and they would be permitted to take the donkey. That is exactly what occurred (vss. 4-6).

The two disciples brought the colt to Jesus and put their garments on it to form a saddle. He then sat on it. This event fulfilled the promise of Zechariah 9:9 and testified clearly that Jesus was indeed the promised King, the Messiah of Israel. Riding an unbroken colt demonstrated to all that Jesus was the Lord over all creation.

2. The presented King (Mark 11:8-10). As Jesus rode into Jerusalem, the people gave Him honor. They "spread their garments in the way." Putting down garments for a king to walk on occurred earlier in Israel. When Jehu became king, the people did the same for him (II Kings 9:13). We do a similar thing today when we roll out the red carpet for important people.

Some of the crowd went ahead of Jesus, and others were behind. All of them cried out, "Hosanna; Blessed is he that cometh in the name of the Lord" (Mark 11:9, quoting from Psalm 118:25-26). The word "hosanna" is a transliteration of the Hebrew words "save now" in Psalm 118:25. Jesus certainly knew the psalm and its messianic importance. The fact that He permitted the crowd to shout it at His entrance to Jerusalem testifies to the reality that He was indeed the Promised One who came to save and be the Lord's King.

The crowd continued its acclamation by shouting, "Blessed be the kingdom of our father David, that cometh in the name of the Lord" (Mark 11:10).

3. The King's inspection tour (Mark 11:11). The impact of Jesus' arrival at Jerusalem with this triumphal procession was great. Would He deliver Israel from Rome and set up David's kingdom? Instead of taking that sort of action, Jesus conducted Himself in a manner that must have puzzled the Jews. He went into the temple area, looked around, and then, since it was evening, left Jerusalem and returned to Bethany with His disciples to spend the night. He did not enter the temple as a pilgrim to worship. He entered it, instead, as its Lord on an inspection tour. This resulted in His actions the next day when He cast out the money changers and those who sold doves (vs.15). He also did not call for a revolt against Rome to set up an earthly kingdom at that time. Instead, He was on His way to the cross as the Lamb of God. Imagine the puzzled hearts and minds of the onlooking Jews who expected far more.

ILLUSTRATING THE LESSON

In His triumphal entry, Jesus came as the humble King. One day He will return as the reigning King.

THE KING

Humble   Triumphant

HE HAS COME AND WILL RETURN

CONCLUDING THE LESSON

Jesus Christ was the center of the most crucial parade in the world's history. He came as God's promised King and presented Himself as the King. The issue for us is whether we are willing to accept Him as the Saviour, the Lamb of God, who gave His life for us. One day He will return and set up His kingdom. Until then, we must allow Him to reign over our lives.

ANTICIPATING THE NEXT LESSON

Our next lesson looks forward to our Lord's return and the accompanying resurrection that is guaranteed for all those who believe in Him.

—R. Larry Overstreet.

PRACTICAL POINTS

1. Believers should always be ready to follow where God leads (Mark 11:1-2).
2. As we obey Christ, He supplies the answers and resources we need (vss. 3-4).
3. We can obey confidently, knowing that we will find things just as Jesus has said (vss. 5-6).
4. Our mission is certain when we offer Christ whatever we have for His use (vss. 7-8).
5. The crowd will worship Christ on good days, but the committed follow Him always (vss. 9-10).
6. Be alert to the presence and work of God, even though He may not come as you expect (vss. 9-11).

—Cheryl Y. Powell.

RESEARCH AND DISCUSSION

1. How was Jesus' entry different from that of other leaders of the time? How is that difference significant (cf. Zech. 9:9)?
2. Why was Jesus coming to Jerusalem? How is it significant that He was coming to Jerusalem at that specific time (cf. Exod. 12:1-14)?
3. What did the shouts of "Hosanna" mean to the crowd (Pss. 118:25-26; 148:1-14)? Did that mean they understood He is the Messiah?
4. How could this crowd praise Jesus Christ on His triumphal entry and demand His crucifixion a few days later?
5. As Jesus looked around the temple at the beginning of Passover Week, what did He see?

—Cheryl Y. Powell.

ILLUSTRATED HIGH POINTS

Go your way

There are many so-called paths in life that a person can take. For instance, there is the vocational path (which career to pursue) and the marital path (which person to marry). But there is one path that stands out above all others. It is the path of life. It is the path the Lord provides for us in His Word and ultimately through His death, burial, and bodily resurrection.

When the Lord told His disciples to go fetch the colt that was in a certain village and to bring the colt to Him, they obeyed, found the colt, and took it to Jesus. They were on the path of life because they obeyed the Lord. Are you walking spiritually on the path of life?

They that followed

My father used to tell about some of his friends in his younger days who went to church but showed no evidence that what was said there had any effect on their lives. They talked piously for a brief time in church but then acted just like people who never went to church.

What was transpiring here? Their faith, if there was any, was only form. They went through the motions and perhaps emotions, but there was no change in their lives spiritually—no life-changing experience through faith in Christ.

Those who hailed Jesus as the Blessed One coming in the name of the Lord were like my father's friends. They had a lot of form, and they even knew some Scripture. But at the end of Passion Week, they would be shouting to have the Lord crucified.

Looked around

What do we see when we observe people at a mall? Do we see just people—or people needing a Saviour? Jesus looked around in the temple. What did He see?

—Paul R. Bawden.

Golden Text Illuminated

"They that went before, and they that followed, cried, saying, Hosanna; Blessed is he that cometh in the name of the Lord" (Mark 11:9).

Jesus and those who traveled with Him were greeted by a large crowd of people as He entered Jerusalem less than a week before His crucifixion. The presence of the crowds was a result of the coming celebration of Passover.

First, the ministry of the seventy, just a few months prior to this, had probably convinced many people that the kingdom was indeed near (Luke 10:1-17; 19:11). Second, the recent raising of Lazarus from the dead in nearby Bethany caused many of the Jews to believe in Him (John 11:45). Third, the healing of two blind men in Jericho just days before increased the anticipation of Jesus' arrival in Jerusalem and no doubt increased the number of people who were traveling with Him.

As Jesus began His approach to Jerusalem, He very deliberately secured a colt on which to ride in fulfillment of messianic prophecy (Mark 11:1-7; cf. Zech. 9:9). As Jesus came to the city, people began to spread their garments and branches in the way before Him. This was an act reserved for people of the highest rank (cf. II Kings 9:13).

As Jesus entered Jerusalem, those who came out from the city to greet Him and went before Him joined with those who followed in crying out, "Hosanna; Blessed is he that cometh in the name of the Lord." This is a direct quote from Psalm 118:25-26. Psalm 118 was one of the so-called Hallel (praise) psalms (chaps. 113—118), which were traditionally sung on Passover. It was fresh on the minds of the people, and in shouting these words in reference to Jesus, they were acknowledging Him as the Messiah.

Quite in contrast to His earlier ministry, Jesus now was boldly, publicly, and officially presenting Himself as Israel's Messiah. Everything together—the context, the approach, the time, the response—providentially and clearly declared Jesus the Messiah. When called upon to rebuke the crowd's proclamation, Jesus refused (Luke 19:39-40).

The people rightly affirmed that Jesus was Israel's Messiah and King. Their response, however, was greater than their understanding. Their cries of "Hosanna," meaning "Save now," probably focused on the physical idea of His sending prosperity now (Ps. 118:25). In other words, they still did not grasp the spiritual nature of the salvation Christ would bring.

To acknowledge Christ by faith means to follow Him, submit to Him, and conform to His Word. Our words of faith will ring true only when our actions confirm them.

—Jarl K. Waggoner.

Heart of the Lesson

1. Jesus prepared for His appearance (Mark 11:1-7). We see how Jesus gave His disciples instructions to prepare for His public appearing. It was a pivotal point in His public ministry. The ordinary, common people received Him gladly and saw Him as the Messiah who had been promised to them. Notice also how specific the instructions were that were given to His disciples to prepare for the event. They had to go to a certain village. The donkey was one that had never been ridden before.

We also learn how the disciples prepared the donkey for their Master. They put their garments on the animal so that Jesus could be seated; this was in preparation for the very public event that was soon to begin. When God gives us instructions, it is very important that we follow them closely, even if they do not make sense to us at the time. Many of the prophecies in Scripture were given so that we might be ready for His coming again. We are to pay heed and prepare for it.

God's presence in our midst calls for prior preparation so that we might be ready to receive Him. The disciples followed the instructions to the letter, and so must we when we read His Word.

2. The crowd responded to Jesus (Mark 11:8-10). In our lesson this week, we see the value of the simplicity of the crowd that recognized Jesus as the promised Messiah. Their minds were not clogged with trite theological arguments. They saw Jesus, knew who He was immediately, and then gave Him the respect and the adoration He deserved. After all, they saw Him as the Messiah who was to come.

We find that the crowds also praised Him in the name of the God they knew, the God of their ancestor David. They saw Him as the One who came in the name of their God and the One who was ushering in the coming kingdom of their ancestor David. The word "Hosanna" was a word of praise to God. It meant "Lord, save us now." Their deliverance from all kinds of bondage, even from that of Roman rule, was there, they thought. It caused them to praise God. It was a collective, national dream come true.

Only those in bondage know what it means to have freedom. Jesus came to set us free from our sins. The Messiah is here for us and seeks our response.

3. Jesus went to the temple (Mark 11:11). We see the priority of Jesus. After the public acclaim He received, we see Him going into the temple at Jerusalem. He set the example for us. Then He went out with His disciples to be with them. Jesus shows us that our ministry begins with our worship of God; then we are to relate to those around us so that we might use the opportunity to minister to others of the grace of God. We are called to reveal God's presence to others.

—A. Koshy Muthalaly.

World Missions

Not all peoples of the earth are unaware of their need for redemption. In the following two stories, we meet tribesmen in different parts of Africa who had been waiting to hear about how they could be reconciled to God. They were truly blessed, because they believed the message of those who came in the name of the Lord.

The Gedeo

The Gedeo people live in the hill country of Ethiopia. These many-faceted tribesmen were held together by their common belief in a good god, whom they call "Magano." However, they were more concerned about appeasing the evil being they called "Shei'tan." A foreigner among them once asked, "How is it that you regard Magano with profound awe and yet sacrifice to Shei'tan?"

An elder replied, "We sacrifice to Shei'tan not because we love him but because we simply do not enjoy close enough ties with Magano to allow us to be done with Shei'tan!"

However, one man, Warrasa Wange, sought out Magano and asked him to reveal himself to the Gedeo people. Magano answered his request by giving Warrasa a vision.

In the vision, he saw two white-skinned strangers. These two men built makeshift shelters under the shade of a sycamore tree near the town of Dilla. At the end of the vision, Warrasa heard a voice say, "These men will bring you a message from Magano. Wait for them."

Eight long years passed. Then, on a hot and sunny day in December 1948, Canadians Albert Brant and Glen Cain reached the plains outside of the town called Dilla.

Scanning the countryside, they spotted a large sycamore tree and decided to pitch their tents under its sprawling branches. Hearing the sound of a motor, Warrasa turned to the plain and watched with his own eyes as the images of his vision from so many years before began to unfold in reality.

Thirty years later, a Spirit-filled Warrasa, along with Albert and others, counted more than 40,000 followers of Jesus Christ among the Gedeo people.

The Mbaka

Among the tribes living in Central

African Republic are the Mbaka. Deep in the tribal memory lay the Creator God, Koro. An elder once told a missionary the following story about Koro: "Koro, the Creator, sent word to our forefathers of long ago that He has already sent His Son into the world to accomplish something wonderful for all mankind. Later, however, our forefathers turned away from the truth about Koro's Son" (Richardson, *Eternity in Their Hearts,* Regal).

Eventually, messengers did come in the form of Ferdinand Rosenau and his colleagues in the 1920s.

The Mbaka were so excited to finally receive this long-forgotten truth that they believed the gospel message wholeheartedly.

—Christina Futrell.

The Jewish Aspect

Our theme this week, "Coming in the Name of the Lord," implies a significant historical background and draws on weighty Old Testament symbolism and prophecies. At the first Passover Feast in Egypt, the Israelites were on the brink of a break for freedom from slavery. On the tenth day of the Hebrew month Nisan, each family was to take a lamb or goat from the flock. It had to be the best animal, free of sickness, blemish, and broken bones (Exod. 12:3, 5). It was placed alone in a pen so that it could be guarded until Nisan 14, when it would be sacrificed "in the evening" (vs. 6).

God's presentation of His Son as the Messiah, the King of Israel, is deeply imbedded in Scripture. Abraham was promised a land forever (Gen. 17:8). David was promised an eternal King (II Sam. 7:16). The kingdom was proclaimed at Mount Sinai just before Israel received the Law (Exod. 19:6). The people of Israel would be a "kingdom of priests, and an holy nation." And if you were not aware that you were in God's plans for that kingdom, Revelation 1:5-6 says that Christians are made "kings and priests unto God and his Father."

Daniel explained that the future kingdom would be so strong that it would lay waste all earthly kingdoms (Dan. 2:44-45). Daniel also received a prophetic vision of the coronation of the King-Messiah, the Lord Jesus Christ (7:13-14).

John the Baptist also preached this message of a coming King (Matt. 3:1-4). After John was imprisoned, Jesus preached the same kingdom message (Mark 1:14-15) and even had His disciples carry that message to the cities and towns of Israel (Matt. 10:5-7; Luke 10:1-3).

Now the time had come to make a formal offer of the kingdom the Jews had heard so much about. Jesus was a marked man. Going to Jerusalem was not safe, for the religious leaders were plotting to kill Him (John 11:53). Jesus rode into Jerusalem, "and when he was come near, he beheld the city, and wept over it, saying, If thou hadst known, . . . the things which belong unto thy peace! but now they are hid from thine eyes" (Luke 19:41-42).

Nevertheless, an enthusiastic crowd welcomed the Lord, "saying, Blessed be the King that cometh in the name of the Lord: peace in heaven, and glory in the highest" (Luke 19:38). The Pharisees angrily called upon Jesus to rebuke the worshippers. But Jesus said, "If these should hold their peace, the stones would immediately cry out" (vs. 40).

The first night of Passover this year is next Saturday. It is Nisan 14, when the passover lamb should be offered in the evening. However, the lamb in the story of the Exodus is totally missing from Jewish worship. There is no animal described as sacrificed. No mention is made of the blood of the lamb that was applied to the doorposts of Jewish homes in Egypt. Lamb is rarely served at traditional Passover Feasts.

It is time to weep, as Jesus did, over the children of Israel. They are not experiencing the kingdom God offered. They need to be saved, for "except a man be born again, he cannot see the kingdom of God" (John 3:3).

—Lyle P. Murphy.

Guiding the Superintendent

DEVOTIONAL OUTLINE

1. Preparation for a triumphal entry (Mark 11:1-6). For the third time, Jesus told His disciples of His imminent death and resurrection (cf. 10:33), but it appears that they still did not fully grasp what He was saying. Jesus and His disciples were traveling to Jerusalem at the time of Passover, but this time He would become the sacrificial lamb as He was crucified just outside the city gates. His disciples mistakenly thought that He was going to set up an earthly kingdom there.

The location of the villages of Bethphage and Bethany at the Mount of Olives was not a coincidence. Jesus confidently directed the disciples regarding the colt with the knowledge that if they did as instructed, the mission would be carried out just as He intended. The virgin colt typified the nature of ceremonial sacrifices made in keeping with the Mosaic Law.

2. Celebrating the coming of the Messiah (Mark 11:7-10). To honor their King and make His entry into Jerusalem as noble and dignified as possible, the disciples and other followers either placed their coats on the back of the donkey's colt for Christ to sit on or spread their coats in the path along with tree branches. The multitude surrounded Jesus and shouted "Hosanna" as Jesus triumphantly approached the city. Jesus would indeed save them; but He would not know joy or prosperity, for soon He would hear men shouting, "Crucify him. . . . Crucify him" (15:13-14).

3. Christ visited the temple (Mark 11:11). It was Jesus' custom to visit the temple upon entering the city. This time was no different. Whether it was the same day or the next day that Jesus cleansed the temple of those who defiled it, He will always set things in order in relation to God and the things of God. The temple of our bodies, like the temple at Jerusalem, must be reverenced and held as sacred; otherwise, the Spirit of the Lord will not inhabit it.

AGE-GROUP EMPHASES

Children: Assure them that there is a place for them in kingdom work and that God needs them to make themselves available to Him.

Youths: Teach them that while they cannot predict their future, their life's purpose is not a mystery to God. He will reveal it to them if they keep their hearts open to Him.

Adults: Some adults may be waiting for the fulfillment of a promise that God made them some time ago. Encourage them to wait patiently on the Lord but to rejoice as if it were already done.

—Jane E. Campbell.

LESSON 6	APRIL 5, 2015

Scripture Lesson Text

I COR. 15:1 Moreover, brethren, I declare unto you the gospel which I preached unto you, which also ye have received, and wherein ye stand;

2 By which also ye are saved, if ye keep in memory what I preached unto you, unless ye have believed in vain.

3 For I delivered unto you first of all that which I also received, how that Christ died for our sins according to the scriptures;

4 And that he was buried, and that he rose again the third day according to the scriptures:

5 And that he was seen of Ce′phas, then of the twelve:

6 After that, he was seen of above five hundred brethren at once; of whom the greater part remain unto this present, but some are fallen asleep.

7 After that, he was seen of James; then of all the apostles.

8 And last of all he was seen of me also, as of one born out of due time.

9 For I am the least of the apostles, that am not meet to be called an apostle, because I persecuted the church of God.

10 But by the grace of God I am what I am: and his grace which *was bestowed* upon me was not in vain; but I laboured more abundantly than they all: yet not I, but the grace of God which was with me.

11 Therefore whether *it were* I or they, so we preach, and so ye believed.

20 But now is Christ risen from the dead, *and* become the firstfruits of them that slept.

21 For since by man *came* death, by man *came* also the resurrection of the dead.

22 For as in Ad′am all die, even so in Christ shall all be made alive.

NOTES

Resurrection Guaranteed

(Easter)

Lesson: I Corinthians 15:1-11, 20-22

Read: I Corinthians 15:1-22

TIME: A.D. 55   PLACE: from Ephesus

GOLDEN TEXT—"For as in Adam all die, even so in Christ shall all be made alive" (I Corinthians 15:22).

Introduction

Factual reality is essential to the conduct of our daily lives. To question the factual reality of whatever is clearly real seems absurd.

Yet when discussing matters of "religion," many assume that each world religion, including Christianity, has evolved its own beliefs, none of which are factually true. If this were true, we would have to discard the central event in our faith, the resurrection of Jesus. Easter would be better spent simply with eggs, bunnies, and new clothes. The resurrection would be a mere myth invented to make us feel better.

Paul too lived in a world with many religions and many skeptics concerning truth. In the Greek city of Corinth, the thought of bodily resurrection was laughable. Our lesson this week shows how Paul proved its truth.

LESSON OUTLINE

I. THE GOSPEL AND CHRIST'S RESURRECTION—I Cor. 15:1-4

II. EVIDENCES OF CHRIST'S RESURRECTION—I Cor. 15:5-11

III. FUTURE IMPLICATIONS OF CHRIST'S RESURRECTION—I Cor. 15:20-22

Exposition: Verse by Verse

THE GOSPEL AND CHRIST'S RESURRECTION

I COR. 15:1 Moreover, brethren, I declare unto you the gospel which I preached unto you, which also ye have received, and wherein ye stand;

2 By which also ye are saved, if ye keep in memory what I preached unto you, unless ye have believed in vain.

3 For I delivered unto you first of all that which I also received, how

that Christ died for our sins according to the scriptures;

4 And that he was buried, and that he rose again the third day according to the scriptures.

The gospel and salvation (I Cor. 15:1-2). The reason Paul wrote so fully of the resurrection in this chapter is not revealed until verse 12: "How say some among you that there is no resurrection of the dead?" Some within the Corinthian church were asserting that there was no such thing as bodily resurrection.

It was commonly believed among the Greeks, following Plato's teaching, that after death the soul lived on but the body did not. The body was an evil prison that kept one confined to a world of shadows. But at death, the soul was freed to enter the world of reality. Thus, it made no sense to them to have the body restored. Paul had encountered mockery in Athens when he preached Jesus' resurrection (Acts 17:18, 32), and the Greek mind-set in Corinth was no different.

The Corinthian believers had initially accepted Paul's message concerning Christ, including His resurrection. But error had crept in, asserting that for Christians who died, there was no resurrection (I Cor. 15:12), no matter what the case might have been with Christ. So Paul found it necessary to return to gospel basics to reveal this inconsistency.

"I declare unto you," wrote Paul, "the gospel which I preached unto you, which also ye have received, and wherein ye stand" (I Cor. 15:1). He should not have found it necessary to do this, for they knew what the gospel (good news) was. They had not only heard it but also received it, embracing its truths. They had taken their stand on those truths.

This gospel had wrought a miraculous work in them; it was the means by which they were being saved. The verb tense used here is present, which in Greek frequently implies continuous action. Salvation was a process being worked out in their lives. The only condition for them to fulfill was that they hold firmly to the truth of what Paul preached to them. The conditional clause in the Greek assumes that they really were holding firmly to Paul's message.

Everything hinged on the truth of that message. The cautionary "unless ye have believed in vain" in I Corinthians 15:2 hypothetically casts doubt not on the Corinthians' faith but on the validity of the gospel itself. All the faith in the world is useless if the message believed is false. This was the issue Paul dealt with in verses 12-19. If the dead are not raised, as some said, both Paul's preaching and their faith were in vain (vss. 14, 17).

The essentials of the gospel (I Cor. 15:3-4). Paul now set out the facts of the gospel to prove it is a message that does save. "For I delivered unto you" reminded the Corinthians that Paul's gospel had not changed. "First of all" should be understood as first in importance, rather than first in time. "That which I also received" probably includes both what Paul had heard from eyewitnesses and what God had revealed to him personally (Gal. 1:11-12, 15-19).

The gospel consists, first, of the truth "that Christ died for our sins according to the scriptures" (I Cor. 15:3). The death of Christ was, in itself, not good news. It seemed a double tragedy because He was sinless and undeserving of death. But it was good news because it was for our sins. He hung on the cross on behalf of all sinners and satisfied the justice of a righteous God. No message can claim to be the gospel unless it presents Christ's death as God's exclusive remedy for sin.

Paul took care to remind the Corinthians that this had happened exactly as the Scriptures had foretold. No one would question the *fact* of Jesus' death, but the *meaning* of it was not evident to all. This is where the testimony of the Old Testament prophetic Scriptures was essential. The same testimony was also given concerning Jesus' resurrection.

Before Jesus died, He referred to these prophecies (Matt. 12:40; 26:24, 53-54; Mark 9:12). After His resurrection, He revealed their meanings more fully to His disciples (Luke 24:25-27, 44-47). After He left the earth, His spokesmen continued to unfold the words that foretold His redemption. Peter did so at Pentecost (Acts 2:29-32); Philip when speaking to the Ethiopian (8:32-35); and Paul whenever he proclaimed Christ (13:35; 17:2-3; 26:22-23; 28:23).

What Old Testament passages pointed to Christ's death for sin and resurrection to new life? Many could be cited, but noteworthy were two passages from the Psalms—Psalm 16:10 and all of Psalm 22. Also crucial was Isaiah 53, which portrays the Lord's Servant suffering for His people's sins and finally being rewarded by the knowledge that many would be justified thereby. These prophets did not fully understand "the sufferings of Christ, and the glory that should follow" (I Pet. 1:11), but God confirmed their words at the appointed time.

The gospel Paul preached would have been incomplete if it had included only Christ's death for sin, for a Saviour who stays dead is no Saviour at all. So he also preached "that he was buried, and that he rose again the third day" (I Cor. 15:4). Christ's resurrection was crucial. But why should His burial be emphasized? The burial is important because it confirms the reality of both His death and His resurrection.

Witnesses saw Jesus' corpse taken down from the cross, wrapped in linen, and placed in a tomb. They also observed that a stone was placed at its entrance (Mark 15:42-47). Witnesses subsequently learned that the stone was rolled back and that the tomb was now empty. They knew that no one could have stolen the body (Matt. 28:1-4, 11). Apart from the resurrection, the empty tomb remains a mystery, for Jesus was truly dead and buried there.

EVIDENCES OF CHRIST'S RESURRECTION

5 And that he was seen of Cephas, then of the twelve:

6 After that, he was seen of above five hundred brethren at once; of whom the greater part remain unto this present, but some are fallen asleep.

7 After that, he was seen of James; then of all the apostles.

8 And last of all he was seen of me also, as of one born out of due time.

9 For I am the least of the apostles, that am not meet to be called an apostle, because I persecuted the church of God.

10 But by the grace of God I am what I am: and his grace which was bestowed upon me was not in vain; but I laboured more abundantly than they all: yet not I, but the grace of God which was with me.

11 Therefore whether it were I or they, so we preach, and so ye believed.

Earliest appearances (I Cor. 15:5). No eyewitnesses of Jesus' death are cited, for that event was common knowledge. But His resurrection was supernatural, and it had to be confirmed by those who saw Him afterward. Such persons were still living, since I Corinthians was written within their generation (A.D. 55). Paul's "and that" tells us that he considered Jesus' appearances as much a part of the gospel as His death and resurrection.

Paul did not recount all the eyewitnesses enumerated in the Gospels—only those who might be significant to the Corinthians. So of those who saw Jesus on the first day, he mentioned only "Cephas" (Peter) and "the twelve" (I Cor. 15:5). The Corinthians knew Peter, and some even claimed to be his followers (cf. 1:12). They would respect his testimony as an apostle. "The twelve" (15:5) refers to the closest disciples, though they no longer included Judas, and Thomas was absent at the first appearance.

Later appearances (I Cor. 15:6-7). The first two cited appearances confirmed Jesus' resurrection for the apostolic band. But there were also later ones. Paul spoke of "above five hundred brethren at once." He no doubt included these to emphasize the sheer numbers who saw Christ at one time. Most were still living, and the Corinthians could verify their experience if they wished. "Fallen asleep" was the usual way to depict believers' deaths.

Still later, Christ was seen by James. This was the half brother of Jesus (cf. Matt. 13:55), who, along with his brothers, had joined the early believers (Acts 1:14). He became a leader in the Jerusalem church (15:13; 21:18) and wrote the epistle bearing his name. Then, just before His ascension, Jesus appeared to all the apostles together, giving them their final commission (Matt. 28:16-20; Acts 1:4-9). Thus, all the founders of the church had seen the risen Christ.

Appearance to Paul (I Cor. 15:8-10). One more appearance was crucial to Paul's argument for the resurrection: "And last of all he was seen of me also." To deny resurrection is to deny the validity of an eyewitness's experience and thus his message. In considering his status next to the other apostles, Paul compared himself to "one born out of due time." The Greek term for "born" here means "abortion," or "miscarriage"—a violent, untimely birth. Unlike the other apostles, who were nurtured gradually by Jesus, Paul was suddenly torn from the womb of militant, anti-Christian Judaism when he met Jesus.

For this reason, Paul always considered himself unworthy to be an apostle. He declared himself not fit to be called one. His apostleship had indeed been questioned by some, and he would later address this problem (II Cor. 10—12). He did not deny his apostleship, and for the sake of the gospel, he defended it against attackers. But he recognized that he was unworthy of it.

The reason for Paul's sense of unworthiness was that he had "persecuted the church of God" (I Cor. 15:9). "Church of God" stresses how bad his crime was: in persecuting God's church, he had persecuted God Himself (cf. Acts 9:4-5). Paul knew God had forgiven him for this, but he could not erase it from his past. This sin seemed to be forever in his memory (cf. Acts 22:4; 26:9-11; Gal. 1:13; I Tim. 1:12-16).

Paul freely confessed, "By the grace of God I am what I am" (I Cor. 15:10). God's grace had not only saved him; it had also made him an apostle with a special ministry to the Gentiles (cf. Eph. 3:8). This bestowal had not been wasted, for it enabled him to work harder than the other apostles. He traveled more miles, suffered more hardship, founded more churches, and wrote more letters than they (cf. II Cor. 11:23-29). This was done only by grace.

Summary (I Cor. 15:11). Paul thus placed his witness of Christ's resurrection alongside that of the other apostles. Having done so, he stated, "Whether it were I or they, so we preach, and so ye believed." In the final analysis, the message, not the messenger, was important. The gospel—Christ's death for our sins, burial, and resurrection—was the single apostolic message, and it had been believed by the Corinthians.

FUTURE IMPLICATIONS OF CHRIST'S RESURRECTION

20 But now is Christ risen from the dead, and become the firstfruits of them that slept.

21 For since by man came death,

by man came also the resurrection of the dead.

22 For as in Adam all die, even so in Christ shall all be made alive.

Although our text from I Corinthians 15 does not include verses 12-19, their significance should be noted. Paul here argued that if Christ did, in fact, rise from the dead and if that resurrection is crucial to the gospel, it is illogical to say that the dead cannot be raised. If that were so, Christ would still be dead, the apostolic message would be false, sins would not be forgiven, and Christians who had died would have perished eternally. Their condition would be "most miserable."

Christ as the firstfruits (I Cor. 15:20). With "but now," Paul sharply contrasted the hypothetical implications of existence without Christ's resurrection with the real implications of life based upon it. Christ is, indeed, risen, and is the "firstfruits of them that slept." As a first, ripe sheaf of grain guarantees a harvest to follow, so Christ's resurrection is the pledge of a future resurrection of deceased believers (cf. Col. 1:18; Rev. 1:5).

Christ as the Last Adam (I Cor. 15:21-22). Paul now drew a parallel between the effects of the actions of Adam and Christ. Adam, the progenitor of mankind, through sin brought death to all his descendants. None are exempted because of the solidarity of all in him (cf. Rom. 5:12). But the Son of Man, Jesus Christ, initiated resurrection from the dead, and those united with Him as a new creation will join Him in new life.

The principle that both death and resurrection have a human progenitor (I Cor. 15:21) is made concrete in the next verse: "For as in Adam all die, even so in Christ shall all be made alive." There is a question about how inclusive the second "all" is. We know that there are no exceptions to the first "all," for all die. But did Paul also mean that all mankind will be given new life?

Jesus Himself taught that there would be a resurrection for both the good and the evil (John 5:28-29), each to their final fate (cf. Rev. 20:5-6, 12-13). But here Paul was dealing with the question of whether deceased *believers* will be raised (I Cor. 15:18, 23, 53-58). It is also hard to see how unbelievers could be "in Christ" (vs. 22). Thus, Paul seems to have been focusing on the resurrection of believers only.

There are other implications of Jesus' resurrection. But even this glimpse of our future life with Him should cause us to rejoice anew and to be, as Paul counseled, "stedfast, unmoveable, always abounding in the work of the Lord" (I Cor. 15:58).

—*Robert E. Wenger.*

QUESTIONS

1. Why did Paul find it necessary to write at length about Christ's resurrection?
2. What experience had the Corinthians had with the gospel? Why did Paul have to repeat it?
3. What is the first essential of the gospel?
4. Did Old Testament writers know the gospel message? Explain.
5. Why is the mere fact that Jesus died not the gospel?
6. What eyewitnesses to Jesus' resurrection did Paul include?
7. How did Paul's conversion differ from those of other apostles?
8. Why did Paul have such a strong sense of God's grace in his life?
9. What did Paul mean when he called Christ the firstfruits of those who slept (I Cor. 15:20)?
10. What parallel did Paul draw between Adam and Christ?

—*Robert E. Wenger.*

Preparing to Teach the Lesson

The word "Easter" is thought by many to come from the worship of a Teutonic spring goddess, "Eostre," who was worshipped in what is our March. This dates to before the time of Christ. Christians took the word and applied it to the annual celebration of Christ's resurrection, which was observed as early as A.D. 154. The Council of Nicea (A.D. 325) determined that the date for Easter would be the first Sunday after the first full moon after the vernal equinox, except when the full moon fell on a Sunday, when Easter would be one week later.

TODAY'S AIM

Facts: to accept the evidence for and guarantee of Christ's resurrection.

Principle: to understand that our resurrection is totally dependent on that of Christ.

Application: to believe in the resurrected Christ for eternal life.

INTRODUCING THE LESSON

The date of Easter is not like that of Christmas; it varies yearly. If I want to know the date of Easter, I look at a printed calendar. Regardless of what the specific date is for any given year, the fact is that without Christ's resurrection, there is no Christian calendar. There is no Christianity without the resurrection! As Paul wrote, "And if Christ be not risen, then is our preaching vain, and your faith is also vain" (I Cor. 15:14).

DEVELOPING THE LESSON

1. Christ's resurrection proved by Scripture (I Cor. 15:1-4). Paul began by reminding the believers at Corinth of what he had told them before when he preached the gospel to them. He then reviewed what he knew of their response to the gospel. They had received it in the past, and they took their present stand in it. He knew they were saved by that gospel.

The verb "saved" is in the present tense, which stresses their continuing sanctification in their salvation, leading to their future life in Christ.

Those believers also had a need to examine their lives (I Cor. 15:2). The phrase "if ye keep in memory" emphasizes Paul's assumption that they would do this—that they would hold fast to their faith. Another possibility existed, however. They might have "believed in vain." The words "in vain" mean "to no purpose." Paul knew that it was possible to have a belief that is not centered on the purpose of the gospel (cf. II Cor. 13:5). In that case, a person is not saved. Each believer must examine himself on this matter.

Paul next concisely defined the gospel he had preached to them (I Cor. 15:3-4). The words "first of all" refer to first in importance. Paul had received the gospel directly from God, so it had His authority (Gal. 1:11-12). The main points of the gospel are that Christ died on behalf of our sins; He was buried, which proved He died; He rose the third day; and He is still the risen Saviour. All of this came about in accordance with the Scriptures. The Scriptures Paul had in mind doubtless included ones such as Psalms 2:7, 16:8-10, 22:22, and Isaiah 53:4-12.

2. Christ's resurrection proved by witnesses (I Cor. 15:5-11). The testimony of Scripture should be enough to satisfy anyone. Paul, however, assured the Corinthians that many witnesses had also seen the risen Christ. Paul first identified Peter's witness ("Cephas") (cf. Luke 24:34), followed by all the apostles (cf. John 20:19-29).

April 5, 2015

Exactly when the five hundred saw Christ, Paul did not say, probably because he had already told the Corinthians earlier. It may have been at the time of Matthew 28:18-20. James, the half brother of Christ, had also seen Him, followed by the apostles (cf. Acts 1:4-11). The last person to witness the resurrected Christ was Paul (cf. chap. 9). He considered himself "one born out of due time" (I Cor. 15:8), a phrase used in ancient Greek literature of a dead, miscarried child.

Paul regarded himself spiritually as one who had no right to be in the society of the apostles. He remembered his past life of persecuting the church persistently. God's grace, however, forever changed Paul's life. Because of God's grace, he labored for Christ unceasingly and more diligently than any of the other apostles. The Corinthians could look at Paul—or any of the apostles—and see the same thing: they all preached the gospel of the resurrected Christ.

3. Christ's resurrection guarantees future resurrection (I Cor. 15:20-22). Christ rose from the dead, which means that preaching and faith are not vain (cf. vs. 14), the apostles testified truly (vs. 15), we are not in our sins (vs. 17), the dead have not perished (vs. 18), and we are not to be pitied but envied (vs. 19). All this is because Christ is the "firstfruits" (vs. 20). The firstfruits of harvest were the earliest pickings of the season, and they pointed to the promise of the greater harvest soon to come. Christ's resurrection was the first to a total new life, and it remains the promise of the resurrection of all believers in Him. Paul proceeded to show what believers can anticipate.

Paul set forth a startling double contrast (I Cor. 15:21-22). The first emphasis is on two men. It was by a man (Adam) that death came into the world (cf. Rom. 5:12). It was by a contrasting man (Christ) that resurrection from both physical and spiritual death came into the world. The second emphasis is on two classes of people. Those people who are in Adam die, and that includes everyone in the world. In contrast, those who are in Christ—that is, those who are saved by faith in Him—shall be made alive through resurrection to eternal life with God.

ILLUSTRATING THE LESSON

The fact that Christ rose from the dead assures us that all believers shall also rise to new life.

CONCLUDING THE LESSON

We have a glorious prospect of resurrection life, but it is only because of the work of Christ. Jesus is not dead in some Jerusalem tomb; He is alive forevermore. This is why we have Easter, the grand climax of God's story of salvation. Give the opportunity for your students to make salvation real in their lives by trusting Christ as their Saviour.

ANTICIPATING THE NEXT LESSON

Next week we will see that because we have new life in Christ through God's grace, we can love each other with God's love.

—R. Larry Overstreet.

PRACTICAL POINTS

1. Those who know the Lord are thoroughly convinced of the gospel of Jesus Christ (I Cor. 15:1-2).
2. Keep it simple: Christ died for our sins, was buried, and rose again (vss. 3-4).
3. Do not be discouraged by those who doubt the resurrection. There were many witnesses to the event (vss. 5-8).
4. We are unworthy, but God is gracious to do great works through us (vs. 9).
5. God's grace gives our lives value and purpose (vss. 10-11).
6. The resurrection of Christ gives us hope for this life and the next (vss. 20-22).

—Cheryl Y. Powell.

RESEARCH AND DISCUSSION

1. What made Jesus Christ an acceptable sacrifice for our sins?
2. Is it possible to be a Christian, yet not believe in the bodily resurrection of Christ? Why or why not?
3. How does it encourage you that Paul, a former persecutor of Christians, eventually became one of Christ's most effective witnesses (cf. Acts 8—9)?
4. How does the resurrection relate to Leviticus 23:9-14?
5. What effect did the sin of Adam have on all mankind?
6. Who does "all" in I Corinthians 15:22 include? Is anyone excluded (cf. Matt. 5:29; II Thess. 1:9; Rev. 20:15)?

—Cheryl Y. Powell.

ILLUSTRATED HIGH POINTS

He was seen

I was presiding at the graveside service for a believer in Christ who had passed away. I mentioned that although his body was being buried in the ground, his personality was now with the Lord. I went on to say that someday, when the Lord returns, He would bring the individual's personality with Him to be joined with his body, which would be raised from the grave. He would then go, as a new person, to be with the Lord forever.

Of course, the bodily resurrection of the believer in Christ hinges on the bodily resurrection of Jesus Christ. If He did not rise from the dead, then the believer in Christ will not rise from the dead, either.

The reality is that science cannot prove or disprove the bodily resurrection of Jesus Christ. The eyewitnesses have given us the evidence that Christ conquered the grave bodily. The bodily resurrection of Christ is as real as you are.

We preach

I was in my study one day when the local sheriff came by and gave me a subpoena to appear in court on a certain date. Before our second daughter was born, the doctor and the anesthesiologist had a scuffle in a room next to where my wife was waiting. I happened to overhear what happened and was now being subpoenaed to appear in court to testify on behalf of the doctor. In court, I was an eyewitness for the doctor. I told what happened, and it was entered into the record.

When we preach the gospel to unbelievers, we do not struggle to convince them. We simply testify to what happened—on that first Easter and in our own lives.

—Paul R. Bawden.

Golden Text Illuminated

"For as in Adam all die, even so in Christ shall all be made alive" (I Corinthians 15:22).

The golden text states a comforting truth. However, it is preceded by a lengthy and detailed argument.

Some within the Corinthian church were denying the future resurrection of believers, even while they accepted the bodily resurrection of Christ (I Cor. 15:12). They were willing to accept Christ's resurrection "as a strange and unusual fact pertaining to a very unusual Person. Yet they were saying there is no such thing as a resurrection of the *Christian's* body" (Boyer, *For a World Like Ours*, Baker). Perhaps in this they were being influenced by Greek philosophy, which was so prevalent in this Greek city.

Paul argued that Christ's resurrection necessarily guarantees the resurrection of every believer. He stated that denial of a resurrection in general is a denial of Christ's resurrection. To deny Christ's resurrection is to reject the very gospel of Christ (I Cor. 15:12-17; cf. vss. 1-8).

Paul then stated again what he and many other witnesses testified to: "Now is Christ risen from the dead" (I Cor. 15:20). This undeniable fact was not an exception to the rule but a guarantee that all believers will likewise be resurrected, for Christ is the "firstfruits" of all believers who now sleep.

The spirits of believers who have died are in the presence of the Lord (II Cor. 5:6-8); yet their bodies "sleep," awaiting a new, resurrection body. Just as the firstfruits of the harvest promise there is more to come, so Jesus' resurrection assures all believers a future resurrection.

The resurrection of Christ reversed the sentence of death for all who trust in Christ. Death entered the world through one man: Adam. His sin brought the sentence of death; and since his sin was passed on to all his descendants, all stand condemned (Rom. 5:12). Those who are in Adam, that is, all who are born physically, die, or, literally "go on dying." They are dead spiritually, and they will die physically.

However, those who are "in Christ," that is, those who are born again spiritually by faith, will be made alive. They will be raised up in new bodies to dwell forever with the Lord. The sentence of death has been reversed through Christ's resurrection.

As we contemplate the resurrection of Christ, we should remember at least two things. First, Christ rose bodily from the grave, and this guarantees a bodily existence for us in eternity. To "be made alive" involves both body and spirit. We are not spirit beings like angels. We have been made to have bodies, and we will have glorified resurrection bodies in the eternal state.

Second, the hope Christ's resurrection offers is a reversal of the sentence of death. He conquered death, and in Him we have new life, eternal life, and resurrection life. Death no longer holds us captive in fear (cf. Heb. 2:15). We still must deal with physical death as a reality, but the greater reality is that while these physical bodies wear out and die, in Christ we are assured of eternal resurrection bodies suited for heaven.

—Jarl K. Waggoner.

Heart of the Lesson

This quarter we see the significance of the idea of the Christian community in the New Testament. It centered around the undeniable fact of Jesus' resurrection. There is no Christian community without an acceptance of this wonderful event.

First Corinthians 15 has often been referred to as the "resurrection chapter" of the Bible. Paul taught us that because Christ died for us and rose again, we too will surely be made alive.

1. Stand firm (I Cor. 15:1-2). These verses give us the hope of Christ because of His resurrection from the dead. It is why Jesus died and is at the very core of our faith. Paul taught the Corinthian believers that they needed to get this teaching right in their hearts, for without it there is no hope of salvation. Paul built on a firm foundation of truth about the resurrection of Jesus. He is alive today.

For those of us who may be searching for the truth about salvation, Paul reminds us here that we first need to recognize that Jesus loved us so much that He died for us. He did not stop there. He also rose again to show us that we can follow the same path as He did and be victorious as He was.

2. God's grace (I Cor. 15:3-9). We see Paul's absolute humility. He showed that he was a sinner and that he too, by the grace of God, came into that community of the faithful because God revealed to him a singular truth about the resurrection. Others had the opportunity to see the risen Christ. Paul too had a vision of the risen Jesus, though much later in time. He did not deserve this after persecuting the church, but God was gracious.

What makes us an integral part of the Christian community is the clear recognition that Jesus died and rose again for each of us. As part of the faithful, we are called to live for Him, a reflection of His resurrection power in the world.

3. Resurrection power (I Cor. 15:10-11). Paul stated two important things. First, he wrote that he worked hard to tell others about the resurrection of Jesus. But he backed this up by saying that he could not have done that effectively except through the grace of God. Second, it was important that his hearers respond to the message of the resurrection of Jesus. This is the heart of the gospel.

Paul affirmed here that what is really important is the end result of the gospel that goes out to all others in the world. He wanted to see all turn to Christ and believe in Him. There is a message here for modern Christians. We need to share the resurrection of Christ with others we meet so that they too will put their trust in Him.

4. The firstfruits (I Cor. 15:20-22). The message is a simple one. Adam was the example of death. Jesus is the example of the resurrected life. We died in sin because we have the Adamic nature of sin. But now, in Christ, we can live again because Jesus is risen from the dead. We can follow Him because we have put our faith in Him.

As Christian believers, we need to take this message to heart. The world needs to know that in Christ we can live again. Our sins are washed away because of the blood of Jesus.

—A. Koshy Muthalaly.

World Missions

Beginning in December 2010, the world witnessed what became known as the Arab Spring. While this movement in the Arab world began with the desire for better treatment and opportunities, along with hope for a better future, the outcome of this movement is still unclear at the present time.

Though only time will tell what the future holds, one thing is clear. The replacing of secular governments with a hard-line Muslim authority has not been kind to Christians of the region.

Many people may forget that before the conquest of Islam, the Middle East was home to a vast number of Christians. Even today, there are large pockets of believers in many of the Muslim nations, even those like Iran. The majority of these Christians are the spiritual descendants of the disciples and apostles of Jesus' earthly time.

The civil war in Syria has been raging unabated. While we can disagree on the politics of the situation, one thing cannot be denied—the torment and despair of the innocent lives affected by brutality and bloodshed.

Syria is home to approximately 2.1 million Christians. Hundreds of thousands have fled their homes in an attempt to escape the violence.

The majority of refugees have been denied entry into the United States and the European Union, which has caused confusion and also a sense of abandonment, for they had always deemed these countries friendly and sympathetic to their plight.

Interestingly, it is the Kurds who have welcomed them into their autonomous region of Iraq. It is my prayer that the Lord will move among these Iraqi Kurds, no strangers themselves to heartache and persecution, and that they will be receptive to the love and light of Jesus.

Even with such high numbers of believers trying to flee the area, there are those who choose to stay behind. They are workers in indigenous ministries.

Sadly, they are often targets of attack. Below is an excerpt from a letter written to a church's pastor, who was away at the time of the tragedy.

"It is with great sadness that I write this email to tell you about brother Sami and his wife and three children. We were meeting for worship in his house church. Yesterday a group of fanatic Muslims came to our meeting. They broke down the door and started to shoot all over the place. . . . Then they asked us to leave the house and told Sami to stay with his family. We left the house. We heard people shouting and then they killed Sami and his family."

Pastor Ammad's response ties in directly with this week's Bible passages, the key verse being I Corinthians 15:22: "For as in Adam all die, even so in Christ shall all be made alive."

Here is a portion of his wise response. "Remember brother that Jesus has been through death and overcame it with His resurrection. Remember that we will all be with Jesus and we are not afraid to die for His glory. Sami was a man of God and loved Jesus with all his heart" (Christian Aid Mission, www.christianaid.org, October 19, 2012).

In times of struggle and hardship, our natural instinct is to run away and seek a place of refuge. However, this is not always God's plan.

God makes no mistakes. Sometimes He purposely places us in the center of the fire not just to be a witness to those who are perishing without Him but also to refine our faith in the sacred fire of His love.

—Christina Futrell.

The Jewish Aspect

Last Friday evening at sundown began the first day of Passover this year (Nisan 14 of the Jewish calendar). Passover was celebrated during the Lord's last week of earthly ministry. If the Jews today understood the truth about Jesus, they would mourn His crucifixion during the Passover.

Only believers can truly rejoice in the resurrection this morning. The resurrection of Jesus is the best-attested fact of ancient history. This week we read in our text about the overwhelming number of witnesses to this great event (I Cor. 15:5-8).

Most Jews in the first century were well-versed on the doctrine of the resurrection of the righteous. As a case in point, take Jesus' friend Martha of Bethany. Before Jesus awakened her brother, Lazarus, from death, she said, "I know that he shall rise again in the resurrection at the last day" (John 11:24). She deserved an A for her grasp of God's plan for the righteous saint after death.

Job also spoke warmly of resurrection: "If a man die, shall he live again? all the days of my appointed time will I wait, till my change come" (Job 14:14).

Reform Judaism considers itself an evolutionary faith—that is, one that changes with time. Bear in mind that their forebears were the only people in the world who knew that resurrection was a secure hope.

Jesus took away Martha's confusion about death and the assurance of life everlasting with the seventh of the "I am" statements in the Gospel of John. He declared, "I am the resurrection, and the life: he that believeth in me, though he were dead, yet shall he live" (11:25).

Did the Jews of Jesus' day have a hard time believing God could reverse death? The Bible's testimony for divine control of life and death was so strong that it was impossible to deny. Three Old Testament passages speak of individuals who died but, through His servants, God restored to life.

A mother in Israel had her son fall fatally ill (I Kings 17:17). Elijah stretched himself upon the boy and cried, "O Lord my God, I pray thee, let this child's soul come into him again. . . . And he revived" (vss. 21-22).

Another righteous woman lost her son in death (II Kings 4:20). The Prophet Elisha was undaunted. After praying and stretching himself upon the boy, Elisha saw God give renewed life.

Sometime after Elisha's death, men cast a dead comrade into his sepulchre. Touching the body of Elisha, the deceased was revived (II Kings 13:21).

During Jesus' ministry, He raised the dead son of the widow of Nain (Luke 7:11-15). Lazarus was also raised to added years of life (John 11:43-44).

Admittedly, these five passages cited on the raising of the dead speak of extending physical life. All five individuals had to face death a second time. The important point is that because of these Old Testament incidents and Jesus' work, Jews were especially aware that the power over life belongs to God.

Sadness attends every funeral, but a Jewish funeral in our day is particularly sad, for the very people who knew of bodily resurrection firsthand now deny its reality. In Judaism, it is only "ashes to ashes and dust to dust." Jews speak heroically of accepting death as a natural accompaniment to life. And for the most part, it is borne stoically. But the living see that death always wins. In contrast, we can rejoice. Because of Christ's resurrection, death itself is doomed (I Cor. 15:26).

—Lyle P. Murphy.

Guiding the Superintendent

There are some teachings that the world may question but that the church can never compromise. The teachings of the infallible Scriptures top that list. In his epistle to the Corinthian church, the Apostle Paul was adamant in his declaration of the gospel of Jesus Christ as the only true gospel.

DEVOTIONAL OUTLINE

1. Believe the resurrection (I Cor. 15:1-6). The Apostle Paul was greatly concerned that these new converts hold to the integrity of the gospel. Paul had received and preached this gospel by which many were convinced and saved. He was apprehensive that some in the church had a mistaken view of the gospel and had begun to sway from Paul's preached word to the false teaching of those who opposed the truth. He feared that some believers were rejecting Christ's resurrection entirely, without which the gospel is incomplete.

When teaching the Word of God, the teacher would do well to follow Paul's example of referring to the Word of God. The recurring theme of Christ's death for man's sin and His resurrection from the dead is the fulfillment of the Old Testament message and the basis of our hope and our victory. To support this, Paul recalled the many eyewitnesses to the risen Christ.

2. Accept the resurrection (I Cor. 15:7-11). Among those to whom Christ showed Himself alive was James, His half brother. At the beginning, James lacked confidence that Jesus was the Son of God (cf. Mark 3:31; John 7:5). Humbly, Paul added that Christ, even after His ascension, showed Himself to Paul through the Damascus-road experience. With royal authority in hand, Paul had expanded his persecution efforts against anyone professing the name of "Jesus" (cf. Acts 9:1-3). Regrettably, in his ignorance, Paul severely victimized the church; yet after his encounter with Christ, he served the church with a greater fervor as minister to "the Gentiles, and kings, and the children of Israel" (vs. 15).

In gratitude to God for the mercy and favor He had bestowed on him, Paul ascribed all that he had become to God's amazing grace. The bestowing of mercy was profitable to the kingdom, as seen by the number of people who came to the knowledge of Christ through Paul's ministry. Paul's reminder to these new converts to hold on to God's Holy Word is beneficial to Christians everywhere.

3. Eternal life through the resurrection (I Cor. 15:20-22). Being sensitive to the ambiguous notion of life after death, Paul testified that Jesus' death was not final but rather the climax of the plan of God. As Christ lives as the Firstfruit, never to die again, so shall every believer live in a resurrected body at the greater harvest to follow.

AGE-GROUP EMPHASES

Children: Easter can be exciting to children. Counter the hype with the truth that Christ suffered in His body and spirit to pay a debt He did not owe.

Youths: This age-group questions many things as their minds are exposed to a multiplicity of what the world has to offer. Teach them that there is no question that Jesus lived, died, and rose again; and since Christ lives, we all are guaranteed eternal life.

Adults: Ask your adults whether anyone doubts the resurrection; further teach and expound on this foundational truth.

—Jane E. Campbell.

LESSON 7   APRIL 12, 2015

Scripture Lesson Text

I JOHN 3:11 For this is the message that ye heard from the beginning, that we should love one another.

12 Not as Cain, *who* was of that wicked one, and slew his brother. And wherefore slew he him? Because his own works were evil, and his brother's righteous.

13 Marvel not, my brethren, if the world hate you.

14 We know that we have passed from death unto life, because we love the brethren. He that loveth not *his* brother abideth in death.

15 Whosoever hateth his brother is a murderer: and ye know that no murderer hath eternal life abiding in him.

16 Hereby perceive we the love *of God,* because he laid down his life for us: and we ought to lay down *our* lives for the brethren.

17 But whoso hath this world's good, and seeth his brother have need, and shutteth up his bowels *of compassion* from him, how dwelleth the love of God in him?

18 My little children, let us not love in word, neither in tongue; but in deed and in truth.

19 And hereby we know that we are of the truth, and shall assure our hearts before him.

20 For if our heart condemn us, God is greater than our heart, and knoweth all things.

21 Beloved, if our heart condemn us not, *then* have we confidence toward God.

22 And whatsoever we ask, we receive of him, because we keep his commandments, and do those things that are pleasing in his sight.

23 And this is his commandment, That we should believe on the name of his Son Je'sus Christ, and love one another, as he gave us commandment.

24 And he that keepeth his commandments dwelleth in him, and he in him. And hereby we know that he abideth in us, by the Spir'it which he hath given us.

NOTES

Love One Another

Lesson: I John 3:11-24

Read: I John 3:11-24

TIME: about A.D. 90–95

PLACE: probably from Ephesus

GOLDEN TEXT—"For this is the message that ye heard from the beginning, that we should love one another" (I John 3:11).

Introduction

When asked what the greatest commandment was, Jesus answered, "Thou shalt love the Lord thy God with all thy heart, and with all thy soul, and with all thy mind, and with all thy strength" (Mark 12:30). But He went beyond this to speak of the second as well, which He said was like the first: "Thou shalt love thy neighbour as thyself" (vs. 31). He declared that these two are inseparable. Indeed, He told His disciples that the one vital sign by which men would know that they were His would be their love for one another (John 13:34-35).

It may be time to refocus on love, the most basic evidence of our faith. "Love one another" is more than a sentimental expression. It is a call to active, unselfish service.

LESSON OUTLINE

I. LOVE MARKS THE CHILDREN OF GOD—I John 3:11-15

II. LOVE IS VERIFIED BY GOOD DEEDS—I John 3:16-18

III. CONFIDENCE FLOWS FROM OBEDIENCE—I John 3:19-24

Exposition: Verse by Verse

LOVE MARKS THE CHILDREN OF GOD

I JOHN 3:11 For this is the message that ye heard from the beginning, that we should love one another.

12 Not as Cain, who was of that wicked one, and slew his brother. And wherefore slew he him? Because his own works were evil, and his brother's righteous.

13 Marvel not, my brethren, if the world hate you.

14 We know that we have passed from death unto life, because we love the brethren. He that loveth not his brother abideth in death.

15 Whosoever hateth his brother is a murderer: and ye know that no murderer hath eternal life abiding in him.

A divine command (I John 3:11). Writing to Christian believers in the late years of the first century, the Apostle John was warning them of a serious doctrinal error. Proceeding from the fallacious suppositions that all matter was evil and that superior knowledge could deliver one from material existence, some teachers were spreading erroneous views of Christ, salvation, and morality. So in his first epistle, John combined doctrine with practical guidance in the outworking of his readers' faith.

In the first part of this chapter (I John 3:1-10), he had emphasized righteousness as a distinguishing mark of a Christian. Now he spoke of a second mark—love for others. The command to love one another was part of "the message that ye heard from the beginning" (vs. 11). It was a corollary of the message of salvation (cf. John 13:35).

Though "from the beginning" (I John 3:11) could mean from the beginning of time, it more likely here refers to the beginning of his readers' Christian experience (cf. 2:7-8). False teachers were offering novel ideas, but John emphasized that the teaching of Christ and the apostles is of eternal origin and never needs revision (cf. vs. 24).

The primary Greek word for "love" in the New Testament does not denote a spontaneous, instinctive, emotional love based on attractiveness in the other person. Rather, it describes a love produced by the reason and the will, a love that deliberately chooses its object. It is the word used of God's love for sinners, who certainly are not attractive to Him (John 3:16; Rom. 5:8). It never seeks self-gratification but always the good of the other person (I Cor. 13:4). This is the love God expects of us.

A negative illustration (I John 3:12-13). John had previously identified children of the devil by two traits: they do not practice righteousness or love their brother (vs. 10). Now he named one who manifested both of these characteristics. The example of Cain is set in stark contrast with the selfless love that God demands. Cain belonged to the evil one, the devil, whom Jesus called "a murderer from the beginning" (John 8:44).

Because of this diabolical relation, Cain "slew his brother" (I John 3:12). The word translated "slew" is found only here and in Revelation in the New Testament. It speaks of brutal slaughter. The Greek translation of the Old Testament uses it to describe the butchering of sacrificial animals. The first crime in human history was thus extremely hideous.

And why did Cain do it? Because his own deeds were evil, while those of his brother were righteous. The Genesis 4 account does not specifically tell us what was evil about Cain's works and righteous about Abel's. But Abel, in faith, offered a sacrifice pleasing to God (Heb. 11:4), while Cain, knowing God's will, disobeyed it. Thus was set in motion a chain reaction of jealousy, hatred, and murder. Cain tried to extinguish the witness that condemned him.

With this illustration in mind, John instructed his readers, "Marvel not, my brethren, if the world hate you" (I John 3:13). "The world" here refers to unbelievers who live by standards that do not come from God (cf. 2:15-16). Cain set the pattern for their reaction to the righteous. Jesus warned His disciples of the world's hatred (John 3:19-20; 15:18-19), and He Himself suffered under its wrath. As believers, we should never be surprised at the world's hatred (I Pet. 4:12-13).

A personal application (I John 3:14-15). John now contrasted his Christian readers with the world. Special emphasis is laid upon the pronoun "we" here; the thought is that we, unlike the world, "know that we have passed from death unto life, because we love the brethren." We have taken a transforming journey out of the realm of spiritual death into that of spiritual life, and the proof of it is that we love other Christians. The present tense of "love" indicates that it is a habit of life.

The opposite also is true. The person who does not love his brother remains in the spiritual death in which he was born. He has never been transformed and thus does not possess divine love. This does not mean unbelievers cannot show kindness and love to one another. But they do not have the divine capacity to love Christian believers or their God.

Lest some think this judgment is too harsh, John went on to prove his point. He asserted that whosoever hates his brother is a murderer and reminded his readers that no murderer possesses eternal life. Hatred is the seed from which murder germinates, for the hater wishes his enemy did not exist. He may not have the courage or the opportunity to murder, but it is in his heart (cf. Matt. 5:21-22, 27-28). Cain's actions prove the point.

The second part of the assertion in I John 3:15 is a general principle that the readers already knew. Murderers are not godly people; they do not have eternal life (cf. John 8:40-44; Rev. 21:8). This does not mean that murderers cannot be saved but that one who is saved will not commit murder. Thus, since a murderer is an unbeliever, and since a hater is a murderer, a hater is not a believer.

LOVE IS VERIFIED BY GOOD DEEDS

16 Hereby perceive we the love of God, because he laid down his life for us: and we ought to lay down our lives for the brethren.

17 But whoso hath this world's good, and seeth his brother have need, and shutteth up his bowels of compassion from him, how dwelleth the love of God in him?

18 My little children, let us not love in word, neither in tongue; but in deed and in truth.

A supreme challenge (I John 3:16). How will we recognize genuine love when we see it? The essence of love is self-sacrifice for the sake of another. And its supreme example is Jesus' death for us. "Hereby perceive we the love" ("of God" is not in the original), wrote John, "because he laid down his life for us." Jesus laid aside what was most precious to Him so that we might become partakers of His resurrection life. Love knows no greater expression than giving one's life for another (Rom. 5:6-8).

The sacrifice of Christ not only provides our atonement; it also sets before us our example and challenge. The apostle continued, "And we ought to lay down our lives for the brethren" (I John 3:16). We can never do for others what Christ did for us, but in a finite way we ought to be willing to make the supreme sacrifice. While hatred leads to the destruction of another's life, love leads to the sacrifice of one's life to save that of another.

A legitimate question (I John 3:17). If love can impel the sacrifice of one's life, how much more should it motivate the sacrifice of one's goods for another? John asked concerning one who refuses to do this, "How dwelleth the love of God in him?" He pictured a person not just glancing but gazing at length at his brother's need. But instead of helping him, he shuts his heart against him. Surely there is no love of God in such an individual!

A pointed exhortation (I John 3:18). Addressing his readers fondly as "little children," John exhorted them to exhibit genuine love. It cannot be a love merely of "word" or "tongue"—an empty verbal expression. Instead, it must be manifested "in deed and in truth." The evidence of God's love is action. Our actions will prove that we have passed from death to life (vs. 14). But because actions can be done with hypocritical motives, we must take care to act in truth. Love is sincere, never a pretense.

CONFIDENCE FLOWS FROM OBEDIENCE

19 And hereby we know that we are of the truth, and shall assure our hearts before him.

20 For if our heart condemn us, God is greater than our heart, and knoweth all things.

21 Beloved, if our heart condemn us not, then have we confidence toward God.

22 And whatsoever we ask, we receive of him, because we keep his commandments, and do those things that are pleasing in his sight.

23 And this is his commandment, That we should believe on the name of his Son Jesus Christ, and love one another, as he gave us commandment.

24 And he that keepeth his commandments dwelleth in him, and he in him. And hereby we know that he abideth in us, by the Spirit which he hath given us.

Confidence and the condemning heart (I John 3:19-20). John now addressed the problem of doubt that Christians often encounter, and he found its solution in the teaching he had just given. "Hereby we know that we are of the truth" refers back to the divine love believers manifest "in deed and in truth" (vs. 18). Thus, if we love, we can be confident that we are of the truth—that is, people of God.

On this basis, we can reassure our hearts before God. The heart (by which John meant the conscience) is not infallible. It either approves or condemns on the basis of our knowledge. Sometimes our knowledge of ourselves betrays us into thinking God has condemned us. We then need to reassure ourselves with the knowledge that He has transformed us and implanted His love in us. Love does not save us, but it gives us the assurance that God dwells in us.

The Greek construction of I John 3:20 is somewhat unclear, and perhaps it should be translated "in whatever our heart condemns us," continuing the thought of verse 19. We can reassure our hearts before God in whatever condemning thoughts we have because "God is greater than our heart, and knoweth all things" (vs. 20). His omniscience keeps Him from misjudging us. Of course, we must always allow room for self-examination, and if we discover unconfessed sin, we need to confess it promptly (cf. 1:9).

Confidence and answered prayer (I John 3:21-22). Having assured ourselves before God, we have an uncondemning heart. John brought out the implication of this: "Beloved, if our heart condemn us not, then have we confidence toward God." The word for "confidence" means "freedom of speech." The reassured believer no longer has to cower before God as a criminal before a judge. Instead, he may come with the openness of a child approaching a father (cf. Heb. 4:16; I John 2:28).

Such boldness should not be equated with brash disrespect. One who has experienced God's saving grace knows he deserves no audience with God at all (Eph. 2:1-3). He knows that his only means of access is Jesus Christ, the Mediator who shed His blood for sinners (Eph. 3:11-12; I Tim. 2:5; Heb. 10:19). But combined with this humility is the assurance that in Christ he has all the privileges of sonship (Rom. 8:15-17).

The confidence bred by an uncondemning heart assures us not only of access to God but also that "whatsoever we ask, we receive of him" (I John 3:22). The present tense of "ask" and "receive" suggest that both are regular occurrences in our lives. We cultivate the habit of asking, and with the same regularity He grants our requests (cf. 5:14-15).

But His answers are not automatic. It is true that Jesus promised that one who asks receives (Matt. 7:7-8) and that God responds to the prayer of faith (Mark

11:24). Yet we must interpret these promises in the light of all scriptural teaching on prayer. Our own text lays down the conditions of keeping God's commands and doing what pleases Him.

Confidence and God's command (I John 3:23). What were God's "commandments" in the preceding verse now are summed up as one "commandment." There are two aspects to it, but each is impossible to fulfill without the other. The two are to "believe on the name of his Son Jesus Christ, and love one another."

Confidence and the divine presence (I John 3:24). Reverting to the plural "commandments," John declared, "And he that keepeth his commandments dwelleth in him, and he in him." The one living the obedient life of love enjoys a mystical union with God described as a mutual indwelling. John may have been recalling Jesus' teaching on the union of the vine and the branches (John 15:1-7). This close union explained how one can practice daily the loving deeds that can originate only with God.

—Robert E. Wenger.

QUESTIONS

1. How long had John's readers known the command to love one another?
2. What is the nature of the love that God commands?
3. According to John, why did Cain kill his brother?
4. How was Cain a prototype of the world Christians face?
5. In what sense is a hater a murderer? What does this prove about his spiritual condition?
6. What is the supreme manifestation of love that God showed humanity?
7. What question arises about a person who will not help a person in need?
8. What should we do if doubts arise about our spiritual condition?
9. On what basis can we approach God boldly and expect Him to answer our prayers?
10. What is the Holy Spirit's role in giving a believer confidence?

—Robert E. Wenger.

Preparing to Teach the Lesson

In our previous lessons we focused on the pledge of God's presence in His Son and through the Holy Spirit. Because of God's presence, we are united as a community of believers. Jesus said that a crucial characteristic that demonstrates that we are His is our love for one another (John 13:35). Early Christians demonstrated this love, as testified by Tertullian (about A.D. 160 to after 220), who reported that pagans said about Christians, "See how these Christians love one another" (*Apologeticus*).

TODAY'S AIM

Facts: to learn how love is the evidence and demonstration of true Christian living.

Principle: to have God's love be the controlling factor in our daily interactions with one another.

Application: to make God's standard of loving one another our constant habit in life.

INTRODUCING THE LESSON

The Apostle John, known as the "disciple whom Jesus loved" (John

21:7), set forth God's teaching on what true brotherly love is. We see that clearly in this week's lesson.

DEVELOPING THE LESSON

1. What brotherly love is not (I John 3:11-15). John first reminded his readers of their obligation to love one another. They had heard that message from the beginning of their salvation. It spoke of their duty to love other believers. Loving one another was to be their habit. To love is to desire the very best for someone else, especially that their lives are in accord with God's will and obedient to His Word.

To reinforce his meaning, John gave the potent negative example of Cain. Cain's actions were motivated by Satan. Cain killed Abel. The idea is that this was a very violent death. Men learned how to kill when they learned how to slay sacrificial animals. The conflict Cain had with Abel was a religious one. God established the way of sacrifice, but Cain wanted to follow his own evil way of religious observance. Abel followed God's righteous way.

The application of that principle was for John's day and for today. If we see such a spirit of hate in brothers over a religious matter, then it should not surprise believers that the unsaved world hates us because of our commitment to Christ and His way of worship.

John then expanded his teaching for his readers. There is a way to have full assurance of eternal life, to know that a person has passed from spiritual death to spiritual life. The evidence of being a child of God is habitually loving the brethren. In contrast, any professing Christian who does not habitually love his brother in Christ is in the sphere of spiritual death. That truth led John to emphasize that this is actually the same as hating another person.

John next asserted that hatred of another is equal to murder in God's sight. The Greek word translated "murderer" in I John 3:15 is used elsewhere only in John 8:44, where the devil is called a "murderer." No true child of God can have such hatred in the heart.

2. What brotherly love is (I John 3:16-18). John next detailed what true Christian love is. He began by stressing the enormous limits of that love. Christians can know true love, as the word "perceive" indicates. This is a common Greek verb that refers to knowledge gained by experience. John said that his readers could know in their own experience the true love of God. It began when Christ so loved them that He "laid down his life" for them. They had experienced that love when they trusted Christ as Saviour. Now they were to willingly give their lives for one another.

John was practical enough to realize that the vast majority of Christians are never called upon to actually die for another believer. He went on to give a more commonplace way to demonstrate love (I John 3:17). John's readers had earthly possessions of food, clothing, and shelter ("this world's good"). If they saw (the idea is to deliberately contemplate) a brother in need of some basic necessities, they were not to respond negatively. The verb "shutteth up" was used of slamming a door, and no believer should do that to his compassion. How is it possible for the love of God to dwell in a person with no compassion?

Martyrdom certainly seems heroic and noble, but it is often harder for believers to do the little, daily things in life that show love for one another. John encouraged his readers not to merely talk about love but to let it be practically demonstrated in their lives.

3. What brotherly love does (I John 3:19-24). John's previous words could easily result in his readers having feelings of failure and spiritual discouragement. So he wrote next to assure them of what brotherly love does. By loving in deed and in truth, believers could know they were children of the God of truth. What happened when they failed? Their hearts could condemn them for not loving as they should. They needed to be assured that "God is greater than our heart." Our worst is always known to Him, and still He loves us. God knew David's sins, but He still said he was a man after His heart (Acts 13:22).

ILLUSTRATING THE LESSON

Our obedience to Christ's command to love others must be manifest in our lives.

OUT OF THE OVERFLOW IN OUR LIVES

(illustration of an overflowing cup labeled "God's Love")

MINISTER TO OTHERS

CONCLUDING THE LESSON

A godly love is the evidence of being a child of God. If a person's heart is constantly filled with hate, he cannot be God's child. Even those of us who are His children, however, may still commit the sin of not loving others as we should. God is willing to restore us when we confess, determine to obey His commands, and live for His glory. This enables us to pray effectively and be assured of His abiding presence.

ANTICIPATING THE NEXT LESSON

Next week we continue the theme of God's love being expressed through our love for others.

—R. Larry Overstreet.

PRACTICAL POINTS

1. Christian love must be genuine—not superficial (I John 3:11-12).
2. The believer cannot allow hatred to take root and destroy himself and others.
3. The love of God sets us apart from the world and for His service (vss. 13-18).
4. Christian love is action—not just an emotion or attitude.
5. Christian love is evidence of genuine faith (vss. 19-21).
6. Obedient living leads to confidence in prayer (vs. 22).
7. Genuine faith is the basis of obedience to God's Word (vss. 23-24).

—Cheryl Y. Powell.

RESEARCH AND DISCUSSION

1. How did Cain's relationship with God compare with that of his brother Abel (I John 3:12)?
2. Why does the world hate Christians?
3. What does it mean that "whosoever hateth his brother is a murderer" (vs. 15)? How should a Christian respond if he finds he feels hate toward another?
4. In what ways do Christians "lay down [their] lives for the brethren" (vs. 16)? How is this kind of sacrifice a standard for genuine Christian love? How is this kind of love different from the love that the world offers?
5. How is confidence in prayer one of the benefits of obedience? How does obedience to God affect our witness in the world?

—Cheryl Y. Powell.

ILLUSTRATED HIGH POINTS

The love of God

A true story is told about a husband who found a note from his wife on the refrigerator door. It read "I hate you. Love, Martha." Evidently this wife was expressing a deep feeling of not liking her husband at that instant. Yet at the same time she was still committed to him. She had a faint understanding that God's love is a commitment, although that understanding was clouded by impulses of the old nature.

The love that God expressed to us through Calvary is completely pure, unconditional, and sacrificial. It is love that is willing to suffer and die for sinners who have no love for God whatsoever. God's love is His act of will to love us regardless of what we have done to Him. God's love is an amazing, lasting love. Just think—He sent His Son to die for us!

Let us love . . . in deed

In one of my pastorates, a portion of our benevolent fund was used to help those who came to us from the community with different needs. We had the stipulation that we would help a person every three months.

One individual kept coming back, expressing a real need for clothing, which we did not provide. Finally, feeling sorry for him, I gave him an old, leather coat. When talking to another pastor in the area, I later discovered that this man had also been at his church asking for help. I began to realize that this fellow was out to take advantage of people. At the same time, he did have a need. I have learned that in helping those in need, sometimes it is better to err on the side of grace. We must always seek God's heart and wisdom.

—Paul R. Bawden.

Golden Text Illuminated

"For this is the message that ye heard from the beginning, that we should love one another" (I John 3:11).

Many who profess to know Jesus Christ as Saviour have doubts from time to time about whether they truly belong to the Lord. They question whether their profession of faith was—or is—genuine. Such doubts often arise when a believer falls into sin.

It is quite appropriate for someone who professes faith in Christ but is controlled by sin to have doubts. Such doubts should at least cause him to examine himself to see whether he is truly in the faith (II Cor. 13:5). However, continual doubts should not plague a Christian.

The book of I John presents a number of very practical tests of the genuineness of a person's Christian faith. One of these tests is set forth negatively in I John 3:10—the person who does not practice righteousness or love his brother is not a child of God. The positive side of this test is that the child of God is revealed by the fact that he practices righteousness and loves the brethren.

"Righteousness" speaks of one's conduct toward others. Upright conduct, as well as love for others, marks one's faith as genuine. Righteousness and love are the fruits that indicate that spiritual life is present.

The verbs in I John 3:10 indicate an ongoing practice. In other words, they do not speak of *perfect* love and righteousness but of lives that are *characterized* by these qualities.

We can look particularly at love for others as a test of Christian faith because the message "from the beginning" was that "we should love one another." The "beginning" probably refers to the time when John's readers first heard the gospel.

These believers, like all born-again believers in Christ, were taught that they were to love one another. Indeed, it is inherent in the gospel message itself that those who are saved and transformed by the grace of God are to love one another. Jesus Himself emphasized this, commanding His followers to love one another, even as He had loved them (John 13:34). This mutual love would, in fact, be what uniquely identified them to the world as Jesus' true disciples (vs. 35).

In loving one another, we make ourselves known to the world as followers of Christ—Christians. By the same token, our love for one another also assures us that we belong to Christ. When we consistently love other believers, it gives assurance to our hearts, because this is a mark of true Christian faith.

Our desire as Christians should be to point others to Christ, to show them what our Saviour is like. One way we do this is by loving one another as He loves us.

—Jarl K. Waggoner.

Heart of the Lesson

This week we touch upon the core of our Christian faith. We explore the matter of loving one another. There is no Christian faith if we do not love others. Love is the natural outcome of following our Lord Jesus.

1. The message of love (I John 3:11-13). John brought out the idea that this message of love has been there since the dawn of time. But loving is hard work. In the Old Testament, Cain hated and killed his brother Abel because what the latter did was right, causing his older brother to be infuriated with him. John makes us think about the possibility that if we do what is right, the world will hate us. So is it worth following Jesus? Sometimes this will cause others to hate us.

2. Loving involves sacrifice (I John 3:14-17). Loving others takes effort, and we often have to give up something and reorder our priorities in order to do this effectively. Love is the mark of the regenerate Christian. Hate and murder are the opposites of love. Love calls us to sacrifice for other people, especially those whom we see in need. Helping those in need is what we Christians do for one another. Refusing to help is a mark of an unregenerate person.

As Christians, we are called to love one another to the point of sacrifice. After all, was this not the mark of the ministry of Jesus, even to the point of giving up His earthly life for us? This is what makes our Christian faith visible in the world. It is an effective witnessing tool that cannot be denied by the eyes of the world.

3. Love in action (I John 3:18-20). Christians who talk a lot about their faith get a lot of criticism when their actions fail to keep in line with their words. This is also a big reason that nonbelievers do not take that important step of reaching out in faith to our Lord Jesus. The Christian believers around them have failed to make their mark on them. Lip service is easy.

John has shown us that if we are to be authentic followers of our Lord, we must show our faith through our actions. John reminded us that our actions need to line up with our words in order for us to be effective witnesses of Christ. God knows our hearts, and we are first accountable to Him above all else. Belief in Jesus and love for others must go hand in hand. John called us to be genuine and true in our walk with Jesus so that it will impact the world around us.

4. Coming boldly to God (I John 3:21-24). John tells us that a loving heart is quick to obey God's commands. Obedience paves the way to come boldly into the presence of God. When we come boldly into God's presence, we can ask Him anything, for our hearts are clean and in the truth. We then ask according to His will, and our God is only too eager to hear and respond and grant our wishes. We can come boldly before Him.

John also reminds us that when the Holy Spirit resides in the heart of believers, He lets us know that we are the children of God and He is indeed our Father. This makes all the difference.

—A. Koshy Muthalaly.

World Missions

Long ago, people came to believe that what we did in our lives would determine where and how we would live in the next life.

Eventually, this belief system took this idea even further and created a system used to classify everyone. People were put in a caste, or category. The most righteous and enlightened people were born into a life of privilege—they deserved it for some good they had done in previous lives.

People born into the lowest class were destined to work out their lives in hard labor and ill treatment. They were looked down on and had very few rights.

As bad as that may be, there was a group even lower than they were. They were the lowest of the low—the untouchables, as they were called, or "dalits." They were mistreated by everyone. To abuse a dalit or even to kill one for no reason was perfectly acceptable.

What would you say if this system were still alive and well today—that millions of people are mistreated and abused every day simply for whom they were born to?

This is still the condition of the social system of India—one of the most populous nations on earth.

The Hindu Indian caste system is made up of four classes of people, with the Dalits (untouchables) coming after the lowest fourth class. They are so low that they do not even have a class of their own. They are outcasts—literally, "out of caste."

This belief system is so ingrained in every aspect and person of society that often even former Hindus who have come to Christ view the Dalits with scorn and ridicule.

One Indian Christian, Neel, grew up with this mind-set but felt convicted by the Holy Spirit that this was not right and was actually hindering God's work among his people.

He reached out to Dalit communities and partnered with Dalit Christian leaders to bring relief and assistance. But

April 12, 2015   94

most important, he brought them hope—hope in Jesus. Only through Jesus is God's love for all men manifested in perfection. Only Jesus can bring true freedom to those in bondage. And only in Jesus are all made equal in the sight of God. This wonderful news has never reached the majority of the untouchables of India.

Neel is working to bring education, health care, and meals to thousands of Dalit children. He and others are also working to bring training and education to Dalit leaders in order to share the gospel.

The freedom and love brought to them through Jesus has proved stronger than any man-made system designed to keep millions of souls in bondage and darkness.

—Christina Futrell.

The Jewish Aspect

People of Jewish heritage have certainly been blessed in their ability to reach the top in many fields of endeavor. Nobel prizes have been awarded to a significant number of Jews. In higher education, government, science, and industry, Jews have held leading roles. A 2013 best-selling book in the nonfiction field was written by a billionaire Jew.

Nevertheless, God's love for His people was manifest when they were among the fewest of all peoples (Deut. 7:7-9). To this day, Jews are comparatively few in number—only about .2 percent of the world population. In the space of a few years, six million Jews were massacred in Central Europe.

God is faithful in His love for His own, even though they may turn away from following Him and refuse to give Him His rightful place in their hearts.

The Apostle John, a Jew, understood God's love for the children of Israel. But John leads us to the conclusion that God has an identical love for His Gentile children: "Hereby perceive we the love of God, because he laid down his life for us" (I John 3:16).

Oh, that Jews would resolve to follow God's commandment expressed in the words "This is his commandment, That we should believe on the name of his Son Jesus Christ" (I John 3:23)!

Just before the fall of Jerusalem in A.D. 70, there was a growing resentment toward the Nazarenes, the Jewish followers of the Messiah Jesus. The Christians of the city understood Jesus' words recorded in the Gospel of Luke as a warning to the faithful: "And when ye shall see Jerusalem compassed with armies, then know that the desolation thereof is nigh. Then let them which are in Judaea flee to the mountains; and let them which are in the midst of it depart out; and let not them that are in the countries enter thereinto" (21:20-21).

The Roman juggernaut began to roll through northern Israel in A.D. 67, bent on the destruction of the Jewish state. The Christians took Jesus' warning seriously. Christian tradition says that Simeon, apparently Jesus' cousin, led the Christians out of Jerusalem to Pella across the Jordan.

The word of Christ to believers had to be obeyed. The Jews' unwillingness to trust Christ continues to this day.

After the fall of Jerusalem, a Pharisaic rabbi was given permission by the Romans to begin a new Judaism without sacrifices in Jabneh, west of Jerusalem. They changed their religion to the priestless faith of the Jews today. They required that a prayer called "Eighteen" (referring to the number of blessings recited in it) be said daily by all Jews. However, they added a new blessing calling for divine retribution against "heretics," a word understood to mean "Nazarenes" (Messianic Jews). They used it as a litmus test, reasoning that no Jewish Christian would recite this and condemn Jesus' followers.

Pray that God will move Jewish hearts today to obey His command to believe in Jesus (I John 3:23).

—Lyle P. Murphy.

Guiding the Superintendent

DEVOTIONAL OUTLINE

1. Obedience ensures fellowship with God (I John 3:11-15). John the beloved disciple was encouraging the saints to seek to have fellowship with God. We have fellowship with God when we have fellowship with one another. God's Word teaches us to edify one another (cf. I Thess. 5:11) in love.

As God's chosen people, we cannot dismiss His command to love. That is what the children of darkness do. "God is love" (I John 4:8), and His desire is that His children manifest His love in the body of Christ.

This selfless love springs from righteousness and truth, which offend the world. Sinners can neither comprehend nor appreciate such compassion. They despise the saints because of it. Godly love sets the believer apart to eternal life; to the sinner who rejects God's love, it is death.

2. Christ's perfect love (I John 3:16-19). Christ as the ultimate example of unfeigned love showed us that no sacrifice of love is too great—no, not even undeserved suffering and death. Can today's Christian make such a sacrifice? We are taught that "because he laid down his life for us: . . . we ought to lay down our lives for the brethren." John 13:34-35 says, "A new commandment I give unto you, That ye love one another; as I have loved you, that ye also love one another. By this shall all men know that ye are my disciples, if ye have love one to another."

3. Obedience results in God's favor (I John 3:20-24). Every believer can be assured that God does indeed know the heart, and He honors those who set their hearts and minds to love Christ and to love their neighbor as themselves (cf. Matt. 22:39). Living a godly life in an ungodly world requires an uncommon power that exceeds man's ability. Being aware of man's vulnerability, Christ prayed to the Father that He would send the Holy Spirit, our Comforter and Teacher, to be God's continual presence with us, making plain God's good pleasure. To those who love and obey our Father's commandments, there are countless untold blessings that are ours for the asking.

AGE-GROUP EMPHASES

Children: A pure, innocent love is innate in children. Nurture it by teaching them that showing love and kindness to others pleases God.

Youths: Today's young people are faced with many new philosophies and theories about what is right and what is wrong. Assure them that God's Word has not changed. The command to love God and to love one another still stands.

Adults: Remind them that God's children who give to those in need out of a sincere heart never lose. In fact, they gain.

—Jane E. Campbell.

LESSON 8 — APRIL 19, 2015

Scripture Lesson Text

I JOHN 4:13 Hereby know we that we dwell in him, and he in us, because he hath given us of his Spir'it.

14 And we have seen and do testify that the Father sent the Son *to be* the Saviour of the world.

15 Whosoever shall confess that Je'sus is the Son of God, God dwelleth in him, and he in God.

16 And we have known and believed the love that God hath to us. God is love; and he that dwelleth in love dwelleth in God, and God in him.

17 Herein is our love made perfect, that we may have boldness in the day of judgment: because as he is, so are we in this world.

18 There is no fear in love; but perfect love casteth out fear: because fear hath torment. He that feareth is not made perfect in love.

19 We love him, because he first loved us.

20 If a man say, I love God, and hateth his brother, he is a liar: for he that loveth not his brother whom he hath seen, how can he love God whom he hath not seen?

21 And this commandment have we from him, That he who loveth God love his brother also.

5:1 Whosoever believeth that Je'sus is the Christ is born of God: and every one that loveth him that begat loveth him also that is begotten of him.

2 By this we know that we love the children of God, when we love God, and keep his commandments.

3 For this is the love of God, that we keep his commandments: and his commandments are not grievous.

4 For whatsoever is born of God overcometh the world: and this is the victory that overcometh the world, *even* our faith.

5 Who is he that overcometh the world, but he that believeth that Je'sus is the Son of God?

NOTES

Believe God's Love

Lesson: I John 4:13—5:5

Read: I John 4:1—5:21

TIME: about A.D. 90–95   PLACE: probably from Ephesus

GOLDEN TEXT—"Whosoever believeth that Jesus is the Christ is born of God: and every one that loveth him that begat loveth him also that is begotten of him" (I John 5:1).

Introduction

Some of us have become so familiar with John 3:16 that we quote it almost glibly. The truth it expresses is the cornerstone of the gospel, and we recognize that fact. But do we appreciate the depth of the love God displayed when He sent His only Son to be our Saviour?

The Apostle Paul described what God's love could do but admitted he did not understand it. He marveled that it led Christ to die for us while we were sinners (Rom. 5:8). Yet he had to admit that the love of Christ surpasses all knowledge (Eph. 3:19).

Of all the apostles, however, it is John who expounded the implications of God's love most fully. Remembering vividly what Jesus had said in His Upper Room Discourse, he wrote at length about how God's love applies to the lives of believers. But in the end, we must accept it by faith, thank Him, and realize we will never understand its fullness.

LESSON OUTLINE

I. LOVE AND DIVINE INDWELLING—I John 4:13-16

II. LOVE AND REMOVAL OF FEAR—I John 4:17-18

III. LOVE AND THE FAMILY RELATIONSHIP—I John 4:19—5:1

IV. LOVE AND OVERCOMING THE WORLD—I John 5:2-5

Exposition: Verse by Verse

LOVE AND DIVINE INDWELLING

I JOHN 4:13 Hereby know we that we dwell in him, and he in us, because he hath given us of his Spirit.

14 And we have seen and do testify that the Father sent the Son to be the Saviour of the world.

15 Whosoever shall confess that Jesus is the Son of God, God dwelleth in him, and he in God.

16 And we have known and believed the love that God hath to us.

God is love; and he that dwelleth in love dwelleth in God, and God in him.

The nature of God's presence (I John 4:13). Throughout his first epistle, John emphasized certain proofs that one's salvation is genuine. These are obedience to God's commands (2:5-6; 3:22-23), love for one another (2:7-10; 3:10-11), and faith in Jesus Christ (2:22-23). In this present passage he wove them together, showing how they are related.

John had just pointed out that even though none have ever seen God, they can observe His primary characteristic, love, as it is brought to completion in us (I John 4:12). Our love is proof that He dwells in us. Our text then becomes more specific about this indwelling: "Hereby know we that we dwell in him, and he in us, because he hath given us of his Spirit" (vs. 13). The spiritual union we have with God is mutual—we in Him and He in us (cf. 3:24)—and the Spirit assures us of its reality.

It is the Holy Spirit who produces in us the ability to trust in Jesus Christ (I John 4:1-3; cf. I Cor. 12:3). He also enables us to love one another and keep God's commands (I John 3:23-24; cf. Gal. 5:22-23). Thus, His presence is evidence that we are true sons of God (Rom. 8:14-16).

The basis for God's presence (I John 4:14-16). The reciprocal indwelling to which John referred has been made possible by faith in the historical facts of Christ's life, death, and resurrection. John spoke of his own personal experience with Him: "And we have seen and do testify that the Father sent the Son to be the Saviour of the world." The emphatic "we" here refers to John and his fellow apostles, eyewitnesses to all that Jesus did (cf. 1:1).

What John had seen convinced him that God the Father had sent the Son to be the Saviour of the world. This is the heart of the gospel (cf. John 3:16-17). The saving work of Christ for the world (lost sinners) includes deliverance from both the penalty of sin and slavery to it. This was the purpose for which the Father sent Him.

John moved from his own faith and confession to that of all Christian believers: "Whosoever shall confess that Jesus is the Son of God, God dwelleth in him, and he in God" (I John 4:15). "Confess" is more than mental assent to a fact. It is a public, wholehearted acknowledgment. John's choice of "Jesus" instead of "Christ" is important. False teachers of his day were claiming that Jesus was a mere man who came to be indwelled by a divine spirit that left him before he died (cf. Burdick, *The Epistles of John,* Moody). But John insisted that Jesus, even in His humanity, is the Son of God. The present tense, "is," declares that He *still* is God's Son and will be forever.

Whoever receives Jesus as such and declares faith in His saving work has God's life and power dwelling in him. He also dwells in God, enjoying security and fruitfulness. Thus, three things combine to give us assurance of eternal life. The first is the apostolic witness concerning Jesus Christ, accepted by faith (I John 4:14-15). The second is the internal witness of the Holy Spirit (vs. 13). The third is our love for one another (vs. 12), the sign that God's love has reached its fulfillment in us.

This last evidence is expanded upon in I John 4:16: "We have known and believed the love that God hath to us." The tense of the verbs "known" and "believed" emphasizes the continuing impact of our knowledge and faith. We learned of God's love through the gospel and trusted that love to meet our needs. "To us" can be translated "in us." The very love that brought us to God has been implanted in us to be exercised toward others.

John explained further that because God is love, whoever dwells in love dwells in God—and God in him. Earlier he drew a negative implication from the fact that God is love—the one who does not love does not know God. Here he looked at the positive side of the same truth—whoever is dwelling in love dwells in the God of love, and this God dwells in him.

LOVE AND REMOVAL OF FEAR

17 Herein is our love made perfect, that we may have boldness in the day of judgment: because as he is, so are we in this world.

18 There is no fear in love; but perfect love casteth out fear: because fear hath torment. He that feareth is not made perfect in love.

Stated positively (I John 4:17). "Herein" most naturally refers to the outworking of God's love in our lives that John has just talked about. That love is made perfect, that is, brought to completion, as we dwell in Him. As a result, we can "have boldness in the day of judgment."

The judgment to which John referred is not that of the great white throne (Rev. 20:11-15), which seals the fate of unbelievers. It is, rather, the judgment seat of Christ (I Cor. 3:12-15; II Cor. 5:10), where the issue is rewards for believers. One who allows God's love to be completed in him will stand there in confidence, having nothing to hide.

This boldness is possible "because as he is, so are we in this world" (I John 4:17). "He" refers to Christ, who manifested God's love through the sacrifice of Himself. The Father testified that He was well pleased with Him. So if we follow Christ's example of love, the Father will be pleased with us as well. Our growing likeness to Christ in this life is the basis for our confidence in the future judgment.

Stated negatively (I John 4:18). "There is no fear in love," wrote John, "but perfect love casteth out fear." Love and fear are incompatible; the one who lives in terror of God's disapproval shows that love is lacking from his life. "Perfect love" should be understood as love brought to completion (cf. 2:5; 4:12). This kind of sacrificial love casts out fear.

John's observation that fear lives in torment points to the punishment that fear is wrapped up in and focused on. The one who fears standing before God is even now experiencing punishment.

LOVE AND THE FAMILY RELATIONSHIP

19 We love him, because he first loved us.

20 If a man say, I love God, and hateth his brother, he is a liar: for he that loveth not his brother whom he hath seen, how can he love God whom he hath not seen?

21 And this commandment have we from him, That he who loveth God love his brother also.

5:1 Whosoever believeth that Jesus is the Christ is born of God: and every one that loveth him that begat loveth him also that is begotten of him.

The divine source (I John 4:19). John now traced the logic of how God's love comes to be seen in Christian relationships. He stressed, first, that God must be the source of Christian love: "We love him, because he first loved us." Some manuscripts omit "him" and read, "We love because He first loved us." Our very capacity to love (God or man) comes from His prior love for us. Our love, of course, is to be ongoing, habitual. God's love for us is most clearly seen in one decisive act—sending Christ to die for us—although His love is certainly ongoing and eternal.

The empty claim (I John 4:20). If God, the source of love, showed it by giving a Saviour for unworthy sinners and shed that love abroad in their hearts (Rom. 5:5), they will logically love their brothers and sisters in Christ. But John, possibly targeting false teachers, spoke of one who claims to love God but hates his brother. This, he wrote, is impossible; that person is a liar.

The apostle's assertion is based on the simple logic of eyesight: "He that loveth not his brother whom he hath seen, how can he love God whom he hath not seen?" (I John 4:20). If one hates a person who is the visible image of God (Gen. 1:26-27), how can he claim to love the God whose image he bears (cf. Jas. 3:8-10)?

The divine command (I John 4:21). Even if a person cannot follow the logic in verse 20, he has no excuse for hating his brother, for God commanded that everyone who loves God must love his brother as well. These commands are found in Deuteronomy 6:5 and Leviticus 19:18, and Jesus brought them together in His teaching (Matt. 22:37-40). Jesus also said that love for one another is the mark of disciples (John 13:35).

The logic of spiritual rebirth (I John 5:1). The fact that Christians are spiritual brothers and sisters is a powerful argument for loving one another. John reminded us that "whosoever believeth that Jesus is the Christ is born of God." Trusting Jesus as God's Anointed makes God our spiritual Father, and all of us share His life in common. It is natural for us to love our Father ("him that begat"). It should be just as natural for us to love "him also that is begotten of him"—that is, every believer—for we all share His nature.

LOVE AND OVERCOMING THE WORLD

2 By this we know that we love the children of God, when we love God, and keep his commandments.

3 For this is the love of God, that we keep his commandments: and his commandments are not grievous.

4 For whatever is born of God overcometh the world: and this is the victory that overcometh the world, even our faith.

5 Who is he that overcometh the world, but he that believeth that Jesus is the Son of God?

The tie between love and obedience (I John 5:2-3a). John continued his theme of love for God's children by connecting it with obedience to God's commands. He declared, "By this we know that we love the children of God, when we love God, and keep his commandments." This seems to invert the argument of 4:20—that love of the brethren proves love for God. Here he seems to say that love of God proves that we love the brethren. Is this a case of circular reasoning?

John had two different purposes in the two passages. In I John 4:20, he was giving an *outward test* by which we can tell whether someone loves God. In 5:2, he was giving an *inward assurance* to us ("by this we know") that our love for fellow believers is genuine. If we demonstrate our love for God by keeping His commands, we can rest assured that our love for others is genuine as well. But if our affection for others leads us away from His commands, it is not the kind of love that pleases Him.

John explained further that loving God means keeping His commandments. Many people look at love and obedience as separate issues, but in reality love is inseparable from keeping God's commandments. To claim to love Him and yet not obey Him is a lie (cf. I John 2:3-4).

The tie between rebirth and obedience (I John 5:3b-5). John assured his readers that God's commandments are not "grievous." This word means "burdensome" or "oppressive" (cf. Matt. 11:28-30). That does not mean God's standards are lax. They are indeed demanding, but He provides the ability necessary for His children to keep them.

John addressed this provision when he said, "For whatsoever is born of God overcometh the world" (I John 5:4). The use of the neuter "whatsoever" is noteworthy. Overcoming power is not attributed to the individual believer but to the divine life and power in him through the new birth. The new life God has placed within us is superior to the "world," which is Satan's evil kingdom (cf. 2:15-17). We practice (and will continue to practice) what is natural to our transformed character.

Victory over the world, however, is not automatic. John made the point that the victory that overcomes the world is our faith. It is likely that he had in mind here a decisive act—the initial profession of faith in Jesus, by which we are born again.

In I John 5:5, the apostle explained more fully the nature of this faith. It is not faith in general, for faith placed in an unworthy object is useless. The overcomer is the one "that believeth that Jesus is the Son of God." This is the same as believing that "Jesus is the Christ" (vs. 1).

—Robert E. Wenger.

QUESTIONS

1. What evidences does the Spirit give that we are sons of God?
2. What convinced John that Jesus was sent to be the Saviour of the world?
3. What error about Jesus' Person was John seeking to combat?
4. What three elements combine to assure us of eternal life?
5. What truth about those who dwell in love did John draw from the fact that God is love?
6. Why does love in our lives give boldness in the Day of Judgment?
7. Why is a person who claims to love God while hating his brother rightly called a liar?
8. Why should it be normal for children of God to love one another?
9. In what sense are God's commandments not burdensome?
10. What is necessary for a person to overcome the world?

—Robert E. Wenger.

Preparing to Teach the Lesson

Do you believe God loves you? Christians correctly respond that God does indeed love us and refer to such Scripture texts as John 3:16 for support. Do you love God? Christians may answer that a bit more slowly, but most likely respond that they do love God.

A final question then arises: How often do you tell God you love Him? If we told our spouse, or our children, or our grandchildren, that we love them as often as we tell God that we love Him, would they be satisfied? Would they believe us? John calls us to believe God's love and to love Him in return.

TODAY'S AIM

Facts: to grasp the depth of God's love for us and the impact it should have on our lives.

Principle: to understand how God's love is demonstrated through the loving expressions of believers.

Application: to demonstrate consistent love to God and to others.

INTRODUCING THE LESSON

Two men walking through the countryside saw a barn with a weather vane on its roof. At the vane's top were the words "God Is Love." One man said it was not appropriate, since weather vanes change and God's love is constant. His friend disagreed. He said, "You misunderstand. That sign is indicating that regardless of which way the wind blows, God is love." Our lesson this week stresses this truth. God is love, and our responsibility is to believe it.

DEVELOPING THE LESSON

1. Assurance of God's love (I John 4:13-16). John gave three specific evidences of our confident assurance of God's love. First, he said that we have the evidence of His Spirit. The Spirit gives assurance to our hearts by implanting within us a new appetite for spiritual things, a desire for prayer, a consciousness of new standards of life, new hope, new joy, and new obligations that please God.

Second, we have this assurance because of the evidence of eyewitnesses. John was the last living apostle of Christ, and he was still testifying that Jesus is the "Saviour of the world" (I John 4:14).

The third evidence of our assurance is our own confession of faith. To confess means to agree with God completely concerning the deity of His Son, Jesus Christ, whom we accept as Saviour (cf. I John 4:2-3). As a result of our salvation, we are assured that God dwells in us and that we dwell in God.

The evidences of assurance lead to our certainty. We know by experience and believe by faith God's love for us. Our faith and experience are grounded in the reality that God is love in His nature.

2. Boldness in God's love (I John 4:17-18). As we dwell in God and He dwells in us, our love is "made perfect." The idea is that it is brought to completion, resulting in boldness in the Day of Judgment (cf. II Cor. 5:10) so that we fear no condemnation. When we have God's love, we can live for Him boldly in this world.

John built on that idea to explain that if we show God's love in our lives, we have no fear, like that of a criminal before a judge. Only an immature Christian has that kind of fear.

3. Demonstration of God's love (I John 4:19-21). Before we can fully demonstrate God's love, we must realize that we can love God only because He first loved us. God took the initiative; we simply respond to what He has done.

That response must be more than mere words. A man may say that he loves God, but he demonstrates it by loving others. A Christian brother is visible to human sight, while God remains invisible. No Christian can truthfully say that he loves the unseen God when he has a continuing hatred for a brother.

The authority for this declaration is none other than Christ Himself. John wrote this with a tone of finality. Jesus said this (cf. John 13:34; 15:12).

4. Power in God's love (I John 5:1-5). A nagging issue still looms in our minds. There are some people we know who are truly unlovable. How can we love them? Where can we get the power to do it? God's love provides the power, through our faith, to do what He requires.

Faith brings new relationships. All those who trust Christ as Saviour are born of God. This means that every child of God is in the same family, as all are children of God. To deny love to another child of God is to deny the family relationship we have in Christ.

Our love for God and our love for His children are like two sides of the same coin; together they lead us to keep God's commands. Whenever a Christian disobeys God's commands, he is acting in an unloving way toward all the children of God.

John expanded on this theme by showing how faith brings obedience. When we love God, we discover that His commands are not burdensome (cf.

Matt. 11:30). Loving Christ makes His burden light—not because He has low standards but because He gives supernatural strength.

The Lord's loving power is gained through faith. Victory is certain. The struggle is in progress and will continue as long as we walk this earth.

ILLUSTRATING THE LESSON

God's love in Christ should flow through us to others.

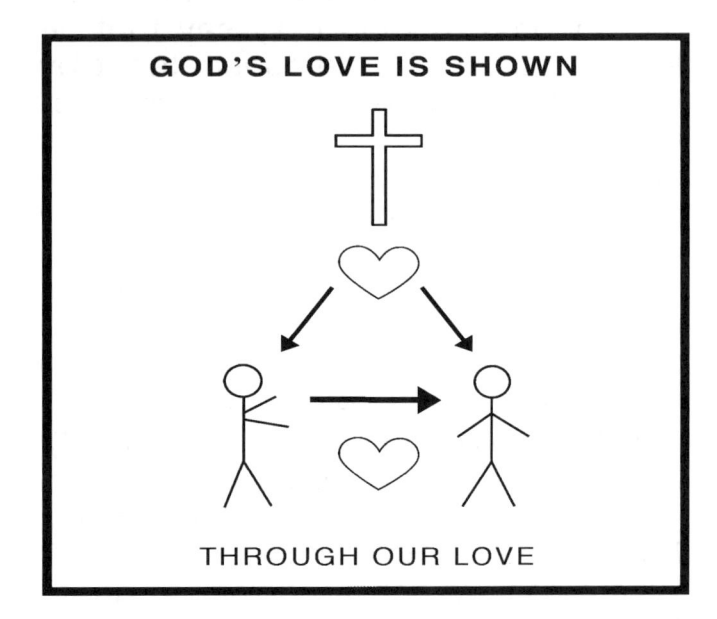

```
GOD'S LOVE IS SHOWN



THROUGH OUR LOVE
```

CONCLUDING THE LESSON

A true child of God can reap the benefits of His love. To reap those benefits fully requires maturing in His love. We demonstrate that maturity by expressing our love for Him in obedience to His commands. We also demonstrate it through our love for one another. God's love brings with it the power of faith, which leads us to the new birth into God's family and victory in our walk with Him.

ANTICIPATING THE NEXT LESSON

While we love God's children, we must also be consciously aware that false teachers exist. Next week we study the equally important necessity of watching out for deceivers.

—R. Larry Overstreet.

PRACTICAL POINTS

1. The Holy Spirit at work in the believer's life proves that person belongs to God (I John 4:13).
2. The Holy Spirit reveals the gospel of Christ so that we may witness to the world (vss. 14-15).
3. Believers can trust the love of God, who lives within us (vs. 16).
4. With God living within, the believer has no reason to fear judgment (vss. 17-18).
5. As God loves us, He enables us to love Him (vs. 19).
6. If we truly love God, we will love those created in His image (vss. 20-21).
7. Faith in Christ gives us victory over the world (5:1-5).

—Cheryl Y. Powell.

RESEARCH AND DISCUSSION

1. How does the relationship between the Father, the Son, and the Holy Spirit impact the believer as described in I John 4:13-15?
2. How does the love that God has for us relate to the love that we have for one another?
3. When I John 4:18 says that "perfect love casteth out fear," does this mean that the believer will never be afraid? Explain.
4. Explain how love for God enables us to obey His commands without feeling burdened.
5. How would you explain the victory that we have in Christ to an unbeliever? How would 5:1-5 help you encourage a struggling Christian?

—Cheryl Y. Powell.

ILLUSTRATED HIGH POINTS

The Son

Having been in the pastorate for a number of years, I have had different experiences with those who deny that Jesus Christ is God.

One lady came into my office, concerned that an individual she had been in touch with had started coming to our church. That individual had come to know Christ as her Saviour and no longer wanted to meet with this lady.

Our conversation soon touched on the deity of Christ. Of course, the lady denied that Jesus was God. So I asked her why she was like the liberal pastors in town who also denied the deity of Jesus Christ. I will always remember her answer: "They must be very wise men."

Wise? To deny the deity of Christ is to deny who He said He was, the I AM. And apart from the deity of Christ, there is no eternal salvation available to anyone. Jesus Christ is God. He and His Father are one (John 10:30).

Son of God

As I mentioned, I have had different experiences with those who deny the deity of Jesus Christ. One of the discussions that sometimes takes place is in regard to the title of Jesus—the "Son of God."

Those who deny the deity of Christ will say that this title refers to the idea that Jesus is a created being; He is not God but only the Son of God.

The title "Son of God," when referring to Jesus Christ, is telling us that Jesus is of the same essence or substance as God His Father. The title "Son of God" acknowledges Jesus' essential deity. To deny that Jesus is God is to deny that He is the eternal Son of God. In fact, He always has been and always will be the eternal Son of God!

—Paul R. Bawden.

Golden Text Illuminated

"Whosoever believeth that Jesus is the Christ is born of God: and every one that loveth him that begat loveth him also that is begotten of him" (I John 5:1).

The Apostle John is known as the apostle of love because of the emphasis on love found in both his Gospel and his three epistles. John was one of Jesus' three closest disciples, along with James and Peter (cf. Mark 1:29; 5:37; 9:2), and he referred to himself in his Gospel as the one whom Jesus loved (John 13:23; 19:26; 20:2; 21:7, 20).

In I John, the apostle returned several times to the theme of brotherly love. Love for other Christians is clearly set forth as an obligation (3:23; 4:11-12) as well as an identifying mark of true believers (2:10; 4:7-9). Love for one another, in fact, gives us assurance of eternal salvation (3:10-22).

In I John 4:16, the apostle began to talk about the love of God. It is because of God's amazing love for us that we love Him (vs. 19). And it is also because of God's love for us that we love the brethren (vs. 20). Such love for other believers not only should be natural; it also is commanded by God (vs. 21).

In our golden text, John showed how our relationship with God is connected to our relationship with others. The person who believes that Jesus is the Christ is "born of God." Belief here means "more than assenting to the proposition that Jesus is the promised Messiah; it means personal faith in Him, personal union with Him, who had been revealed . . . as the Christ and Son of God" (Bruce, *The Gospel and Epistles of John,* Eerdmans).

Such belief, or faith, in Christ is the means by which we receive the gift of salvation (Eph. 2:8-9). By faith we are born again; we are saved and transformed into new creations in Christ.

This work of salvation is totally the work of God. He is the one who "begat," or gave birth to, us spiritually as believers. And it is only natural and expected that we would love the God who gave us this new life and "delivered us from the power of darkness, and . . . translated us into the kingdom of his dear Son" (Col. 1:13).

Likewise, John argued, everyone who loves God also must love others who are "begotten of him." Christ's standard is that we love all people, even our enemies (Matt. 5:44-45). But love for the brethren is the identifying mark of every Christian (John 13:34-35). Indeed, we can never learn to love our enemies if we cannot even love our brothers and sisters in Christ. In fact, John stated later in this passage that a lack of love for fellow Christians indicates a lack of love for God (I John 3:17).

All this suggests that the love that should come naturally is a love that must be worked on and developed as we follow Christ. If we truly love Him, the One who saved us, we must love others—particularly our fellow Christians.

—Jarl K. Waggoner.

Heart of the Lesson

This week we continue our study of the community of disciples who share our faith in our Lord Jesus Christ. Our emphasis this week is that if we believe that Jesus came from God, we are to love those in that community of faith. It is a community of faith that is held together by the common bond of trust in Jesus. We are called to love the world around us as God loved us and reflect the love that Jesus has for us.

1. God loves (I John 4:13-16a). It is important to realize that those who are born again are those who can testify to what God has done for them through His Spirit. They have experienced the love of God firsthand and can testify to His goodness to them. They have learned to trust Him in all circumstances. There is something even better here. When a person puts his faith in the Lord Jesus, God dwells in him. It is His Holy Spirit who makes this possible.

2. God's complete love (I John 4:16b-19). There is no love on earth like God's love for us as His children. There is a mutual relationship between God and His children. He lives in their hearts, and they live in Him. This is a mystery, but it shows us how close we can be to God. We have nothing to fear. This mutual relationship grows more comfortable every day and more perfect with time.

This mutual love between man and God also takes away all fear, especially of the Day of Judgment that all men will face. As believers in Christ, we can face Him with boldness, for we are His children. If we are afraid, it may be an indication that we have not fully grasped the nature of His love for us.

As His children, we can live among men in this world as Jesus lived. All His victories are our victories. His love for us provides the basis for the power we need to live as He did. His incarnate life sets the tone for how we are to live here on earth with the attitude of His love. We love each other because He first chose deliberately to love us despite who we are. That is the nature of godly love. We must follow His example.

3. Show love (I John 4:20-21). Love is the hallmark of the Christian's identity with Christ. If we say that we love God, then we must be able to love others around us. Loving others is the natural outcome of loving God. God is invisible. We are able to see our fellow beings. We should be able to love both because of God's love in us. They go hand in hand. As Christians, we must see that loving others is a good way to show those around us that we love our God.

4. Love's obedience (I John 5:1-5). As Christian believers, we have to show others that we are people who respect and keep the laws of God if we want to claim we love Him. Walking with God is not just a Sunday event. It is something we do daily. He has promised us victory if we obey His commands. His blessings follow our obedience to Him.

Trusting in Jesus, the Son of God, is the source of our power for our obedience to the laws He has set forth for us. God loves us so much that He has given us love enough to obey Him daily.

—A. Koshy Muthalaly.

World Missions

The golden text for this lesson is I John 5:1, which says, "Whosoever believeth that Jesus is the Christ is born of God: and every one that loveth him that begat loveth him also that is begotten of him." This verse means that whoever believes that Jesus is the Christ belongs to God and that whoever loves God loves His people, those who are likewise born of God.

Some might think that just believing in Jesus will justify them before the Lord, but this perspective does not take the whole picture into account. As we read further, I John 5:2-3 says, "By this we know that we love the children of God, when we love God, and keep his commandments. For this is the love of God, that we keep his commandments: and his commandments are not grievous."

One example of faith in motion is the story of Edmund. Edmund is from Albania and lives in the town of Lezha. He is pastor to a small congregation with a heart for church-planting.

A few years ago, he felt the Lord was calling him in a different direction—prison ministry. His heart became burdened for the thousands of inmates who would probably never enter through church doors.

"My desire is to reach people everywhere. I saw there was a great need in the prisons for people to know the hope they can have in Christ," said Edmund.

He started out by going to a prison in Lezha that is home to 650 inmates. He has a special affinity for these men because most of them are from the northern provinces, like him, and speak the same Gheg dialect.

Prison officials have given Edmund authorization to visit with all the inmates freely in all areas of the prison compound. This has especially been a blessing because it has allowed Edmund to develop close friendships with the men.

"I never ask a prisoner, 'What crime did you commit?'" he said. "Instead, I tell him, 'I am not here as a judge. I came simply to share the gospel.'"

During these visits, Edmund and his friend Enris do many things. They worship together with the inmates, have a Bible study, and talk with the men. They have been able to give all 650 inmates a New Testament.

Having the assistance of prison officials and guards has been a wonderful blessing. They often ask Edmund to facilitate new sorts of outreach, such as Christmas programs, English classes, and even a computer-skills workshop.

Edmund says, "When you show love in this way, they never forget you." Edmund is living out his belief in Jesus Christ, as commanded by God. Can we say the same for ourselves?

—Christina Futrell.

The Jewish Aspect

It is thrilling for missionaries to see their calling confirmed in Scripture. John wrote, "We have seen and do testify that the Father sent the Son to be the Saviour of the world" (I John 4:14).

The thrust of this week's theme, "Believe God's love," is our cry to the people of the world.

Ron was at the desk at the motel when I checked in. As it turned out, he was the owner. After completing my registration, he was open to talk. We exchanged pleasantries, and then the conversation turned to spiritual things. He listened intently but then excused himself to brief his housekeeping staff before their shift ended. He promised to return and take up our conversation where we left off.

In about twenty minutes, he was back. Ron was clearly ill. I was very surprised when he slowly sagged to the floor and remained there. He seemed to revel in the coolness of the floor. It was nearly 100 degrees outside. I joined him on the motel welcome mat.

Ron was a second-generation Jew of Russian heritage. He explained that he was both sick and lonely. As I slowly presented the gospel, it was easy to emphasize that the plan of God was based on His great love for mankind. What more appropriate verse could I find than "For God so loved the world, that he gave his only begotten Son, that whosoever believeth in him should not perish, but have everlasting life" (John 3:16)?

Though a Jew, Ron was not aware of the special mercy (*hesed* in Hebrew) and grace (*hen*) that God had shown to the people of Israel. I was able to explain to him that while no one has a right to enjoy a relationship with God, His kindness extends to all people, even the worst of sinners. It is God's love that is the first cause of man's salvation.

There on the floor of his motel, Ron placed his faith in the Messiah Jesus. As I left the office, I was startled to have a maid ask me whether I had led Ron to Christ. When I was hesitant to answer, she said, "He cut short our briefing because he said a guest wanted to save him."

Dr. J. Barton Payne pointed to the greatness of God's love for man in what he described as "theological tension." This compassion for man looked forward to the day when Jesus Christ exhibited that love for which there is no equal by laying down His life for His undeserving friends (*The Theology of the Older Testament,* Zondervan).

It is very hard for us to believe that a rabbi could actually teach his flock that there is much uncertainty about God and His will for man or that the Jewish

Bible (the Old Testament) is unreliable. Could he really claim that there is no heaven or hell and deny a mountain of prophecy regarding Jesus the Messiah? Yes, that is the case today. The Lord Jesus also "endured such contradiction of sinners against himself" (Heb. 12:3).

Opportunities like the one with Ron are rare. We must go to people, trusting that the love of God will grant us a witness to the sick and lonely so that they might turn from darkness to light. This is our privilege and obligation.

—Lyle P. Murphy.

Guiding the Superintendent

What joy there is in knowing that every believer born from above shall triumph through faith in the unconditional love of God that has been secured by the precious blood of Jesus Christ, our Redeemer! If we trust His love for us, we shall walk in victory in this world and rest in eternal life, joy, and peace in the world to come.

DEVOTIONAL OUTLINE

1. God's love indwells us (I John 4:13-16). How do we know that we truly live in God's love? Do we demonstrate His love in our daily walk? Is it manifested in our interactions with others? It is easy to profess the belief that God so loved us that He sent Jesus to die a substitutionary death for our sins (cf. John 3:16). But if we confess Jesus, whom God raised from the dead, as our Saviour and Lord, we are obligated to exemplify His attributes in the world—the most notable being His divine love. Love of this magnitude requires total reliance on the indwelling of God's Spirit.

2. God's love is perfect (I John 4:17-19). What does the love of God look like? Can the world recognize it in the lives of His saints? To know God is to know true love; therefore, only those who are in fellowship with God and constant communion with His Spirit can experience it and are progressively made complete in it. Believers in whom our Father's love abides will love God and their fellow man.

3. God's love corrects us (I John 4:20-21). It is an affront to God for man to proclaim a blind affection for Him while rejecting His lordship and His decree to love the brethren. The commandments of God are not negotiable. Anyone desiring the favor of God must do the will of God. Anyone claiming to love God must love his brother also.

4. Faith overcomes (I John 5:1-5). Something as crucial to the salvation of the believer as love for God and Jesus, the incarnate Son of God, cannot be overstated. Our Father has ordained it to be evidence of our love for our brothers and sisters in Christ and our obedience to His perfect will. God did not design His will to be a burden to His children.

AGE-GROUP EMPHASES

Children: Children whose faith may be in the developing stage are usually very trusting. Use this lesson to teach them to trust and believe that God truly loves them.

Youths: Young people can often be rebellious, always asking "Why?" and wanting to have everything their way. Help them to appreciate the benefits of obeying God and embracing life His way.

Adults: Stress to the adults that the appropriate response to God's compassionate love is obedience to God's Word and gratitude for His grace and mercy.

—Jane E. Campbell.

Scripture Lesson Text

II JOHN 1:1 The elder unto the elect lady and her children, whom I love in the truth; and not I only, but also all they that have known the truth;

2 For the truth's sake, which dwelleth in us, and shall be with us for ever.

3 Grace be with you, mercy, *and* peace, from God the Father, and from the Lord Je′sus Christ, the Son of the Father, in truth and love.

4 I rejoiced greatly that I found of thy children walking in truth, as we have received a commandment from the Father.

5 And now I beseech thee, lady, not as though I wrote a new commandment unto thee, but that which we had from the beginning, that we love one another.

6 And this is love, that we walk after his commandments. This is the commandment, That, as ye have heard from the beginning, ye should walk in it.

7 For many deceivers are entered into the world, who confess not that Je′sus Christ is come in the flesh. This is a deceiver and an antichrist.

8 Look to yourselves, that we lose not those things which we have wrought, but that we receive a full reward.

9 Whosoever transgresseth, and abideth not in the doctrine of Christ, hath not God. He that abideth in the doctrine of Christ, he hath both the Father and the Son.

10 If there come any unto you, and bring not this doctrine, receive him not into *your* house, neither bid him God speed:

11 For he that biddeth him God speed is partaker of his evil deeds.

12 Having many things to write unto you, I would not *write* with paper and ink: but I trust to come unto you, and speak face to face, that our joy may be full.

13 The children of thy elect sister greet thee. Amen.

NOTES

Watch Out for Deceivers!

Lesson: II John 1:1-13

Read: I John 5:6-12, 18-20; II John 1:1-13

TIME: about A.D. 90–95   PLACE: probably from Ephesus

GOLDEN TEXT—"Look to yourselves, that we lose not those things which we have wrought, but that we receive a full reward" (II John 1:8).

Introduction

In an age when we can communicate almost instantly with people anywhere in the world, it is hard for us to imagine how difficult this was in the first century. Even if we were restricted to only our postal system, the differences between communication now and in ancient times would still be vast.

The Roman Empire had an efficient postal service, but it was reserved for official business. Everyone else depended on everyday travelers—merchants, servants, or friends. Depending on distance, the letter would be taken by foot, horseback, pack animal, or ship.

All of this required labor, time, and risk. Yet this is the way New Testament epistles were delivered. God oversaw their safe delivery and made it possible for us to profit from them.

LESSON OUTLINE

I. GREETING—II John 1:1-3

II. EXHORTATION—II John 1:4-6

III. WARNING—II John 1:7-11

IV. CONCLUSION—II John 1:12-13

Exposition: Verse by Verse

GREETING

II JOHN 1:1 The elder unto the elect lady and her children, whom I love in the truth; and not I only, but also all they that have known the truth;

2 For the truth's sake, which dwelleth in us, and shall be with us for ever.

3 Grace be with you, mercy, and peace, from God the Father, and from the Lord Jesus Christ, the Son of the Father, in truth and love.

The bond of truth (II John 1:1-2). John began his short letter in the typical Greek fashion, introducing himself first, then the recipients. He did not call himself by his name but by "the elder." The similarities between this letter and I John, however, confirm that the same author wrote both. He may have cho-

Bible Expositor and Illuminator   April 26, 2015

sen the title "elder" because (1) this was his official position; (2) he was advanced in age; or (3) he was more mature spiritually than his readers.

He addressed his letter to "the elect lady and her children, whom I love in the truth" (II John 1:1). A number of views have been expressed as to the identity of these persons (see Stott, *The Epistles of John,* Eerdmans). But the two most natural ones are that they were (1) an unnamed lady and her children or (2) a church and its members.

The second view seems more likely, since John mentioned no personal names and alternated between singular and plural ("thee" and "ye" in II John 1:5-6). It also seems stilted to speak of someone as an "elect lady" (vs. 1) and her sister as "thy elect sister" (vs.13). It may have been prudent for John to use such language of churches because of the danger of persecution.

Whoever the recipients were, for John they were people whom he loved in the truth. Christian love is based on God's truth revealed in Christ. Without His gospel, there can be no love, for it is through receiving Him that God's love is implanted in us (cf. I John 4:15-16; 5:1). Thus, it was not only John who loved these readers but also all others who had come to know the truth.

According to II John 1:2, the love that believers share is "for the truth's sake," that is, because of it. The reason for Christian love is that the truth lives in us. Becoming a Christian entails more than acknowledging the facts about God's salvation. It means making them part of our life and experience. When the truth dwells in us, it makes our character godlike.

Once implanted in us, God's truth will remain with us forever. This should strongly encourage believers, for although false teachers may depart from the truth, the truth will remain secure in the lives of true believers.

The balance between truth and love is always delicate. Some become so zealous to defend truth that they stifle the love that naturally flows from it. Others become so obsessed with love that they compromise God's true message and make peace with error.

The blessings of God (II John 1:3). John's greeting is not a mere invocation. It is a confident assertion: "There shall be with us grace, mercy, and peace" (personal translation). "Grace" refers to God's undeserved favor, freely bestowed. "Mercy" is His tender compassion for us in our miserable condition. "Peace" is the resulting well-being we have with Him, ourselves, and others.

These blessings come from both God the Father and the Lord Jesus Christ, His Son. John assured his readers that whatever blessings come from the Father also come from His Son. And in view of false teaching that minimized Jesus, John stressed that He is the Father's Son.

EXHORTATION

4 I rejoiced greatly that I found of thy children walking in truth, as we have received a commandment from the Father.

5 And now I beseech thee, lady, not as though I wrote a new commandment unto thee, but that which we had from the beginning, that we love one another.

6 And this is love, that we walk after his commandments. This is the commandment, That, as ye have heard from the beginning, ye should walk in it.

A commendation for truth (II John 1:4). "I rejoiced greatly," wrote John, "that I found of thy children walking in truth." If indeed the epistle was written to a church, the "children" were members whom he had met. "Of thy children" means "some of your children," and it may imply no more than that John had not met all of them. But in light of the warnings that follow, it may hint that others of them were in danger of going astray.

To walk in truth means to live daily in faithfulness to God's revealed truth. It includes both soundness of doctrine and obedience in conduct. It is not optional, for we have been commanded by the Father to do so.

A call to love (II John 1:5-6). John had commended saints for walking in truth; now he addressed the need to keep showing love to one another. "And now I beseech thee, lady" reveals that John had chosen to request love rather than command it. He had the apostolic authority to command, but here he placed himself on the same level as his readers and almost pleaded with them.

John based his plea on no new command but rather on the one they had had from the beginning. It is the command Christ Himself gave the apostles (cf. John 13:34-35; 15:12, 17). Love is the mark by which His followers are to identify themselves before the world. Thus, it was a command that John's readers had known since the beginning of their spiritual journey. False teachers brought new doctrine; John urged adherence to the old.

John also stressed love's nature: "And this is love, that we walk after his commandments" (II John 1:6). We love in order to obey a command, but in so doing we are fulfilling *all* God's commands.

Having shown this relationship between love and God's commands, John returned to the single command that encompasses all others. "This is the commandmant," he wrote, "That, as ye have heard from the beginning, ye should walk in it" (II John 1:6). The "it" at the end of the verse is love. Christians are called to walk in love, displaying it daily as a habit of life.

WARNING

7 For many deceivers are entered into the world, who confess not that Jesus Christ is come in the flesh. This is a deceiver and an antichrist.

8 Look to yourselves, that we lose not those things which we have wrought, but that we receive a full reward.

9 Whosoever transgresseth, and abideth not in the doctrine of Christ, hath not God. He that abideth in the doctrine of Christ, he hath both the Father and the Son.

10 If there come any unto you, and bring not this doctrine, receive him not into your house, neither bid him God speed:

11 For he that biddeth him God speed is partaker of his evil deeds.

Being aware of deceivers (II John 1:7-8). "For" reveals a connection with John's previous exhortation. Precisely because "many deceivers are entered into the world," Christian love is essential. Love is necessary in times of false teaching for several reasons. But among the most important are these two. First, love keeps Christians knit in the faith and unlikely to be drawn to falsehood. Second, Christians demonstrate the superiority of the gospel over error by the love it produces.

John called these false prophets deceivers. They led people astray in both doctrine and conduct. They went out into the world as agents of Satan, just as the apostles were sent as delegates of Christ. They refused to confess that Jesus Christ came in the flesh. They denied His incarnation (cf. I John 4:1-3) either by claiming that His physical body was not real or by saying He was a mere man only temporarily linked with a divine spirit.

An error like that is fatal to the faith. Anyone who teaches it is "a deceiver and an antichrist" (II John 1:7), sharing the essence of the great deceiver who will appear in the end times, motivated by Satan (cf. I John 2:18-19, 22; 4:3).

In light of this threat, believers are urged, "Look to yourselves" (II John

1:8). In present-day English, we would say, "Beware!" John warned that following falsehood leads to a loss of reward.

The danger they faced in being led astray was not loss of salvation but loss of reward (II John 1:8; cf. I Cor. 3:13-15).

Identifying deceivers (II John 1:9). "Whosoever transgresseth" could be translated "whoever goes onward," indicating one who goes beyond apostolic teaching. The deceivers took pride in introducing new revelation that would give believers superior knowledge. In so doing, they abandoned Christ's teaching and the apostles' teaching about Him. Such a person does not have God. God is not living in him; the god he worships is a product of his own mind.

Conversely, the person who abides in the doctrine of Christ has both the Father and the Son. The key to the Christian faith is Jesus Christ, the only one to give access to the Father. He claimed, "I and my Father are one" (John 10:30); therefore, "no man cometh unto the Father, but by me" (14:6). To trust Jesus is to know the Father, but to reject Him is to reject the true God and eternal life (8:42).

Dealing with deceivers (II John 1:10-11). The subject of deceivers was not an academic matter to John's readers, for they were sure to encounter them. In a day when itinerant Christian teachers traveled from church to church, false teachers were likely to slip in among them. So John commanded, "If there come any unto you, and bring not this doctrine, receive him not into your house." The "if" in Greek is so certain that it could almost read "when."

The instructions in II John 1:10 are clear: "Receive him not into your house, neither bid him God speed." To receive someone means to show hospitality—food and lodging. "God speed" renders a Greek word usually translated "rejoice," which was the usual term for greeting. Whether spoken upon arrival or departure, it was the normal way of wishing a person well.

John's prohibition does not rule out entertaining unbelievers in our homes—or Christians who interpret Scripture differently from us. His words apply only to those who qualify as deceivers and antichrists—individuals who promote teaching that denigrates Christ and thus leaves out the heart of the gospel. Those who are spreading anti-Christian teaching are to receive neither support nor encouragement in our homes and churches.

Whoever actively spreads error is committing evil deeds—deeds devoted to the corruption of others. To encourage such a person in any way is to share in his evil. We become accomplices to deception. Such a serious charge should cause every Christian to study Scripture carefully and pray for discernment to recognize error when he sees it. All of us need divine wisdom to know whom we can welcome into our homes and pulpits.

CONCLUSION

12 Having many things to write unto you, I would not write with paper and ink: but I trust to come unto you, and speak face to face, that our joy may be full.

13 The children of thy elect sister greet thee. Amen.

Anticipation of fellowship (II John 1:12). John conceded that he still had much to write to his friends. In this short letter he touched on only the most urgent matters. He preferred not to commit the rest to paper and ink but to save them for a personal visit. This is the only instance of the word "paper" in the New Testament, and it refers to papyrus sheets. Ink was usually a mixture of soot and water, sometimes thickened with gum.

John was anticipating a visit to these saints as he wrote. Speaking to them face-to-face (literally "mouth to mouth") would be far more satisfying and would complete the joy of the Lord for both parties.

Greetings (II John 1:13). John closed with a greeting from "the children of thy elect sister." If this referred to a literal family, it would raise some interesting questions. Why is the sister unnamed? Why do the greetings come from her children and not from her? How had John come into contact with these children? It seems better to take this as a "sister church," also chosen of God, and the "children" as members of that church. This is a glimpse of fellowship between congregations in apostolic times.

Second John reminds us to keep our priorities in balance. We must value truth, but not at the expense of love. At the same time, we must not let love overwhelm and compromise the truth at the heart of our faith—Jesus Christ, the incarnate Son of God and Saviour of the world.

—Robert E. Wenger.

QUESTIONS

1. How did John introduce himself to the readers of II John?
2. To whom was II John addressed? What are the two major interpretations of who these people were?
3. What dangers must we avoid in our balancing of truth and love?
4. What does it mean to walk in truth?
5. How are walking in love and keeping God's commandments related?
6. Why is it important for Christians to be knit together in love in times of false teaching?
7. What was the doctrinal error of the deceivers in John's day?
8. Can one worship God without worshipping Christ? Explain.
9. How did John tell Christians to deal with deceivers who came their way? Why?
10. Why did John write such a short letter?

—Robert E. Wenger.

Preparing to Teach the Lesson

This quarter we have seen that Christians have the Lord's pledge of His presence in our lives. Jesus came as God's Lamb to bring this to pass and sent the Holy Spirit as our Comforter and Teacher. Because of the Lord's work, we are a community of disciples who serve God together in His love. This week and next week we see how we must deal with potential dangers to the Christian faith.

TODAY'S AIM

Facts: to learn how to identify deceivers who lead believers away from God's truth.

Principle: to stand firm in God's truth, discerning those in error.

Application: to practice Christian love, realizing it does not include accepting false teachers.

INTRODUCING THE LESSON

A store manager had his laptop stolen and reported it to the police. That night a man phoned him, saying that he was a police officer and that they caught the thief. The officer said the manager's business card was taped to the laptop. If the manager knew the password, the officer would know the

Bible Expositor and Illuminator   April 26, 2015

laptop was his. The manager gave him the password, and the officer thanked him and hung up. When the manager phoned the police station to ask when he would get his laptop, they replied, "What laptop? What officer?"

We are learning to be cautious about deceivers and identity theft. More critical, however, are those deceivers who lead people away from God's truth.

DEVELOPING THE LESSON

1. The participants in truth (II John 1:1-3). Before we can ever be correctly on guard against deceivers, we must be participants in the truth of God's Word. John wrote to "the elect lady and her children." John loved these friends, as did all the other believers who knew them. They were loved because they knew the truth of God. We must never sacrifice God's truth for the sake of so-called love. This truth dwells in us forever, and we must be faithful to it.

John desired that his friends would experience three particular blessings from the Father and His Son. All of us daily need God's grace, His unmerited favor. We also require His mercy, that kindness that relieves our afflictions. Finally, we call to Him for His peace. Peace is tranquillity of heart, enabling us to withstand trials. We will experience grace, mercy, and peace if we stay grounded in truth and love.

2. The pathway of truth (II John 1:4-6). John rejoiced that his friends were walking in the pathway of truth. This included every element of their lives, from their family life, to their social life, to their business endeavors. Their lives were circumscribed by God's truth as revealed in His Word. Our Heavenly Father has given commandments, and His children's responsibility is to receive it.

Walking in God's truth also requires that His children walk in love. It is not an either-or but a both-and command from God. God's commandment to walk in love has applied since the beginning of Christianity. Believers are to love one another continually. But how do we know when God's love is really being expressed through us? We know when it is lived out in obedience to the commandments given in His Word.

3. The peril to truth (II John 1:7-11). Believers who commit themselves to loving others can face a particular peril—the peril of untruth. Loving others never requires us to surrender truth.

John opened with a declarative statement of the peril—that many deceivers are in the world. If that was true in those early days of the church, it is even more so in our world today. These deceivers teach doctrine contrary to God's teaching concerning Jesus Christ. They may be in a pagan religion, or in a cult, or even in a professing Christian church. Whoever teaches falsely about Christ is a deceiver—one who leads others astray. He is also an antichrist, one who opposes Christ Himself.

John next detailed our proper response to this peril. First, we must look to ourselves, keeping a watchful eye on our own beliefs and teachings so that we do not lose any of the rewards God desires to grant us for faithful service.

We must also look at others. Any religious spokesman who goes contrary to the truth of Scripture concerning Christ does not remain in His doctrine. As a result, that person does not have God. He is not redeemed. We should present the gospel to such people.

Knowing what we believe enables us to identify the peril of false teachers. The next step is to reject that peril. False teachers will come. These are not folks seeking a friend; they come to teach what is false. The believer's response is to reject them, to provide no hospitality for them. Inviting them into your house indicates that you desire to learn from them. If a false teacher wants to enter your home to teach you his doctrine, he must not be admitted. Nor should a false teacher be wished "God speed" (II John 1:11).

4. The postscript to truth (II John 1:12-13). John had other things to tell his friends, but they were not the purpose of this letter. He anticipated, instead, that he would see them personally and that they could share their mutual joys in Christ.

ILLUSTRATING THE LESSON

We must evaluate teachers only by the truth of God's Word.

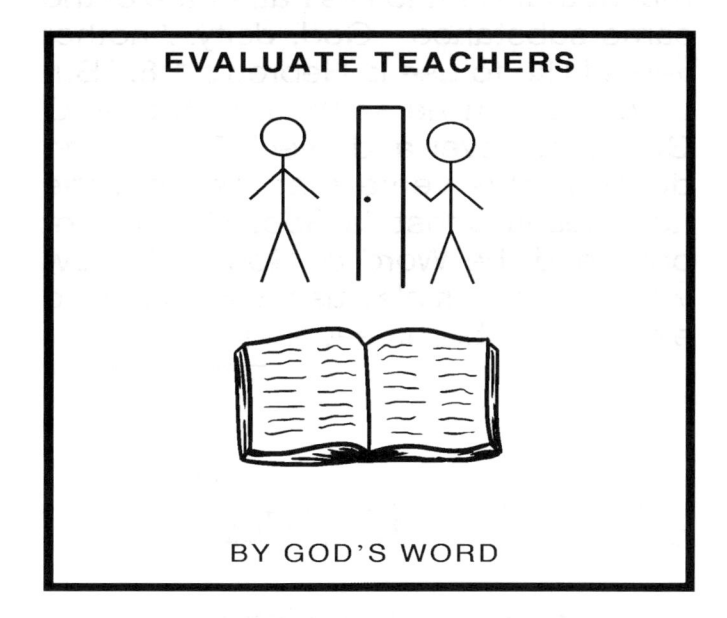

[EVALUATE TEACHERS / BY GOD'S WORD]

CONCLUDING THE LESSON

Do we know enough about God's Word, particularly what it teaches concerning Christ, to recognize false teachers and their teaching? Such knowledge comes only as a result of diligent study of Scripture. When we identify false teachers (and teaching), are we bold enough to stand firmly on God's Word of truth? God will reward us as we serve Him faithfully.

ANTICIPATING THE NEXT LESSON

Serving the Lord connects us with godly Christians. Next week's lesson focuses on the joys of working with godly coworkers in the truth.

—*R. Larry Overstreet.*

PRACTICAL POINTS

1. Christian love is built on truth (II John 1:1-2).
2. Great blessings await those who abide in God's truth and love (vs. 3).
3. Each generation must teach the next to walk in truth and love (vs. 4).
4. As we walk in God's truth, we will have fellowship with and love for other believers (vss. 5-6).
5. Be aware of teachers who promote false ideas about Jesus Christ, and take care not to support or promote them (vss. 7-11).
6. Joy occurs when believers have an opportunity for fellowship with one another (vss. 12-13).

—*Cheryl Y. Powell.*

RESEARCH AND DISCUSSION

1. Give an example of a false teacher who may visit a modern-day church fellowship. What is wrong with welcoming such visitors (II John 1:10)?
2. Does refusing hospitality to a false teacher mean that a Christian is not walking in love toward that individual? Explain.
3. How do believers resist and defend against the deception and malice of today's false teachers?
4. How can believers remain faithful to the truth of God's Word when interacting with family members who reject the gospel?
5. Beyond hospitality in one's home, how might believers today support the work of teachers or missionaries?

—*Cheryl Y. Powell.*

ILLUSTRATED HIGH POINTS

For the truth's sake

My wife and I are reading through the Bible again this year. This morning's reading was about King Solomon. He had just become king of Israel. God had appeared to him in a dream and asked him what he wanted as the king of Israel. Solomon did not ask for riches but for an understanding heart and discernment so that he could judge God's people according to the truth.

That God had indeed given Solomon a discerning heart was first seen when he had to decide to which mother a living baby belonged. By directing the baby to be killed, Solomon found out immediately who the real mother was, for she said to not kill the baby but give it to the other woman. The real mother was given back her own child.

Walking in truth

What provides the believer in Christ the insight to recognize unbiblical teaching? The answer is that the believer needs to know what the Bible teaches.

For example, I use John 8:58, which records the words of Jesus Christ: "Before Abraham was, I am." "I am" echoes the great "I AM" of Exodus 3:14; Jesus was claiming the self-existence of God. John 10:30 is also a great verse. Jesus taught, "I and my Father are one." He meant that He and His Father are of the same substance—God, deity. Another verse I like to use is Hebrews 1:8: "But unto the Son he saith, Thy throne, O God, is for ever and ever." There is no doubt in this verse that the Son, the Lord Jesus Christ, is God. May we not only read the Word of God and know what it says but also use what it says to expose unbiblical teaching.

—*Paul R. Bawden.*

Golden Text Illuminated

"Look to yourselves, that we lose not those things which we have wrought, but that we receive a full reward" (II John 1:8).

Like most of the other authors of the New Testament epistles, John saw the need to confront false teaching that was influencing and even invading the early church. The particular heresy he addressed in the little book of II John is not altogether clear, but it probably involved a denial of the incarnation: that God became man in the Person of Jesus Christ. Whatever the exact nature of the false teaching, it focused on the Person of Jesus Christ and was being promoted by "many deceivers" (1:7).

When Jesus asked His disciples, "Whom say ye that I am?" He affirmed that Peter's answer was correct: "Thou art the Christ, the Son of the living God" (Matt. 16:15-16). John warned that many in his day were denying the truth about who Jesus was. They were not confessing the truth about Him (II John 1:7). "Confess" means to say the same thing. These people were not saying the same thing as God says; they were in disagreement with the truth. It is crucial that we understand who Jesus is—Christ, God, and Man—and thus say the same thing about Him that God does.

John's answer to the problem created by these false teachers was very practical. He offered a brief recipe for protecting ourselves and others from their influence. Interestingly, he indicated that our focus is not to be on the false teachers but rather on ourselves. We are to look to ourselves. That is, we are to guard ourselves against losing what has been accomplished.

John was not referring to salvation here but undoubtedly to the missionary efforts that had taken place in the area where his readers resided. He did not want those efforts to be negated by false teaching. If the false teachers were tolerated, received, and allowed to teach, the truth of the gospel would be compromised and the work lost.

How do we guard ourselves? We do so by knowing and committing ourselves to the truth of God's Word and nothing less. The truth must be upheld if we are to "receive a full reward." This expression refers to a worker's wages—what he has worked for. When we compromise the truth, we jeopardize the reward of God that comes from knowing and following that truth.

Far too often, Christians make small compromises in order not to offend people in the mistaken notion that it will open the door to greater opportunities. Yet we can never sacrifice the truth in all its fullness for the sake of outward harmony and not making waves.

Any teaching that falls short of the full truth about Jesus Christ is in reality opposed to the truth and the God of truth.

—Jarl K. Waggoner.

Heart of the Lesson

The community of godly believers will always have its sense of unity threatened if its core value of love is challenged. The Christian community is marked by the love of Christ and His Person and work. These values are preserved for us in some core teachings of the Christian faith. These are things that Jesus Himself emphasized while He was on earth with His disciples. This being the case, we must watch out for false teachers who desire to break up this community of faith.

1. Preserve the eternal truth (II John 1:1-3). John wrote to one local church, possibly represented by the "elect lady and her children." The lesson for us here is that God's truth will always win. However, it is up to us to know this truth from God and to deliberately preserve what God has put in the hearts of all those who believe in Him. John also reminds us that those who live in the truth of God are those who are preserved by the grace, mercy, and peace that comes from Him alone.

The community of the faithful is kept safe from untruths and even partial truths that seek to come in and destroy young believers in Christ. God Himself will protect His children from the deceitful and corrupt teachings that often creep in if we are not careful. All throughout church history, we find this to be true. It can happen especially in the last days. We are warned of that in these verses. So we have to be on guard to always value and uphold the eternal truth that God Himself has implanted within our hearts.

2. Live in the truth (II John 1:4-6). Here is the testimony of John himself about his visit to the congregation that received his letter. He had found those Christian believers living in the truth, following what the Lord Himself had showed them. He urged them to live in love, proving that they were keeping God's commandments. Love is a reflection of Christ, especially when it comes through the local body of believers. It is very sad to see some of our churches riddled with conflict.

This letter speaks of the danger of having no love in our local congregations. Lack of love takes away from the eternal truth that was given to us from the very beginning by God Himself. We then compromise with the world around us.

3. Be careful of deceivers (II John 1:7-13). Deceivers are there to deceive. They come without warning. We know them because they do not believe that Jesus came in the flesh to be with us. The way to be aware of such false teachers is to stay close to what Jesus taught us, which is found in His Word. We then will not go astray. We are warned not to have anything to do with those who bring false teachings, lest we fall prey to them. John was not telling us that we should not be hospitable to those who need our hospitality.

Rather, the Apostle John was warning us of the danger of those who do not stick with the truth as Jesus proclaimed it when He was on earth. Fellowship with God comes through knowing and following the truth in Jesus Christ. There is a danger that we can lose what we have worked for if we do not stay close to our Lord. Following the teachings of Jesus will keep us safe in Him. We cannot stray far from Him if we do this.

As John intimated here, it is important that we receive face-to-face teaching of the truth. It will keep us on the right track. If we are not careful, we could fall away.

—A. Koshy Muthalaly.

World Missions

Lott Carey was born into slavery in the tobacco country of Virginia around the year 1780. His grandmother was a follower of Jesus, and she had a great conviction that one day he would return to her homeland and preach the gospel there. As a child, he had no schooling but was sent to work in a tobacco warehouse as a young man.

Inclined to profanity and drunkenness, there was little evidence in his life that he would do great things for God.

However, Lott's life changed dramatically when, at twenty-seven, he became a Christian. He took a wife, attended church, and learned how to read in order to understand the Bible for himself. After this, he became licensed to preach.

His first wife died in 1813, leaving him with small children to raise; yet this did not deter him from purchasing freedom for himself and his children with money he set aside from his earnings that same year.

In 1820, when Lott announced that he was leaving for Africa, his employers were surprised. They offered him an additional $200 per year to stay, but Lott refused. Before embarking on the forty-four-day sea voyage to Africa, he said, "I am an African, and in this country, however meritorious my conduct and respectable my character, I cannot receive due to either. I wish to go to a country where I shall be esteemed by my merits, not by my complexion, and I feel bound to labor for my suffering race" (Taylor, *Biography of Elder Lott Cary,* Armstrong & Berry).

Lott ended up in Liberia, a newly founded colony for repatriated American slaves. He founded the colony's first church and also ministered to outlying native tribes.

In addition to his preaching, he also founded and taught a school for children.

Despite all the good he had done, Lott

strayed from his commitment to God's work and participated in an armed insurrection against the ruling government.

Because of his involvement, Lott was barred from preaching. He was not indignant but humbly began to restore his reputation by continuing his mission work and taking care of the sick.

Lott regained the trust of the authorities, and the Liberian colony flourished under his care. People were in good spirits, new schools were founded, and Christianity was being firmly established.

Lott's unexpected death in 1828 was a loss for Liberia and for those who loved him. However, Lott's faith in Christ and his commitment to his people are still remembered today.

—*Christina Futrell.*

The Jewish Aspect

After the close of World War II, a French scholar of Jewish ancestry, Jules Isaac, was granted an audience with Pope John XXIII, who was liberal-minded and had plans to modernize his church. Isaac made the case that the state-sponsored churches of central Europe were largely responsible for anti-Semitism—hatred of the Jews—over many centuries.

Isaac added that the Gospels and epistles of the Apostle John had especially been misused in order to charge the Jews with sole responsibility for the murder of Jesus. Scriptural misapplications, he charged, were calculated to incite the populace against their Jewish neighbors. One such misrepresented passage is John 8:44, where Jesus is quoted as saying to Jews, "Ye are of your father the devil."

Isaac was particularly incensed at the church's use of the words of the letter to Smyrna in Revelation, in which Jesus said, "I know the blasphemy of them which say they are Jews, and are not, but are the synagogue of Satan" (2:9).

If properly interpreted, neither passage impugns the whole Jewish race. In John 8:44, Jesus directed His remark at those Jews in Jerusalem who were scheming to kill Him (vss. 37, 40). He said that since Satan is a murderer, their actions revealed their true spiritual heredity.

"Synagogue of Satan" (Rev. 2:9) describes the Jews in Smyrna who slandered (blasphemed) Christians. "Satan" literally means "adversary," and this group did the bidding of Christ's supreme adversary.

Our theme this week warns "Watch Out for Deceivers!" It is difficult to understand why some professing Christians would twist Scripture in such a way as to attribute to Jesus and the Apostle John a vengeful attitude toward their own Jewish people. John's writings often focused on love. He emphasized again and again "that which we had from the beginning, that we love one another" (II John 1:5).

Satan has exploited anti-Semitism to keep up pressure on the Jews. Russia was defeated by the Japanese in 1905. The embarrassed government of the czar found that a document called "The Protocols of the Learned Elders of Zion" was useful in diverting its people's attention. The pamphlet purported that Jewish bankers from all over the world were conspiring to use their great fortunes to take over the world and impose a one-world government.

A London newsman in 1921 exposed the "Protocols" as pure fiction that had been plagiarized from some rather amusing sources. Despite the lack of evidence for a Jewish plot, thousands of people considered the document to be true. I have a copy of the "Protocols," and its original owner made pencil notations revealing his conviction that the material was factual.

Deceivers abound in the pages of history, just as they do today. Judaism and Christianity have their share. Thankfully, we can know the truth as we study God's Word and are taught by the Holy Spirit.

—Lyle P. Murphy.

Guiding the Superintendent

The debate continues as to whether this book is a letter to a specific woman and her children in a church where John ministered or to the church herself. Either way, the message to modern saints is the same. Walk in the truth, walk in obedience, and walk in love.

DEVOTIONAL OUTLINE

1. Salute one another in truth (II John 1:1-3). The apostle John did not announce himself or flaunt his title as he wrote this epistle to "the elect lady and her children." His greeting, however, is in keeping with being an elderly apostle and with whom he was writing to. It is addressed to followers or a follower of Christ who shared John's devotion to the truth and whom he and many other converts held in high esteem.

2. Exhort one another in the truth (II John 1:4-6). Scripture teaches, "But exhort one another daily, while it is called To day; lest any of you be hardened through the deceitfulness of sin" (Heb. 3:13). Christians who encourage others also encourage themselves. Holding to God's commands is challenging, but an obedient life will not go unnoticed or unrewarded by our Father.

John never strayed from the central theme of his writings. Again he implored Christ's saints to love one another. This commandment encapsulates Christ's teaching, preaching, and healing ministry (Matt. 9:35).

3. Protect the truth (II John 1:7-11). The time of the antichrist is at hand. There will be defectors who once believed but now reject the truth in God's Word. The Spirit of God does not dwell in them, but the spirit of the deceiver does. Be alert, lest these false teachers entrap you and strip you of the advances you have made toward the kingdom.

4. Continually share the truth (II John 1:12-13). When teaching and sharing the Word of God, there never seems to be enough time to communicate all that is in our hearts. The truth is that the Word is so big that we can never tell it all. However, like the elderly apostle, we must strive to convey as much spiritual knowledge as has been revealed to us to the saving of sinners.

AGE-GROUP EMPHASES

Children: Include with this lesson the exercise of having each student say something positive about the student next to him until everyone has participated. This encourages the student speaking as well as the one being spoken of.

Youths: Teach that the Bible is the infallible Word of God and that the young people should embrace it and hold to it.

Adults: More important than trying to define the elect lady is striving to be like her—esteemed and loved for her steadfastness to the truth.

—Jane E. Campbell.

LESSON 10   MAY 3, 2015

Scripture Lesson Text

III JOHN 1:1 The elder unto the wellbeloved Ga'ius, whom I love in the truth.

2 Beloved, I wish above all things that thou mayest prosper and be in health, even as thy soul prospereth.

3 For I rejoiced greatly, when the brethren came and testified of the truth that is in thee, even as thou walkest in the truth.

4 I have no greater joy than to hear that my children walk in truth.

5 Beloved, thou doest faithfully whatsoever thou doest to the brethren, and to strangers;

6 Which have borne witness of thy charity before the church: whom if thou bring forward on their journey after a godly sort, thou shalt do well:

7 Because that for his name's sake they went forth, taking nothing of the Gen'tiles.

8 We therefore ought to receive such, that we might be fellowhelpers to the truth.

9 I wrote unto the church: but Di-ot're-phes, who loveth to have the preeminence among them, receiveth us not.

10 Wherefore, if I come, I will remember his deeds which he doeth, prating against us with malicious words: and not content therewith, neither doth he himself receive the brethren, and forbiddeth them that would, and casteth *them* out of the church.

11 Beloved, follow not that which is evil, but that which is good. He that doeth good is of God: but he that doeth evil hath not seen God.

12 De-me'tri-us hath good report of all *men,* and of the truth itself: yea, and we *also* bear record; and ye know that our record is true.

13 I had many things to write, but I will not with ink and pen write unto thee:

14 But I trust I shall shortly see thee, and we shall speak face to face. Peace *be* to thee. *Our* friends salute thee. Greet the friends by name.

NOTES

Coworkers with the Truth

Lesson: III John 1:1-14

Read: III John 1:1-14

TIME: about A.D. 90–95   PLACE: probably from Ephesus

GOLDEN TEXT—"We therefore ought to receive such, that we might be fellowhelpers to the truth" (III John 1:8).

Introduction

We sometimes have the erroneous idea that conditions in New Testament churches were ideal, or nearly so. It is true that they had the advantage of the presence of the apostles, who had seen Christ and could give them His authoritative teaching.

But John's epistles reflect the problems his readers faced. His first epistle dealt with an early form of Gnosticism, which claimed superior knowledge and promoted a faulty view of Jesus Christ. Second John is concerned with inroads by the same teachers, who sought support from unwary Christians.

Third John is similar to II John in some respects. Both are short; both were written by "the elder"; they have similar conclusions; and both speak of walking in truth. Both also deal with problems related to traveling teachers. But whereas II John warns against receiving impostors, III John urges the support of true messengers.

LESSON OUTLINE

I. THE COMMENDATION—III John 1:1-8

II. THE CENSURE—III John 1:9-10

III. THE CAUTION—III John 1:11-12

IV. THE CLOSING—III John 1:13-14

Exposition: Verse by Verse

THE COMMENDATION

III JOHN 1:1 The elder unto the wellbeloved Gaius, whom I love in the truth.

2 Beloved, I wish above all things that thou mayest prosper and be in health, even as thy soul prospereth.

3 For I rejoiced greatly, when the brethren came and testified of the truth that is in thee, even as thou walkest in the truth.

4 I have no greater joy than to hear that my children walk in truth.

5 Beloved, thou doest faithfully

whatsoever thou doest to the brethren, and to strangers;

6 Which have borne witness of thy charity before the church: whom if thou bring forward on their journey after a godly sort, thou shalt do well:

7 Because that for his name's sake they went forth, taking nothing of the Gentiles.

8 We therefore ought to receive such, that we might be fellowhelpers to the truth.

John's greeting (III John 1:1). The greeting in III John is one of the shortest in the New Testament; yet it is full of meaning. The apostle called himself "the elder," stressing his mature spiritual leadership. He wrote to "the wellbeloved Gaius." Though three men of this name are found elsewhere in Scripture, we cannot know whether he was one of them. This Gaius probably lived in Asia Minor, where John spent his final years.

Being one who was well-beloved, Gaius apparently was held in high esteem by others. We do not know his position, but he must have been a prominent Christian in his community, respected for his good deeds (as indicated later). But John also added his own estimation of Gaius—he loved him in the truth, laying special emphasis on their personal bond. This bond was produced by the truth—the gospel of Christ—which has the power to forge the closest spiritual ties.

John's desire (III John 1:2). John expressed his wish that Gaius might "prosper and be in health, even as thy soul prospereth." "Above all things" can be rightly understood as "in all things." He wished prosperity and health for all aspects of Gaius's life.

It was a compliment to Gaius that John wished him material and physical welfare to match his spiritual stature. The observation that his soul was prospering reflects the fact that Gaius was already spiritually mature.

John's joy (III John 1:3-4). John had good reason to declare that Gaius's soul was prospering. He spoke of the evidence: "For I rejoiced greatly, when the brethren came and testified of the truth that is in thee." The "brethren" were fellow believers who had encountered Gaius while traveling and were impressed with his godliness.

The statement that the truth was in Gaius is a way of saying that he was faithful to it. This was not a matter of mere formality. Gaius walked in the truth. He not only believed true doctrine; he also practiced it. To say that he *walked* in the truth implies that he applied it habitually.

John passed from Gaius's example to a more general observation: there was no greater joy for him than to hear that his children were walking in truth. He had lived long enough to have seen God's truth twisted, rejected, and ignored. How refreshing it must have been to see it received and applied!

The reference to children should be interpreted spiritually. John may have been referring to converts he had brought to Christ. If so, Gaius owed his conversion to the ministry of John. Or perhaps John, as an elder, looked upon all under his pastoral care in a fatherly light.

Rendered word-for-word literally, III John 1:4 reads, "Greater joy than these I do not have." "These" no doubt refers to the numerous good reports about his spiritual children. They gave him great joy because they assured him that his work had been worthwhile and that the gospel was producing fruit.

John's encouragement (III John 1:5-8). John now came to the heart of his letter, complimenting Gaius on his faithful hospitality. He assured him that he was acting faithfully in all that he was doing for "the brethren" and "strangers." "Brethren" and "strangers" refer to the same group—Christian brothers who were strangers to him. They were traveling teachers or evangelists who had stopped at the church of which Gaius was a part, and he had extended hospitality to them.

He apparently needed the reassurance that in taking in these travelers, he was doing a faithful thing. From John's later remarks, we surmise that Gaius had been criticized for his open-handedness. So the apostle reassured him that he had done nothing amiss. Indeed, he was making a valuable contribution to the work of Christ.

Now these men were apparently leaving on another mission, and John urged Gaius to repeat his good deeds (III John 1:6). The expression "thou shalt do well" can be understood as a simple "please." John was politely asking that Gaius bring the men "forward on their journey" again. This implied more than hospitality in one's home and accompanying them for a short distance afterward. It included material support for the next phase of their journey (cf. Rom. 15:24; I Cor. 16:6).

"After a godly sort" (III John 1:6) means "in a manner worthy of God." These servants represented God, and to treat them well was the same as treating Him well (cf. Matt. 10:40). God gave the supreme example of generosity when He sent His Son; His people should be no less generous to fellow children of God.

John gave a twofold reason for continuing support for these Christian messengers. First, "for his name's sake they went forth" (III John 1:7). "His" does not appear in the Greek original; it says that "they went out for the sake of the name." "The name" was an expression in the early church referring to the name of "Christ"—that is, all He is as the incarnate Saviour (cf. Acts 4:12; 5:41; Jas. 2:7). To represent the Name was a high privilege for both the messengers and their supporters.

Second, they were accepting nothing from the Gentiles. The Gentiles were the unbelieving pagans among whom Christians lived. The Roman highways were frequented by advocates of many religions, all soliciting funds from the public for their deity.

But this was not the Christian way. When Jesus sent out the Twelve and the Seventy, He had instructed them not to take provisions but to rely on the hospitality of those who accepted their message (Matt. 10:7-14; Luke 10:3-11). John here upheld the principle that God's work should be supported by God's people.

So he concluded, "We therefore ought to receive such, that we might be fellowhelpers to the truth" (III John 1:8). Because these messengers bore Jesus' name and took nothing from unbelievers, the saints were to underwrite their ministry.

But such support is not just a responsibility; it is also an opportunity. Through it we become partners with the truth. As one who gives aid to a false teacher becomes a "partaker of his evil deeds" (II John 1:11), so the one who supports true ministers is a participant with them in sowing for a spiritual harvest.

THE CENSURE

9 I wrote unto the church: but Diotrephes, who loveth to have the preeminence among them, receiveth us not.

10 Wherefore, if I come, I will remember his deeds which he doeth, prating against us with malicious words: and not content therewith, neither doth he himself receive the brethren, and forbiddeth them that would, and casteth them out of the church.

For usurping power (III John 1:9). Not everyone, however, agreed with this. John spoke of one Diotrephes, who resisted his instructions. "I wrote (something) unto the church." It is very likely that this was not a long letter but one that gave the very instructions he was now giving Gaius. "The church" in this case was probably the congregation to which both Gaius and Diotrephes belonged.

John's letter, however, had been suppressed, for Diotrephes loved having the place of prominence in the congregation and did not acknowledge John's authority. The apostolic instructions should have been obeyed. But Diotrephes used his influence to counteract them. Whether his preeminence was delegated or self-assumed we do not know, but he clearly loved power and refused to bow even to the authority of the apostle.

Diotrephes did not have doctrinal problems, or John would have refuted them. His problem was simple: he was self-centered and determined to dominate the church.

For hindering the work of Christ (III John 1:10). In his desire to exalt himself, Diotrephes was hurting the Lord's people and damaging His work. John did not take this lightly. He declared, "If I come, I will remember his deeds which he doeth." "Remember" means "call attention to." John would confront him in a public meeting and rebuke him for his deeds.

These deeds included, first, indulging in false and wicked innuendo, all of which was baseless nonsense. Diotrephes's criticisms of John were malicious, senseless, and without substance. Second, he was guilty of not receiving the brethren—the traveling missionaries who needed aid.

Third, he stopped those who wanted to welcome the missionaries from doing so. To receive those whom John had sent was to acknowledge John's authority, and Diotrephes could not countenance this threat to his own. But he went even further: he put them out of the church. So complete was his desire for control that he usurped the power of excommunication.

THE CAUTION

11 Beloved, follow not that which is evil, but that which is good. He that doeth good is of God: but he that doeth evil hath not seen God.

12 Demetrius hath good report of all men, and of the truth itself: yea, and we also bear record; and ye know that our record is true.

Exhortation to good (III John 1:11). John used this occasion to remind Gaius of a broader spiritual lesson: "Beloved, follow not that which is evil, but that which is good." "Follow" means "imitate," and the present imperative could be taken as "stop imitating" but more likely is intended as a general precept. Was Gaius, in spite of his good deeds, tempted to follow Diotrephes's wicked example? Probably not, but John's caution would bolster his resolve to stay on the good path.

Good and evil deeds have opposite origins. The person who does good is from God; the person who does evil has never seen God. Of course, we all fall into sin at times, but John had habitual behavior in mind. To be from God or one of His means having Him as one's spiritual Father. To have seen Him implies having come to know Him through the eyes of faith. One who habitually commits evil reveals that he does not have God's life or a vision of who He really is.

Praise for Demetrius (III John 1:12). One person worthy of imitation was Demetrius, who had a "good report." We know nothing else about this man, but since he was being introduced for the first time, he might have been the carrier of this letter. His "good report" came from three sources. It came, first, from "all men"—believers and unbelievers alike. Second, it came from "the truth itself." His life was consistent with God's truth embodied in His Word. Third, "we also bear record (witness)," said John. He added his personal and apostolic recommendation, which Gaius knew was true.

THE CLOSING

13 I had many things to write, but I will not with ink and pen write unto thee:

14 But I trust I shall shortly see thee, and we shall speak face to face. Peace be to thee. Our friends salute thee. Greet the friends by name.

John had many things to write about but found ink and pen inadequate to express them. He intended to visit Gaius shortly and talk to him in person.

He concluded with a benediction of peace to Gaius and greetings to the other believers. The expression of peace follows the greeting Christ Himself used (cf. John 20:19, 21, 26). The designation of believers as friends instead of brethren is unique to John. But Jesus had once called the apostles friends (15:13-15).

This brief letter reminds us that the church's mission is not carried out primarily by professionals. All of us have an opportunity to be coworkers with those who carry the message full-time. Let us do so through prayer, hospitality, and financial support.

—Robert E. Wenger.

QUESTIONS

1. To whom was III John written? What was John's estimation of him?
2. John had heard that Gaius was walking in the truth. What does this mean?
3. For what godly deeds did John commend Gaius?
4. Why was receiving God's messengers the same as receiving God?
5. On what source did Christian missionaries depend for support?
6. What was Diotrephes's chief motive in rejecting John's authority?
7. What did John vow to do when he was able to visit the church?
8. What things was Diotrephes doing that hindered the work of Christ?
9. What do good or evil practices reveal about the spiritual condition of those who do them?
10. What was the threefold character witness Demetrius had?

—Robert E. Wenger.

Preparing to Teach the Lesson

Loving other believers is a priority for God's church. However, love must be discerning, for there are deceivers outside the church who want to lead believers astray from God's truth. This week we see that when we demonstrate love and care for others, we may face opposition even from within the church. Even if that occurs, we should never stop being coworkers in the truth.

TODAY'S AIM

Facts: to learn how important godly fellowship is in God's work.

Principle: to know that each of us can be an effective coworker in the ministry of God's Word.

Application: to put into practical use the pertinent lessons about fellowship seen in III John.

INTRODUCING THE LESSON

Churches often have a fellowship time after a service. This commonly means that food will be served and that time will be spent talking about items of interest to those attending. When the Bible speaks of fellowship, however, it stresses sharing spiritual things that we have in common (Acts 2:42), sharing the gospel (Phil. 1:5), or sharing our finances to assist in the ministry of God (II Cor. 8:4). This week's text instructs us in this proper fellowship with other coworkers in God's truth.

DEVELOPING THE LESSON

1. True practice of fellowship (III John 1:1-8). John began by asserting his joy in Gaius. Joy can be defined as the state of mind during a pleasurable experience. Gaius caused this delight in John. John knew him well and loved him deeply; they were united in the truth.

John's joy in Gaius led to a prayerful desire for him. John wanted Gaius to do well in his pursuits and to be in good physical health. However, this was not a health-and-wealth prosperity-gospel desire. John wanted Gaius to prosper physically and materially in proportion to how his soul was prospering.

Gaius needed this prosperity because of the willing support he gave to those ministering God's Word. Whenever these brothers saw John, they eagerly testified that Gaius was walking according to the truth of God's Word. John had no greater joy than to hear such words.

John explained in detail why he had such joy: Gaius demonstrated faithful service for our Saviour. Many of the inns of that time were known for their evil. Traveling preachers could not be comfortable in such places. Whenever such preachers came to Gaius's town, even when they were strangers, they could count on him. He showed them true Christian fellowship as he gave them housing, food, and financial assistance. They testified about the love Gaius had shown them.

The church today needs people who are determined to serve God faithfully, just as Gaius was. Gaius's ministry was providing financial assistance to the traveling preachers, which is the meaning of the phrase "bring forward on their journey" (III John 1:6). These preachers were proclaiming the free gospel of grace found in Jesus Christ. They went forth only for the sake of God's name. They could not ask for support from unbelievers, so they trusted God to supply for them through people such as Gaius.

2. Troublesome practice of rejected fellowship (III John 1:9-11). In stark contrast to Gaius was Diotrephes. John had written to the church where both Gaius and Diotrephes worshipped. He was a leader in that church. He had apparently suppressed the letter, so Gaius did not know about it. Diotrephes was motivated by his love for the supremacy that only Jesus should have (Col. 1:18). He had not distinguished love for Christ and for His church from love for his own place in it.

According to III John 1:10, Diotrephes was guilty of three sins. First, he was "prating" against John and the other preachers. He uttered malicious gossip, seeking to ruin their reputations. Second, he refused to "receive the brethren," the traveling preachers who ministered God's Word. He also endeavored to stop anyone else in the church from providing hospitality to them. Third, Diotrephes sought to cast out of the church anyone, like Gaius, who showed such Christian hospitality toward others.

In light of these circumstances, John advised Gaius not to imitate the bad. Gaius could have capitulated to keep the peace, to not interfere with the church, to not rock the boat. The difference between doing right and doing wrong, however, is irreconcilable.

3. Trustworthy practice of fellowship (III John 1:12). As another example of a godly servant, John mentioned Demetrius, who probably took this letter to Gaius. Believers consistently spoke well of his life, as did John himself. That is because he lived according to God's truth.

4. Anticipation of future fellowship (III John 1:13-14). John quickly closed his letter because he anticipated visiting Gaius in the near future. He wrote, "Peace be to thee." This included the internal peace of a good conscience, the external peace of universal friendship, and the heavenly peace of future glory, which begins even in this life.

ILLUSTRATING THE LESSON

We must open hearts and homes to God's servants.

CONCLUDING THE LESSON

How easy it is for us to think more highly of ourselves than we should, like Diotrephes! We must remember that only Christ is to be preeminent in our personal lives and in our church. Let us determine to imitate that which is good, follow godly examples, and share our loving fellowship with those who are faithfully serving our Lord.

ANTICIPATING THE NEXT LESSON

Next week we begin the third unit of our series, "Woven Together in Love." We open with a focus on the gifts of the Spirit that unite us.

—R. Larry Overstreet.

PRACTICAL POINTS

1. Believers must love and pray for fellow Christian workers (III John 1:1-2).
2. We rejoice when God uses us to draw others to faith and Christian service (vss. 3-4).
3. Hospitality is one evidence of Christian love (vss. 5-6).
4. Christian churches and believers are responsible to support those who are called to full-time ministry (vss. 6-8).
5. Believers must confront and oppose the actions of leaders who set a bad example (vss. 9-10).
6. Believers must support and imitate the deeds of those who provide a good example (vss. 11-14).

—Cheryl Y. Powell.

RESEARCH AND DISCUSSION

1. What can we pray for missionaries who carry the gospel to foreign lands? In what other ways can we support their work?
2. How has news about the selfish or evil motives of some Christian pastors or leaders affected your view of the church or ministers in general? How can a believer ensure that those feelings of disappointment or anger do not hinder God's work through legitimate ministries?
3. How should the church address the behavior of leaders who have set a bad example without damaging her witness in the world?
4. How can churches encourage and support good leaders? Why is this necessary?

—Cheryl Y. Powell.

ILLUSTRATED HIGH POINTS

The brethren

I remember going on a mission trip to Mexico with a group of about twenty people from the church I pastored. One of the individuals was a teacher who also painted houses in the summer. Knowing the mission compound needed painting, he went around to different paint stores and gathered paint that had been returned. He mixed it all together into an off-white color using five-gallon cans. We also prepared for giving testimonies and teaching God's Word.

When we arrived in Mexico, we all worked together. Some painted the mission compound; others went out into the country to help build a church building. In the evenings, we went to different churches to share the gospel of Jesus Christ.

Have you ever been on a mission trip? If not, I encourage you to go.

Thy charity

During New Testament times, there were no hotels or motels as we know them now. Believers who traveled usually stopped by another believer's place, where they were received warmly and provided overnight lodging.

Diotrephes . . . Demetrius

Having served in the pastorate for some forty-five years, I have been through a lot. One of the things that can grieve the Spirit of God is seeing people lose the vision of what God's church is all about. We are to glorify God by worshipping Him, by building up the believers, and by reaching out with the gospel of Jesus Christ. When that vision becomes clouded, people become prideful and start picking at each other, like Diotrephes, rather than worshipping and serving God, like Demetrius.

—*Paul R. Bawden.*

Golden Text Illuminated

"We therefore ought to receive such, that we might be fellow helpers to the truth" (III John 1:8).

First-century evangelists, what we would call missionaries, seem to have followed the pattern of Paul, traveling from place to place planting the gospel and instructing believers. As they did this, they were dependent on fellow believers for food, shelter, and provisions. In fact, they made a point of *not* seeking the help of "the Gentiles" (III John 1:7), a term here used for non-Christians.

The Apostle John commended a man named Gaius (III John 1:1) for taking upon himself the ministry of providing for these traveling servants of the Lord (vss. 5-7). John said Gaius was doing "well" in doing this work. This word suggests that he was doing something not only useful and right but also appropriate and even beautiful.

In our golden text, the apostle stated explicitly what he had implied in his prior words to Gaius. As Christians, we are, in fact, obligated to support those who are ministering for the Lord. The word "receive" can also mean "support." The two ideas are very close in meaning, and this particular word may have been chosen because both ideas are present here. John was saying that those who have proved their unselfish service to Christ are worthy of acceptance and support by their fellow believers.

Here we see the other side of the principle at play in II John 1:10-12. John said there that those who do not faithfully teach the truth are not to be received and supported. However, those who are true to God's Word are worthy of our support.

Not only is such support proper; it also makes us "fellowhelpers to (or for) the truth." The idea is that we are supporting the truth, or participating in the ministry of truth. Thus, supporting others in the work of ministry is not just an obligation; it is an opportunity to participate in their ministry as "fellowhelpers," or "companion[s] in labour," as this same word is translated in Philippians 2:25.

Here is the wonderful principle that lay behind John's words: Any ministry we have makes us participants in a wider ministry. If we give toward the support of missionaries, that in itself is ministry. But our ministry does not stop there. We participate in the work of those missionaries as they minister to others, perhaps in remote regions of the world.

We are indeed connected to every other part of the body of Christ. What a blessing it is to know that our humble and simple ministries and support of other servants of God can have an impact on the worldwide church and the world itself now and even beyond our lifetimes!

—*Jarl K. Waggoner.*

Heart of the Lesson

This week we reject deceivers in the world, from whom we should turn away, and encourage those who are spreading the truth of Jesus. We are encouraged this week to work closely with them, for they are doing what is right. We are called to be close associates of those who possess the truth of God and help them in the good work that they are doing to introduce the life of Jesus to the world.

1. Living in the truth (III John 1:1-4). In this letter, addressed to his friend Gaius, John commented on a good report that he had received about his friend's living in the truth of Jesus Christ. There is no greater testimony than this. It brings joy to our Lord. John himself rejoiced in this. As believers in Jesus, we must always remember that our Lord rejoices when we live in the truth of His Word and thus proclaim Him to the world around us.

It is important to realize that in a pluralistic society, this truth is often distorted. It takes hard work to preserve the truth and live within its boundaries. What was once considered sinful is now often accepted as the norm. This is a dangerous path that we see many taking in our society today. John reminds us of the permanence of God's truth, which does not change. He was happy that those he had taught were still following the absolute truth in Jesus.

2. Support the truth (III John 1:5-8). The Bible teaches us that we are to care for those who bring us the truth of God's Word and who feed us spiritually. It is the primary responsibility of the local church to take care of those preachers and teachers who are passing through during the course of their ministry. Christians must show hospitality, especially to care for those who teach the Word. They do not look to non-Christians to take care of them, so it is our task to do what is needed.

It is important to understand that this

can be done by giving through church channels or by direct giving. Churches need to set priorities to spread the gospel and take care of those who do the work of ministry. They are spreading the truth of the Word of God and the good news of the gospel of our Lord Jesus to the world. If we truly believe in God's love for us, we will invest in our coworkers with the truth. They are useful to the cause of the ministry.

3. Opposition to truth (III John 1:9-14). John raised the possibility and provided a concrete example of someone who did not take care of the work of the ministry. Diotrephes was not willing to submit to authority in the church. As a result, he prevented others from doing what was hospitable and caused people to go astray. Sadly, this is sometimes true of our local congregations even today. Scripture calls us to follow what is good and avoid such bad examples.

In striking contrast, we find John citing Demetrius, a shining example of truthfulness. He was an example worth following. In order to prove that we are good disciples, we ought to be doing good. This goodness includes taking care of those who have given themselves to the work of the ministry. It is the Christian responsibility to honor and care for such teachers of the truth of God.

We all are in the same ministry. As coworkers in the truth, we are called to care for one another.

—A. Koshy Muthalaly.

World Missions

The country of Colombia is a land of rough and rugged terrain, poor infrastructure, violence, poverty, and instability. These difficulties contribute to Colombia's lack of law and order. In many rural areas, there is no government. This gives rise to individuals taking matters into their own hands with little to no consequence if an injustice is committed.

Two families claimed rights to one piece of land. One day, two brothers, Felix and Rigoberto, were having an argument with a man from the other family. The man pulled out a gun and killed Rigoberto without just cause.

After the murder, the man left the village with his family. But his absence did not lessen the feelings of rage that consumed Felix over his brother's death. Felix would have carried out his desire for revenge had it not been for the intervention of a stranger.

Diego works with a ministry whose main goal is to preach the gospel and plant churches in isolated jungle villages in Colombia. Travel is often on horseback or by boat because there are no roads. Paramilitary groups and armed bandits traverse the country. Thankfully, Diego set out from his home church and arrived safely at Felix's village.

Diego began meeting with the families of the village to share the gospel. When he came to the home of Felix, he found a family still grieving over Rigoberto's death. Felix told Diego about the hate and bitterness in his heart. Diego prayed with him and promised to come back again on his next visit.

When Diego returned, he shared with Felix the freedom he could experience through forgiveness. He did not have to be a prisoner to the darkness that consumed him.

Felix thought about everything Diego said. Tired of the despair, Felix chose to give his life to Jesus and begin life anew and fresh.

Over time, Felix was filled with a profound sense of peace. The thoughts of revenge ebbed, finally replaced by that great sea of forgiveness.

God was moving among the rival family as well. They had moved away, but they could not leave what had happened behind. Their family was also visited by missionaries. The man's wife accepted Christ, and the hardness of the man's heart was softening.

Violence and hatred do not end with death. They live on, multiplying within the hearts of those who are touched by them. Only one thing can end the vicious cycle—a healing so profound that it cannot be found anywhere but through the gentle release of forgiveness.

—Christina Futrell.

The Jewish Aspect

The great war of A.D. 70, which reduced Jerusalem and the temple to ashes and stones, sent thousands of survivors into exile and slavery. Jewish slaves flooded the markets of the Mediterranean basin.

Our theme this week, "Coworkers with the Truth," speaks to us of life within the church—historically, that of Asia Minor, where the Apostle John labored. It is highly likely that somewhere near the church John was writing to was a synagogue of displaced Jews.

The Jews of what was called the Diaspora, or Dispersion, were generally tolerated and sometimes even well treated by their Roman rulers. Life for Jews revolved around the home and the synagogue. They placed themselves under the major obligation to ransom every enslaved or deprived Jew. That commitment holds to this day.

After 1989, the Soviet Union began to evolve into a more democratic entity. The Jews of Russia, numbering in the millions, were at last free to leave the country. The Jewish community in my city, numbering 20,000, raised thousands of dollars to bring impoverished Russian Jews to our city. It was hoped that they would join one of our fifteen synagogues. Hundreds came; few joined. They had not been free to practice Judaism in Russia, and it had no appeal for them here.

In Jesus' day, one of the largest concentrations of Jews was in Alexandria, Egypt. They had beautiful houses of worship and their own governing body. The Jews of Rome were also well organized in that time and generally well treated.

The synagogue was an institution born in Babylon. It was essentially for prayer, Scripture study, and communal gatherings. Worship rituals were not added until after the destruction of the temple. This institution then became the center of Jewish religious and cultural life.

In Jesus' day, a two-drachma temple tax was collected by the Jewish authorities for the upkeep of the temple (cf. Matt. 17:24-27). After the Jewish revolt, however, Emperor Vespasian charged this tax as a punishment to all Jews (including women, children, and slaves) all over the empire. These revenues were sent to support the upkeep of the temple of Jupiter in Rome.

In spite of the fact that Judaism was a protected religion under the laws of the Roman Empire, it was viewed negatively. Even in the first century B.C., Cicero called it a "barbarous superstition."

The Romans also held strange views of Jewish history. The Exodus was portrayed as a group of lepers forced out of Egypt. The Jewish symbol of the golden vine was said to be the emblem of Bacchus, the drunken debaucher of ancient mythology (Schurer, *A History of the Jewish People in the Time of Christ*, vol. II, Hendrickson).

Obviously, the lives of Jews in ancient times were not easy. As a result, they helped each other. Can we as Christians do any less to help our brothers in Christ (III John 1:5-8)? Demetrius is a wonderful example (vs. 12).

—Lyle P. Murphy.

Guiding the Superintendent

In the workplace, employee team efforts have a better outcome when there is a common goal. In this week's lesson, this concept seems to have been apparent to John, Gaius, and Demetrius, as they shared not only love for one another but also the pursuit of the truth. Together they contributed to the edification of the saints and the spread of the gospel.

DEVOTIONAL OUTLINE

1. Acknowledge evangelism (III John 1:1-2). Another colaborer in the truth is identified in this letter personally addressed to him. Gaius was a beloved friend of John and a fellow believer. He was renowned as one who demonstrated the love of God through extraordinary benevolence in the form of hospitality, especially toward traveling evangelists.

2. Support evangelism (III John 1:3-8). Some of the evangelists to whom Gaius had offered assistance testified of the loving-kindness Gaius had shown to them as well as to strangers who were also ambassadors for Christ. John highly commended Gaius.

Missionaries and evangelists laboring to win souls for the kingdom need the support of other believers. Who better to support the ministry of Christ our Saviour than men and women who have been saved by His grace? While it is true that every believer is not called to the ministry of evangelism, we all can do something to assist those who are called. We can love them, pray for them, write to them, and assist them financially.

3. Sinners against evangelism (III John 1:9-12). Sadly, there will be those who try to usurp God's power. It will not work! Ask Lucifer. God has set everything in motion.

John encouraged us to follow the pattern of those who do good works. He singled out Demetrius as a role model. John had knowledge of Demetrius's work, as did other believers.

4. Face-to-face sharing (III John 1:13-14). John desired to see his friend Gaius and continue to instruct him in the things of God, face-to-face. Face-to-face sharing is very effective and always meaningful. It has the power to send a stronger, more passionate message than can be expressed in writing.

AGE-GROUP EMPHASES

Children: This lesson can be used to teach children the benefits of working together to do the work of ministry.

Youths: At this age, young people are usually very impressionable and will often pattern themselves after whoever happens to be popular at the moment. Teach them why Jesus is who they should emulate.

Adults: Remind the adults that we are charged to carry the gospel. Challenge them to commit to witness face-to-face to someone who seemingly has no personal relationship with God.

—Jane E. Campbell.

LESSON 11 MAY 10, 2015

Scripture Lesson Text

I COR. 12:1 Now concerning spiritual *gifts,* brethren, I would not have you ignorant.

2 Ye know that ye were Gen'tiles, carried away unto these dumb idols, even as ye were led.

3 Wherefore I give you to understand, that no man speaking by the Spir'it of God calleth Je'sus accursed: and *that* no man can say that Je'sus is the Lord, but by the Ho'ly Ghost.

4 Now there are diversities of gifts, but the same Spir'it.

5 And there are differences of administrations, but the same Lord.

6 And there are diversities of operations, but it is the same God which worketh all in all.

7 But the manifestation of the Spir'it is given to every man to profit withal.

8 For to one is given by the Spir'it the word of wisdom; to another the word of knowledge by the same Spir'it;

9 To another faith by the same Spir'it; to another the gifts of healing by the same Spir'it;

10 To another the working of miracles; to another prophecy; to another discerning of spirits; to another *divers* kinds of tongues; to another the interpretation of tongues:

11 But all these worketh that one and the selfsame Spir'it, dividing to every man severally as he will.

NOTES

Gifts of the Spirit

Lesson: I Corinthians 12:1-11

Read: I Corinthians 12:1-11

TIME: A.D. 55　　　　　　　　　　　　　　　PLACE: from Ephesus

GOLDEN TEXT—"The manifestation of the Spirit is given to every man to profit withal" (I Corinthians 12:7).

Introduction

Our quarter's theme of the Holy Spirit's ministry in the church concludes with a unit of four lessons on the love that knits together the body of Christ. These lessons are taken from I Corinthians.

If any church needed instruction on the unity love produces, it was the church at Corinth. Although apparently a gifted church, its effectiveness was hindered by a host of carnal practices. Factions were rampant, with members dividing over which Christian leader to follow. Sexual immorality was widespread, with little consciousness of its seriousness. Some of their marriages and families were dysfunctional. And Christians with disputes were taking each other to court.

Another major issue was the misunderstanding and misuse of spiritual gifts. This prompted the Apostle Paul to devote much space to this subject. This week's lesson reveals the source of these gifts and the reason they are given.

LESSON OUTLINE

I. THE SOURCE OF SPIRITUAL GIFTS—I Cor. 12:1-3

II. THE UNITY OF DIVERSE SPIRITUAL GIFTS—I Cor. 12:4-11

Exposition: Verse by Verse

THE SOURCE OF SPIRITUAL GIFTS

I COR. 12:1 Now concerning spiritual gifts, brethren, I would not have you ignorant.

2 Ye know that ye were Gentiles, carried away unto these dumb idols, even as ye were led.

3 Wherefore I give you to understand, that no man speaking by the Spirit of God calleth Jesus accursed: and that no man can say that Jesus is the Lord, but by the Holy Ghost.

The need for instruction (I Cor. 12:1-2). Beginning in chapter 7, Paul addressed issues about which the Corinthians had written to him (cf. vs. 1). These included marital questions (vss. 1, 25), meat offered to idols (8:1), a collection for poverty-stricken saints (16:1), and the role of Apollos (vs. 12). Also included was the proper use of spiritual gifts, and it is introduced here with the same formula that introduces other issues: "now concerning" (12:1)

In I Corinthians 12:1, the word "gifts" does not appear in the Greek text. The word for "spiritual" can mean either "spiritual persons" or "spiritual things." Although Paul eventually spoke of spiritual gifts (using a different word), the word here means "spiritual things." It is a general reference to things related to the spiritual realm.

Although Paul's readers were brothers in Christ, they still had much to learn about this, and some apparently were confused. Thus, Paul did not want them to remain ignorant. This was a mild rebuke, for the Corinthians, like most Greeks, prided themselves on their knowledge. Earlier, Paul had warned them of the inadequacy of earthly wisdom (cf. I Cor. 1:18-29; 3:18-20).

Paul reminded them about what they once had been: Gentiles who had been swept away into the worship of mute idols, easily led astray. They had been unbelieving pagans, caught up in the false worship of speechless idols. Unlike the true God, who has spoken to reveal Himself, these physical objects stood mute and powerless (cf. Ps. 115:4-8; I Cor. 8:4-6).

Yet the idols' impotence did not rule out a malignant power behind them that had carried off and influenced the Corinthians. They had been caught up in a whirlwind of false ideas promoted by satanic forces (cf. Deut. 32:17; Ps. 106:36-37; I Cor. 10:20; Rev. 9:20).

But these believers had not yet learned to distinguish between demonic manifestations and those of the Holy Spirit. Adding to this problem were false teachers, who came posing as Christians. We get a glimpse of them in II Corinthians, where Paul set his apostleship against their false claims (cf. 11:3-4, 13-15, 19-20).

The test for the Spirit's presence (I Cor. 12:3). How could a person discern which spiritual forces were from God? Paul laid down a simple test: "No man speaking by the Spirit of God calleth Jesus accursed: and . . . no man can say that Jesus is the Lord, but by the Holy Ghost." This test revolves around Jesus, the Nazarene who was crucified and rose from the dead. On Him rise or fall all claimants to spiritual authority.

No one speaking under the Holy Spirit's influence, wrote Paul, can call Jesus accursed. "Anathema," the word for "accursed" in the Greek translation of the Old Testament, referred to objects or persons devoted to God for destruction (cf. Josh. 6:17-18). It is unthinkable that the Holy Spirit, sent into the world to represent Jesus, would inspire this kind of utterance.

It may seem incredible that an assertion that Jesus is accursed would be made in a setting of Christian worship. Could Paul have been referring to what the Corinthians had heard from pagans or unbelieving Jews? But in that day, some false teachers posing as Christians actually taught that Jesus was a mere man whose humiliating death proved He was accursed by God. In fact, Paul later wrote of one who came preaching "another Jesus" (II Cor. 11:4).

Conversely, no one can affirm that Jesus is Lord, except by the power of the Holy Spirit. This confession is at the heart of the church's faith. Though Jesus died a humiliating death, He triumphed over it and has been raised to the highest position in the universe. To say that He is Lord acknowledges, first, that He is deity (the same word is translated "Yahweh" in the Greek translation of the Old Testament). Second, it affirms His sovereignty over the person who makes the confession. This utterance comes only from God's Spirit.

THE UNITY OF DIVERSE SPIRITUAL GIFTS

4 Now there are diversities of gifts, but the same Spirit.

5 And there are differences of administrations, but the same Lord.

6 And there are diversities of operations, but it is the same God which worketh all in all.

7 But the manifestation of the Spirit is given to every man to profit withal.

8 For to one is given by the Spirit the word of wisdom; to another the word of knowledge by the same Spirit;

9 To another faith by the same Spirit; to another the gifts of healing by the same Spirit;

10 To another the working of miracles; to another prophecy; to another discerning of spirits; to another divers kinds of tongues; to another the interpretation of tongues:

11 But all these worketh that one and the selfsame Spirit, dividing to every man severally as he will.

Diversity from a single source (I Cor. 12:4-6). If the Spirit testifies that Jesus is Lord, how does He do it? Direct speech is one way, but the text now unfolds how He does this through the church. We learn first that "there are diversities of gifts, but the same Spirit." "Gifts" is the Greek word *charismata*, which is derived from the word for "grace." It refers to graciously given endowments through which individual believers can glorify Christ. "Diversities" comes from a verb meaning "apportion," or "divide."

Gifts have been apportioned to all believers by the Spirit; so the church has a variety of gifts in operation. Some members may have similar gifts, but no two are identical, since they manifest themselves through differing personalities.

Spiritual gifts, though diverse, should operate in harmony, for they all are given by the same Holy Spirit. All who possess them, if they allow the Spirit to control them, will contribute to His witness that Jesus is Lord.

Paul continued to explain this unity in diversity: "And there are differences of administrations, but the same Lord" (I Cor. 12:5). "Administrations" could also read "services." Just as there are varieties of gifts, so there are varieties of services gifted persons can perform. And since services are by nature unselfish acts for others, there is no room in them for self-exaltation.

The services of believers, though diverse, are unified by the fact that the same Lord is glorified through them. In light of the point made earlier, the Lord here is Jesus. While the Spirit gives the gifts, He does so in order that the ministries they produce may glorify Jesus. That is the purpose for which the Spirit was given (John 15:26; 16:14), and any gift that does not call attention to Him is not being properly used.

But Paul went one step further in declaring the unity of the gifts: "And there are diversities of operations, but it is the same God which worketh all in all" (I Cor. 12:6). "Operations" are the effects that come from the gifts at work in various ministries. This term, which is related to our word "energy," emphasizes the divine power that produces these results.

But, again, diversity is unified into one purpose, for the same God works through all the members. He takes all the gifts and through them produces effects in all the persons who use them. The reference here is to the Heavenly Father; thus, all three Persons of the Trinity are working in the church. The Spirit bestows the gifts; Jesus receives the glory from the service they produce; and the Father empowers the entire operation to produce results.

Diversity with a single focus (I Cor. 12:7). "But" marks a change in emphasis. Though all gifts come from one Triune God, "the manifestation of the Spirit is given to every man to profit withal." The Spirit manifests His power as He operates through individuals. "To profit withal" means "for the common good." Gifts are not given simply to make the gifted person feel good; they are intended to profit the whole church.

The Corinthian church was apparently highly gifted (I Cor. 1:4-7). But in their spiritual immaturity, its members were parading their abilities to glorify themselves. It was as if they were performing on a stage to gain applause from men.

Two dangers to our modern church suggest themselves in our text here. One is the Corinthian tendency to glory in our gifts, robbing the church of their benefit and the Lord of His glory. The other is to deprive the church of God's blessing by failing to use our gifts at all or to ignore some of the gifts possessed by our brothers and sisters.

Unity in diversity illustrated (I Cor. 12:8-10). Paul now named nine gifts to illustrate the principle he had been developing. That this list is only a sampling becomes clear from the list in verse 28, which repeats much of it but contains some differences, as well as from other lists in Romans 12:6-8, Ephesians 4:11, and I Peter 4:10-11. But here Paul made the point that each of these manifestations can be traced to one source—God's Spirit.

The first gift mentioned is "the word of wisdom" (I Cor. 12:8). In the Corinthian context, this was probably the ability to understand and explain the "deep things of God" (2:10), which distinguish His truth from earthly understanding (I Cor. 1:23-24; 2:6-7; cf. Col. 2:2-3).

The second gift mentioned is "the word of knowledge" (I Cor. 12:8). This is the ability to explain God's truth, both in its overall scope and in its relevance to specific situations (cf. Acts 18:25-28).

To another the Holy Spirit gives the gift of faith (I Cor. 12:9). This faith goes beyond the saving faith that is expected of every disciple. It is extraordinary trust that God will work in seemingly impossible settings (cf. Matt. 8:5-10).

To others the Spirit gives "the gifts of healing" (I Cor. 12:9). The original reads "healings," emphasizing the multiple kinds of both gifts and healings. Healing played an important role in the early church to certify the truth of the gospel (cf. Acts 3:7; 5:16; 9:34; 19:12), but it has occurred less often in most recent times. Healing has never been promised for everyone in all circumstances; the Spirit uses it sovereignly as a means of glorifying Christ.

Several more spiritual gifts are listed in I Corinthians 12:10. First among these is "the working of miracles." While this includes healings, it encompasses any extraordinary manifestation of God's power. Scripture includes examples of exorcising demons (Acts 8:7; 16:18; 19:12), striking with disease or death (13:8-11), restoring life (9:36-41; 20:9-10), and warding off the effect of poison (28:3-6). As with healings, the Spirit chooses the circumstances in which miracles are the best means of glorifying Christ.

"Prophecy" (I Cor. 12:10) was a gift especially valuable to the church before the Scriptures were completed. It is the ability to bring direct revelation from God to His people. Sometimes prophets made known some aspect of God's will (cf. Acts 13:1-2); at other times they foretold future events (11:27-28; 21:10-11). Prophecy in this form has now been replaced by scriptural exposition and exhortation.

"Discerning of spirits" (I Cor. 12:10) is an important gift because of the presence of false prophets and teachers. Before the New Testament was completed, Christians were especially vulnerable to hucksters who claimed some new revelation. Although all believers received apostolic guidelines by which to discern true doctrine (cf. I John 4:1-

6), some individuals were gifted with special discernment.

"Divers kinds of tongues" (I Cor. 12:10) is a gift that will receive fuller treatment in lesson 13. Here, however, it may be said that these were most likely actual foreign languages that a person could speak without having studied them. This phenomenon was evident at the church's birth on the Day of Pentecost (Acts 2:4-11). It was an important tool for evangelism, but in the case of the Corinthians, it was dependent on the interpretation of tongues to make the utterances intelligible (I Cor. 14:8-13, 27-28).

Unity in diversity summarized (I Cor. 12:11). All these gifts have unity because they are all distributed by the same Holy Spirit. He apportions to every man according to His will. Since the Spirit has given the gifts, we should not despise anyone using one of them in the church. And since they are sovereignly given, we can neither choose our gifts nor boast of the one (or ones) we have. We ought to give thanks for our abilities and use them fully for the common good of Christ's body.

—*Robert E. Wenger.*

QUESTIONS

1. From what religious background had the Corinthians come? What problem did this pose for them?
2. What test did Paul propose to tell true from false teaching?
3. Where might the Corinthians have heard someone claim that Jesus was accursed?
4. What are the implications of the statement that Jesus is Lord?
5. Why is it logical that all spiritual gifts operate in harmony?
6. How did Paul show that all three Persons of the Trinity are involved in spiritual gifts?
7. For whose profit are gifts to be exercised?
8. How is the gift of faith different from saving faith?
9. How is the gift of miracles different from the gift of healings?
10. What gift was necessary to make the gift of tongues useful?

—*Robert E. Wenger.*

Preparing to Teach the Lesson

Paul wrote I Corinthians because he was concerned about the church's problems. He had heard from members of Chloe's household (1:11) that the church was beset with serious divisions (chaps. 1—4), immorality (chap. 5), lawsuits (6:1-11), and impurity (vss. 12-20). The church also had questions they wanted Paul to answer. These concerned marriage (chap. 7), Christian liberty (8:1—11:1), church worship (11:2-34), spiritual gifts (chaps. 12—14), resurrection (chap. 15), and stewardship (16:1-18).

Our lesson for this week centers on the questions the church asked concerning spiritual gifts.

TODAY'S AIM

Facts: to understand how the Triune God grants spiritual gifts to His church.

Principle: to know that God bestows on each Christian spiritual gifts to benefit the church's ministry.

Application: to show how each Christian should identify and employ his spiritual gift or gifts in church ministry.

INTRODUCING THE LESSON

Tim told his uncle, "Thanks for the harmonica you gave me for Christmas. It's the best Christmas gift I ever got." "That's great," said his uncle. "Do you know how to play it?" "Oh, I don't play it," Tim replied. "My mom gives me a dollar a day not to play it during the day, and my dad gives me five dollars a week not to play it at night."

Like Tim, many Christians never use their God-given spiritual gifts.

DEVELOPING THE LESSON

1. Christ is Lord over the gifts (I Cor. 12:1-3). A spiritual gift can be defined as a God-given ability for service. It is important to observe that it is an ability, not an office or a position where the ability may be used. The problem in Corinth was that they exalted the gifts that made a show.

In speaking of spiritual gifts, Paul addressed his readers as brothers in Christ. They had been unsaved Gentiles, led astray by the voiceless idols of paganism. Those heathen religions regarded visions, oracles, and miracles as proof of a person's relationship with a god.

A person's relationship with the living God of heaven, however, is not based on any such experience. The one great test of possessing God's Holy Spirit in your life is your relationship with Jesus Christ. The Holy Spirit always honors the name of "Jesus." Each person who has the Spirit will acknowledge that Jesus, the man from Galilee, is also the Lord, the sovereign God.

2. God is the source of the gifts (I Cor. 12:4-6). Spiritual gifts are described by three terms. They are "gifts," a word that points out their gracious character. They are also "administrations," a term that shows their purpose—to minister. Finally, they are "operations" (Greek: energies), a word that shows their power.

Paul clearly set forth that all three Members of the Godhead function as the source of the gifts. The diverse gifts are given to believers by the Spirit. Those believers are then placed in the work of the church by the Lord, who is Jesus Christ (cf. Eph. 4:8, 11). The entire process is under the governance of God the Father.

3. The Spirit distributes the gifts (I Cor. 12:7-11). Just as the gifts were united in source, so they were united in purpose. The reason God's Spirit distributes the various gifts is announced first. The "manifestation of the Spirit" varies in those who receive the gifts, as different believers receive different gifts. Regardless of that, all gifts have the same purpose, which is "to profit withal." All gifts are to be used to benefit the church.

Lists of spiritual gifts are found in Romans 12:6-8, I Corinthians 12:28-31, Ephesians 4:11, and I Peter 4:10-11, in addition to the nine specific gifts Paul identified here in I Corinthians 12:8-10. With the exception of the gift of "faith," these are all debated. Are they still in practice in today's church? Four general positions are held on this question.

Some charismatics hold that all these gifts are still in existence and experienced only by those who receive the "baptism of the Holy Spirit." This commonly occurs after salvation, and its required evidence is speaking in tongues. Other charismatics believe that all these gifts are still in existence, but speaking in tongues is not a required evidence of being baptized by the Spirit.

Noncharismatics are those who have not experienced any of the special gifts but withhold judging whether charismatics are correct in their views.

Cessationists believe that all of the "sign" gifts were temporary, foundational gifts (cf. Eph. 2:20) for use only in the early church. They were practiced to provide credentials of authority for

God's servants (cf. Heb. 2:1-4). Those gifts ceased in the first century, when "that which is perfect" (I Cor. 13:10), the completed New Testament canon, came. At that time, the various sign gifts, that which was "in part," passed away.

Paul concluded his list of gifts by asserting that no believer receives any gift by selecting it, by praying for it, or by craving it (I Cor. 12:11). Instead, gifts are given to every man, without exception, as the Holy Spirit wills.

ILLUSTRATING THE LESSON

God sovereignly bestows spiritual gifts as He chooses.

CONCLUDING THE LESSON

In His grace, God gave spiritual gifts to all Christians to advance the work of His church. He expects each of us to use our gifts to profit the church. "As every man hath received the gift, even so minister the same one to another, as good stewards of the manifold grace of God" (I Pet. 4:10).

ANTICIPATING THE NEXT LESSON

The emphasis of next week's lesson is that all believers are members of one body in Christ.

—R. Larry Overstreet.

PRACTICAL POINTS

1. We must understand about spiritual gifts to use them properly (I Cor. 12:1).
2. The Holy Spirit witnesses the truth about Jesus to the human heart (vss. 2-3).
3. Believers have different abilities and areas of service, but there is only one source: God (vss. 4-6).
4. Spiritual gifts are given for the good of the church as a whole (vs. 7).
5. All believers possess gifts that empower them to accomplish the work that God has assigned them in His church (vss. 8-11).
6. Spiritual gifts are given by God and are not to be a source of division or pride within the church.

—Cheryl Y. Powell.

RESEARCH AND DISCUSSION

1. How do Christian churches today show favoritism among believers based on differences in spiritual gifts? How does this harm the church?
2. How does the church respond to a member who feels that he has nothing to contribute to the work of the ministry or to the member who feels superior because of his gift?
3. How does the diversity of gifts in the church illustrate the relationship between the Father, the Son, and the Holy Spirit?
4. Of the spiritual gifts listed, which gifts have you received? How have you used your gifts for the edification of the church? Is the list in I Corinthians 12:8-10 all-inclusive?

—Cheryl Y. Powell.

ILLUSTRATED HIGH POINTS

Diversities of gifts

One of the aims of our culture today is to make us believe that men and women are the same. In spite of man's depraved thinking, God created a man and a woman to be different, although He made each one in His image. When a man and woman are married, in their diversity they blend together to create a greater unity.

It is the same for believers in Jesus Christ. The Spirit of God gives different spiritual gifts—actually, God-given abilities for service—so that His kingdom on earth will be furthered and He will be glorified. As believers use the different gifts God has given to them, out of that diversity comes a unity that brings the Lord glory and causes God's kingdom to expand on earth. Are you using the spiritual gift that God has given you?

Dividing to every man

In a Bible study, we were looking at the subject of spiritual gifts. As we ended our session, I asked how many knew their spiritual gift. People were reluctant to say what they thought their spiritual gift was. They may not have wanted to seem arrogant, claiming too much. Since our group knew each other fairly well, I decided to change direction. Now I asked each member to try to identify the spiritual gift of the person sitting on his right. We took some time doing this, and people were encouraged and sometimes surprised to discover what another person thought his spiritual gift was.

Do you know what your spiritual gift is? If not, perhaps you would like to try what I just described. If you know your spiritual gift, are you using it to glorify the Lord and to give evidence of God's unity in your life and in your local church?

—Paul R. Bawden.

Golden Text Illuminated

"The manifestation of the Spirit is given to every man to profit withal" (I Corinthians 12:7).

With I Corinthians 12, Paul began a lengthy discussion of spiritual gifts, which were the cause of much confusion and pride in the Corinthian church. This brought Paul's rebuke, as well as his correction, with clear, systematic, and step-by-step instructions.

Paul began in I Corinthians 12:3 by reminding the Corinthian believers that every Christian has the Holy Spirit dwelling within and working in his or her life.

The apostle went on to explain that there are many different gifts but that all come from the same Holy Spirit (I Cor. 12:4). And all the gifts have the same basic purpose.

When Paul spoke of the "manifestation of the Spirit," he was speaking of the gifts given by the Holy Spirit. These are special abilities God the Holy Spirit gives for service in the body of Christ, the church. These gifts, some of which are listed in I Corinthians 12:8-10, are, in fact, the visible evidence, or manifestation, of the Spirit's presence among His people. Where God's people are gathered, divinely given gifts will be present and active.

The spiritual gifts are given to "every man." The word "man" actually does not appear in the Greek original, which uses a word that simply means "each" or "every." "Man" is added to complete the thought in English. We could just as easily say "each one" or "every person."

Spiritual gifts are not limited to certain special people. They are given by the Holy Spirit to all Christians. In fact, this seems to say that *every* born-again person has at least one Spirit-given gift.

The modern emphasis on discovering one's spiritual gift is not a biblical concern. The Bible's emphasis is on employing the gifts in service to the church.

All the spiritual gifts are given "to profit withal." That is, they are given for the common good of the church. They are not given for personal pleasure or for drawing attention to oneself, as some of the Corinthians seemed to believe.

The gifts vary greatly. Some are more noticeable and prominent among the gathered church. Others tend to be exercised on a more personal level or behind the scenes. However, one thing all the gifts have in common is that they are designed for the common good of the whole church.

Every believer should be building up other believers. This is the ultimate purpose of all the gifts.

—Jarl K. Waggoner.

Heart of the Lesson

In this third unit we begin to see how God has endowed us with various gifts. They are for the use of the common ministry that we have in leading others to our Lord and then discipling them toward growing and maturing in the Lord Jesus. We are one body, working toward a common end that will glorify the Lord Jesus through the local body of Christ, the church. God's Spirit works in each of us to express His love to the church.

1. Jesus is Lord (I Cor. 12:1-3). Paul set the stage as he spoke to the Corinthian Christians. He told them that in the past, they had worshipped idols that could not respond to them. Now he called them his brothers and sisters in Christ and told them that they had a new understanding of the true God. They had come to know Jesus, and they could now proclaim Him as their Lord. Contrary to what they had believed in their old pagan life, they could do this only because the Spirit of God dwelled in them.

Like them, we can now affirm our new standing in faith as an acknowledgement that we are part of the local believing body of Christ. We are now under His rule. Like them, we can live by His power. Jesus is the Head, and we are all part of the same body, held together by the common bond of love. Like them, we need to see that Jesus is true and that pagan idols are false.

2. One Spirit (I Cor. 12:4-7). Is it not amazing how different we all are? Everyone has a special spiritual gift from God, and these are handpicked by Him for His purposes in the local church body. Many things have to be done in the local church, and God uses each of us in a very special way to get those things done. Each one is given at least one special gift upon salvation. This is how carefully God planned our lives, for even before we were born He planned our avenues of service in the local church.

It must be noted here that there are many things that need to be done in the local body of believers. Our God has placed us with precision in the local church so that we may be used by Him in the area of our special gifting. We must learn to use these gifts so that we can help each other in the work of the church. It is God's Holy Spirit who is the source of these gifts, and He gives them to us as He wills so that the church may benefit and His work continue.

3. Different gifts (I Cor. 12:8-11). God knows where to place us in the body of Christ. He also knows exactly what gifts are needed there. It is with this in mind that our God plans ahead to equip us with the right gifts so that we may serve Him appropriately.

Some people are given the ability to give good advice. They have the wisdom of God. Others have special knowledge. Some have faith, and others can pray to heal the sick. Some can speak to others under God's inspiration. Others can discern between what is genuine and what is false, especially when it comes to distinguishing between the voice of God and that of a false spirit. Some can speak in other languages, and yet others are given the ability to interpret so that the message of God might be proclaimed.

We see that the Holy Spirit is in charge and directs the operation. It is He who gives gifts to each one of us so that we might serve Christ in love for each other.

—A. Koshy Muthalaly.

World Missions

Ruth has dreams that she will never forget. Why? It is because God speaks to her through her dreams. It is almost impossible to forget the words of God when the Holy Spirit dwells inside our hearts.

In her dreams, Ruth sees children. They are not happy children. These children are lame, blind, and alone, with no one to care for them. She hears a voice say, "They are your responsibility."

Another dream shows her walking along a dangerous and treacherous path. But she is not walking alone; the hand of God is guiding her and helping her find the way.

The location of God's work for Ruth and her husband, Nelson, is Gujarat, India, where there is virtually no Christian witness. There she and her husband pluck abandoned children from the grasp of poverty and neglect. The constant love and nourishment the children experience with Nelson and Ruth give them peace. The Bible stories and teachings about Jesus give them hope.

Over fifty children to tend to is not overwhelming for Nelson and Ruth. God shows them more and more places where His Spirit is needed. How will these people know God's salvation when there is no one else to go?

God placed in their hearts the desire to serve. And He put in their spirits the strength to expand their ministry.

They took the gospel to over thirty villages and in eight years' time have trained many believers to be disciples for Jesus. The excitement of salvation is strong among those hearing God's message of redemption, and hundreds of people are turning to Jesus. This has been achieved through faithful perseverance and steady prayer.

In I Corinthians 12, we are told that God gives many gifts but that they all come from one source—His Spirit. And we are also told that the purpose of these gifts is for one thing—to help one another and to bring about a common good for everyone.

And that is one reason there is so much excitement surrounding Nelson and Ruth. They are not using the gifts God gave them for their own selfish ends. They are using them to bring salvation to many. Theirs is a labor that does not end with one soul. It is a work that multiplies the harvest through the help of God's Spirit.

Despite everything Nelson and Ruth have already done, God is not finished yet! Over 800 people attended a prayer and fasting service. Over 250 new teachers have received training for reaching out to children. Churches are growing so fast that they are having trouble finding adequate numbers of teachers.

Despite the surpassing work they see before them, they know that God is faithful and will provide everything they need through His Spirit.

—*Christina Futrell.*

The Jewish Aspect

We often can benefit from the insights of Christian Jews. One such believer is Dr. Arnold Fruchtenbaum, who has written for this feature from time to time. As a young man enrolled in Hebrew University in Jerusalem, Arnold became a witness to Israel's Six-Day War in 1967. He returned home after the war and continued his education in Bible and theology.

The Old Testament provides some examples of people being given special abilities through the power of the Holy Spirit. Bezaleel, for example, crafted all of the tabernacle articles and the robes of the priests in the power of the Holy Spirit (Exod. 35:30-33). The seventy elders of Israel received the Spirit in order to share the burden of judging the people (Num. 11:24-30). David also had a prophetic ministry through the Spirit but was concerned about the possible impermanence of the gift. He wrote, "Take not thy holy spirit from me" (Ps. 51:11).

Each of the several branches of Judaism today has rabbis as spiritual leaders. The word "rabbi" means "master." Jesus was called "rabbi" at times. A woman may be a rabbi in Reform and Conservative Judaism. The Orthodox, however, allow only men.

Rabbis are well trained, particularly in Hebrew and related languages. Studying the Talmud (the sayings of rabbis since the temple's destruction), nevertheless, is the center of their preparation. Through the years, rabbis have taken on more pastoral responsibilities and resemble their Christian counterparts.

Rabbis are free to hold differing views on Jewish life and worship. One female rabbi revealed that she and the other rabbinical staff of her synagogue cannot agree on how kosher a Jew must be in food and diet. As a result, they never dine together, which for her is a disappointing feature of their partnership.

Cantors (singers) are essential for the Jewish worship service. Graduates of cantorial schools are responsible for the chanting of Old Testament and talmudic passages. Often called a *hazzan,* the cantor is also responsible for teaching the children in Hebrew. He prepares them for the Bar Mitzvah service, at which thirteen-year-old boys (and in Reform circles, Bat Mitzvah girls as well) become full members of the synagogue.

One of the most important rituals in Jewish practice is that of circumcision. Jews who are not identified with a synagogue will seek out someone qualified for this service. Called a mohel, this person is qualified in ritual circumcision and is a graduate of a medical program for the surgery. Sometimes the mohel is an actual doctor.

The *soferim* once were teachers, such as the scribes you encounter in the New Testament. Today, their greatest service is in preparing and maintaining the scrolls of the law. Torah scrolls are kept in a cabinet called an ark, which stands by the synagogue wall that is nearest Jerusalem.

These are just a few key roles in a Jewish religious community. The church, however, is blessed with believers who serve each other with Spirit-empowered abilities.

—Lyle P. Murphy.

Guiding the Superintendent

It is God who gives spiritual gifts or expressions of special abilities to His people by His Holy Spirit. In his letter to those in the Corinthian church, the Apostle Paul addressed their lack of understanding and misuse of spiritual gifts. Paul's teachings are relevant today, as God's special endowments of spiritual talents and skills continue to be flaunted and abused.

DEVOTIONAL OUTLINE

1. Understanding spiritual graces (I Cor. 12:1-3). Believers are lifelong learners who never "graduate" because we can never know all there is to know about our great God. The concerned church leader will embrace the Apostle Paul's desire that every believer be taught to unerringly recognize the manifestation of the Holy Spirit especially when He is at work in his life.

Some new converts can be easily swayed in one direction or another, having limited spiritual awareness on which to build. Only God's Spirit can fill us with the spiritual graces necessary to speak as we ought to speak and behave as Christians ought to behave.

2. Varieties of spiritual graces (I Cor. 12:4-6). "Diversities of gifts," "differences of administrations," and "diversities of operations" are reflective of the Holy Trinity and should be understood as spiritual outpourings through which one body ministers in numerous ways. Every gift is significant and designed by God to work for the benefit of the entire body of Christ.

3. The necessity of spiritual graces (I Cor. 12:7-11). Imagine the state of the church without godly wisdom and knowledge. Faith is essential to affect healings and miracles. Prophecy itself, being perceived as mystifying, would be totally dismissed without faith. The rapidity with which false doctrine would spread without the gift of discernment would prove immeasurably divisive, especially among vulnerable converts unfamiliar with the covenant of promise. Possession of the inspired ability to speak in unknown languages or interpret them would be reduced to speculation and controversy except for the intervention of the Spirit.

AGE-GROUP EMPHASES

Children: Point out what each child does well. Explain that this might be his God-given talent to bless others and glorify God.

Youths: Young people generally are not shy about flaunting the skill and know-how they think they have. Teach them that God deserves the credit for whatever abilities they possess.

Adults: Encourage the adults to be thankful for the special gifts that God has entrusted them with and not to be envious of what He has given to others.

—Jane E. Campbell.

LESSON 12   **MAY 17, 2015**

Scripture Lesson Text

I COR. 12:14 For the body is not one member, but many.

15 If the foot shall say, Because I am not the hand, I am not of the body; is it therefore not of the body?

16 And if the ear shall say, Because I am not the eye, I am not of the body; is it therefore not of the body?

17 If the whole body *were* an eye, where *were* the hearing? If the whole *were* hearing, where *were* the smelling?

18 But now hath God set the members every one of them in the body, as it hath pleased him.

19 And if they were all one member, where *were* the body?

20 But now *are they* many members, yet but one body.

21 And the eye cannot say unto the hand, I have no need of thee: nor again the head to the feet, I have no need of you.

22 Nay, much more those members of the body, which seem to be more feeble, are necessary:

23 And those *members* of the body, which we think to be less honourable, upon these we bestow more abundant honour; and our uncomely *parts* have more abundant comeliness.

24 For our comely *parts* have no need: but God hath tempered the body together, having given more abundant honour to that *part* which lacked:

25 That there should be no schism in the body, but *that* the members should have the same care one for another.

26 And whether one member suffer, all the members suffer with it; or one member be honoured, all the members rejoice with it.

27 Now ye are the body of Christ, and members in particular.

28 And God hath set some in the church, first apostles, secondarily prophets, thirdly teachers, after that miracles, then gifts of healings, helps, governments, diversities of tongues.

29 *Are* all apostles? *are* all prophets? *are* all teachers? *are* all workers of miracles?

30 Have all the gifts of healing? do all speak with tongues? do all interpret?

31 But covet earnestly the best gifts: and yet shew I unto you a more excellent way.

NOTES

Bible Expositor and Illuminator

Members of One Body

Lesson: I Corinthians 12:14-31

Read: I Corinthians 12:12-31

TIME: A.D. 55   PLACE: from Ephesus

GOLDEN TEXT—"Now ye are the body of Christ, and members in particular" (I Corinthians 12:27).

Introduction

One of the most important keys to the success of an organization is a proper division of responsibilities. All of us are familiar with the elaborate bureaucratic structures that characterize national, state, and local governments and big-business corporations. Educational institutions also require clear-cut divisions among administrators, faculty, and supporting staff. Bureaucracy, of course, can become dysfunctional, but all recognize a need for organization appropriate to the purpose.

The church of Jesus Christ is more than an organization. It is a spiritual organism deriving its life from God and having Jesus as its Head. Nevertheless, its effectiveness depends on each member recognizing his or her spiritual gift and using it in harmony with others.

LESSON OUTLINE

I. **THE WORTH OF THE MEMBERS**—I Cor. 12:14-20

II. **THE HARMONY OF THE MEMBERS**—I Cor. 12:21-26

III. **THE GIFTS OF THE MEMBERS**—I Cor. 12:27-31

Exposition: Verse by Verse

THE WORTH OF THE MEMBERS

I COR. 12:14 For the body is not one member, but many.

15 If the foot shall say, Because I am not the hand, I am not of the body; is it therefore not of the body?

16 And if the ear shall say, Because I am not the eye, I am not of the body; is it therefore not of the body?

17 If the whole body were an eye, where were the hearing? If the whole were hearing, where were the smelling?

18 But now hath God set the members every one of them in the body, as it hath pleased him.

19 And if they were all one mem-

May 17, 2015

ber, where were the body?

20 But now are they many members, yet but one body.

The principle stated (I Cor. 12:14). After explaining the concept of gifts bestowed by the Holy Spirit to glorify Christ (vss. 1-11), Paul likened the church to a body of many members unified in Christ (vs. 12). It has been brought together in one Spirit from many backgrounds (vs. 13). This spiritual unity is a remarkable phenomenon, unmatched by any human unifying force. But then he began to stress the need for diversity in the unified body in order to achieve its spiritual goals: "For the body is not one member, but many" (vs. 14). The point he was about to develop is that to function as a body, the body needs the contribution of each separate part.

Illustrations from the human body (I Cor. 12:15-17). To illustrate problems that can hinder the church, Paul offered a whimsical but pertinent speculation on what would happen if bodily organs refused to accept their proper functions. The foot, for example, might say, "Because I am not the hand, I am not of the body." The foot would therefore stop functioning as it should and deprive the body of an essential ability.

Something like this was happening in Corinth. Those who had spectacular gifts (tongues) were exalting themselves. Those who lacked such gifts became discouraged and assumed they had nothing to contribute, depriving the church of gifts they *did* have.

Extending his illustration, Paul imagined the ear saying, "Because I am not the eye, I am not of the body" (I Cor. 12:16). As the foot denigrated itself because it considered the hand superior, so the ear sees itself as inferior to the eye. All would agree that hands and eyes are essential. But no one would argue from this that feet and ears are unnecessary. Yet equivalent arguments in the church left some members discouraged or disgruntled and the church impoverished.

Paul showed how nonsensical such thinking is. If the entire body were an eye, where would the hearing be? If the entire body were an ear, what would happen to the sense of smell? Each organ is important, but there would be no point to its ability without the rest.

So it is with members of a church who think their gifts are the only important ones. By despising others' gifts or trying to force them all into one mold, they are actually destroying the spiritual body of which they are a part. Church leaders ought to encourage all their people to discover, develop, and use their gifts.

God's sovereign distribution (I Cor. 12:18). "But now" turns attention from hypothetical illustrations to the actual facts. Instead of fashioning the body of just one or two organs, God has "set the members every one of them in the body, as it hath pleased him." We marvel at the body's efficiency in spite of its complexity. All parts cooperate to achieve what it was intended to do.

If God has the wisdom and power to design our bodies to operate efficiently, can He not fashion Christ's spiritual body, the church, in the same way? It is not our prerogative to question His design or impose our own interpretation of how it should work. We should welcome the diversity of spiritual gifts and seek wisdom in how they can be used.

The summary of the argument (I Cor. 12:19-20). Paul now recapitulated his major point—that the body cannot exist apart from its many members. "And if they were all one member," he asked, "where were the body?" The unstated answer is that there would be no body. But he immediately asserted, "But now are they many members, yet but one body." This is a self-evident truth about the physical body, and it is true of Christ's church as well.

THE HARMONY OF THE MEMBERS

21 And the eye cannot say unto the hand, I have no need of thee: nor again the head to the feet, I have no need of you.

22 Nay, much more those members of the body, which seem to be more feeble, are necessary:

23 And those members of the body, which we think to be less honourable, upon these we bestow more abundant honour; and our uncomely parts have more abundant comeliness.

24 For our comely parts have no need: but God hath tempered the body together, having given more abundant honour to that part which lacked:

25 That there should be no schism in the body, but that the members should have the same care one for another.

26 And whether one member suffer, all the members suffer with it; or one member be honoured, all the members rejoice with it.

The necessity of harmony (I Cor. 12:21-23). Paul now resumed his illustration but shifted the emphasis from body parts that feel useless or deprived to those that feel independently sufficient. If the eye says to the hand or the head says to the feet, "I have no need of thee," they are deceiving themselves. The eye looks at the desirable object, but without the hand to pick it up, the desire is left unfulfilled. The head, with all its reasoning powers, cannot move at all without the cooperation of the feet.

So it is with members of the body of Christ. The Corinthians needed this admonition because some of them were glorying in their gifts and despising all who lacked them. Factions had developed (I Cor. 1:10-11) and were evident even at their observances of the Lord's Supper (11:18-22). Their inordinate emphasis on tongues had led to disorderly services (chap. 14). Their abuse of Christian liberty caused them to wound weak consciences (8:9-12).

Thus, Paul reminded them that, rather than to be despised, those members of the body that seem weak or feeble are all the more necessary. Many bodily organs are not visible and, in fact, need to be protected inside the skin and bone structure—the heart, lungs, digestive organs, and kidneys. Yet they are essential to human life.

Likewise, in the body of Christ, many members who never minister publicly are nevertheless the "lifeline" of the church. They may actually be more important to the church than those who have a public ministry.

Paul went even further: "And those members of the body, which we think to be less honourable, upon these we bestow more abundant honour; and our uncomely parts have more abundant comeliness" (I Cor. 12:23). This describes parts of the body that modesty tells us should not be exposed; so we bestow on them more abundant honor through clothing. Thus, the more presentable members bestow comeliness on those that are unpresentable.

God's provision of harmony (I Cor. 12:24). God recognizes that "our comely parts have no need." To conceal them would be to hinder their effectiveness. But He has put the body together in such a way as to give extra honor to the parts that lacked it. God has interspersed the weaker members with the stronger, the less presentable with the more attractive, so that all members partake of a common honor.

As a result, the entire body presents an attractive, unified appearance. All are blended into a harmonious whole, and all members can rejoice that the body not only works smoothly but also presents a pleasing appearance to others.

The outworking of harmony (I Cor. 12:25-26). God has blended the members together so "that there should be no schism in the body, but that the members should have the same care one for another." In the church, as in our bodies, God has arranged the members in a way that will promote unity, not division. He has given all members the opportunity and responsibility to lavish on one another the same kind of care they bestow on themselves.

Sadly, the Corinthian church was not experiencing this harmony (I Cor. 1:11; 11:18). The members had all the gifts necessary to do so, but their spiritual maturity did not match their giftedness.

The Corinthian church had difficulty experiencing what comes naturally to the physical body. If one part suffers, the rest of the body suffers with it; or if one part is honored, the rest of the body rejoices with it.

The same principle should be true of the church. Paul urged the Romans, "Rejoice with them that do rejoice, and weep with them that weep" (Rom. 12:15). To feel no reaction to either one is evidence of a serious spiritual problem. Ironically, it is often easier for believers to sympathize with those who weep than to rejoice with those who rejoice. Some of us are too self-centered to rejoice when another is honored.

THE GIFTS OF THE MEMBERS

27 Now ye are the body of Christ, and members in particular.

28 And God hath set some in the church, first apostles, secondarily prophets, thirdly teachers, after that miracles, then gifts of healings, helps, governments, diversities of tongues.

29 Are all apostles? are all prophets? are all teachers? are all workers of miracles?

30 Have all the gifts of healing? do all speak with tongues? do all interpret?

31 But covet earnestly the best gifts: and yet shew I unto you a more excellent way.

A listing of gifts (I Cor. 12:27-28). From his use of the human body as an illustration, Paul moved to his intended lesson: "Now ye are the body of Christ, and members in particular." The church is an organism to live out and manifest the life of Christ.

Within this organism, individual believers make up its various members. Each believer has a vital role to fulfill. But each must know that he or she is but one member, not the whole body, and therefore needs the contributions of all the others to make the congregation's ministry glorifying to Christ.

Paul then listed spiritual gifts that contribute to the church's health. The list is not exhaustive, but it gives a good representation of gifts known to the Corinthians. Paul made it clear that God does the giving. He also indicated that there is a definite ranking to the gifts. Paul saw that the Corinthians were exalting lesser gifts precisely because they were showier. He therefore had to set things straight.

The first rank belonged to the apostles. These were the men who had seen the risen Christ and were commissioned by Him to plant churches and give them His authoritative teaching.

Second, God gave the church prophets. These were people who received new revelation from God and passed it on to the churches as occasion required before the New Testament canon was completed. The third group is teachers, who have the ability to expound and apply truth that has already been revealed. These first three gifts are ranked ahead of the others because they are involved in communicating the content of the Christian message.

In the latter part of I Corinthians 12:28, Paul listed gifts such as miracles, healing, helps, governments, and diverse tongues. "Helps" refers to all kinds of ministrations to other members of the body. "Governments" refers to administration, and it is instructive that what is regarded as a high office in human organizations is given a lower ranking in the church. Finally, "tongues" (languages) is pointedly ranked last.

The importance of diversity (I Cor. 12:29-30). Paul now posed a series of rhetorical questions, all of which anticipate a negative answer. Choosing a sampling of the gifts just enumerated, he showed the folly of thinking everyone in the church should have them all. God has bestowed gifts on all His children, but He has left in each of us a vacuum that can be filled only by the gifts of others.

Advice to the church (I Cor. 12:31). Paul ended this discussion with a command: "But covet earnestly the best gifts." He was saying, "You are right in wanting God's gifts, but ask Him for those that are most useful in edifying the church as a whole." These would be especially prophecy and teaching.

But Paul was about to show them something even better: the way of love, which he would expound in the next chapter. So, in effect he was saying, "Desire the most useful gifts. But, more important, show love to one another in using the gifts you have."

—Robert E. Wenger.

QUESTIONS

1. What potential problem in the church did Paul illustrate through the foot and the ear?
2. How were self-important church members destroying the church?
3. Why should we welcome the diversity God has given the church?
4. How were the Corinthians destroying the harmony of the church?
5. How does the vital importance of physical organs that are hidden relate to spiritual gifts?
6. How can a church of diverse elements present a unified witness?
7. Is it easy for Christians to rejoice and sympathize with each other? Explain.
8. In Paul's list of spiritual gifts, which ones did he rank higher? Why?
9. How was Paul's ranking of gifts a rebuke to the Corinthians?
10. What was Paul's advice to believers at the end of this passage?

—Robert E. Wenger.

Preparing to Teach the Lesson

According to some estimates, there are approximately 33,000 Protestant denominations in the world today. How does this variety of denominations correlate to Paul's teaching that all believers are in one body in Christ? What do Paul's words "Now ye are the body of Christ, and members in particular" (I Cor. 12:27) mean?

TODAY'S AIM

Facts: to understand the biblical emphasis on believers being one body in Christ.

Principle: to accept that unity in the church is achieved through the work of God, not people.

Application: to minister effectively in our local churches with oneness of heart.

INTRODUCING THE LESSON

Have you ever watched an orchestra tuning up before a concert? How do all the diverse instruments tune up in order to play in unity? The first-chair oboe player keeps his instrument tuned to A 440, the standard. All the other orchestra members tune their instruments to that oboe.

The body of Christ is similar to an orchestra. The standard for us is the Lord Himself. The Holy Spirit places us, as His instruments, into Christ's body by His baptism. Whether Jew or Gentile, we are united in one body (I Cor. 12:12-13). Each local church should reflect the characteristics of that one body.

DEVELOPING THE LESSON

1. We are the body (I Cor. 12:14-20). Paul used the example of a human body as an analogy for the body of Christ as seen in the local congregation. A human body is not limited to one member but is composed of many that all function together. In a similar way, a church is not one member, but many. Individuals in a church have many different gifts, but together they are one body.

Paul elaborated on his analogy by showing how inconceivable it should be that a person with a particular gift would be envious of another with a different gift. You cannot imagine your foot refusing to cooperate in your body because it is not a hand; nor can you imagine your ear refusing to be recognized as part of your body because it is not an eye. It is just as foolish to think that because you do not have one certain gift, you are not valuable in the local church.

Without question, differences in the members of our body exist, but each has its own purpose. How functional would a body be if it were only an eye, or an ear, or a nose? The differences in the various members are what give advantage to the physical body. The same is true to church members, who have various gifts in the spiritual body.

The whole arrangement of having different members in a human body was God's doing. Differing gifts for those in a local church is likewise God's divine purpose. The gifts are not placed in the body randomly; they are arranged by God for His purposes. Some Christians feel that they are not appreciated because they do not have the gifts that would put them in the limelight. God, however, makes no mistakes. He placed diversity within the church for His purposes, using each part for His glory. There is no inferior gift in God's plan, even if some are not as public as others.

2. We share in the body (I Cor. 12:21-26). Paul continued his analogy of the human body. He showed how unthinkable it is that any one part would think it can function alone. Try to imagine an eye getting any work done without the hands or the head moving anywhere without the feet. In the church, likewise, no one person can fulfill God's purposes without the others functioning alongside in the ministry.

All parts of a human body are essential to its functioning capabilities. This includes parts that seemingly are "feeble" (I Cor. 12:22), "less honourable," "uncomely" (vs. 23), or "comely" (vs. 24). God is the one who put the body together, and He did it for a threefold purpose. His purpose was for harmony, for mutual care, and for mutual sympathy.

3. We function in the body (I Cor. 12:27-31). All parts of the spiritual body are to function like a physical body. The church at Corinth was of the same quality as the whole body of Christ. Just as the human body should work together, so should the church.

As parts of God's church, we must recognize that He gives gifts according to His sovereignty. Paul began by listing the most important gifts according to those who possessed them. Gifts differ in their apparent value, and God chooses which Christians receive which gifts. All Christians, however, must be faithful in exercising their gifts (cf. I Pet. 4:10). The apostles came first, followed by the prophets, and then by the teachers. All these were involved with directly communicating God's truth and establishing His church. After these came the gifts of lesser importance—miracles, healings, helps, governments, and tongues (I Cor. 12:28).

In addition to giving gifts according to His sovereignty, God also gives them in diversity. He gives the gifts to whom He pleases. No Christian receives them all. Since none of us has all the gifts, what should we do? We should "covet earnestly the best gifts" (I Cor. 12:31). The verb "covet" means "to earnestly desire." Corinth exalted tongues, a lesser gift. Paul exhorted them to instead desire to use the better gifts.

ILLUSTRATING THE LESSON

Each person in the local church cooperates to further Christ's work.

WE ARE THE CHURCH

UNITY IN DIVERSITY

CONCLUDING THE LESSON

God gave spiritual gifts as it pleased Him. No matter what your gift may be, you have a vital part to play in your local church. Any attitude of grumbling or of superiority is out of place. The goal is for each of us to exercise our gifts and cause the body to function properly.

ANTICIPATING THE NEXT LESSON

Next week our attention focuses specifically on the gift of languages as used in the early church.

—R. Larry Overstreet.

PRACTICAL POINTS

1. The Holy Spirit unites many members into one body to do God's work (I Cor. 12:14).
2. Believers should neither boast of nor belittle their status in the body of Christ (vss. 15-19).
3. Every gift is critical to the healthy functioning of the church (vss. 20-21).
4. Behind-the-scenes work is often most critical to the success of a ministry (vss. 22-24).
5. The members of Christ's body are inseparably bound to one another (vss. 25-26).
6. Believers must accept God's gifts for them and not envy those of others (vss. 27-31).

—Cheryl Y. Powell.

RESEARCH AND DISCUSSION

1. How does the Christian church respond to the member who really does not feel that he is a part of the church's ministry? Why is it important to address this issue?
2. What, if any, is the difference between a natural ability or talent that God blesses someone with and a spiritual gift?
3. What types of church work are seen as more honorable than others? What types may be considered less honorable? How do the different categories of service work together for the good of the whole?
4. What does it mean that all members suffer with the member who suffers? How does this attitude prevent division in the church?

—Cheryl Y. Powell.

ILLUSTRATED HIGH POINTS

Not one member

The family unit is a wonderful entity that God has created. Although each member has a different personality, each one adds to the whole, which has a personality of its own. When family members know Jesus Christ as Saviour and submit to Him, each individual learns to love, respect, and support the others. Forgiveness is practiced when relationships become strained. Through submission to Christ, the family lives in harmony, and God is glorified.

It should be the same way in the larger family—the family of God, the local church. Having experienced Christ's new life through having faith in Him and submitting to Him, each person learns to love, respect, and support the others. When sin arises, forgiveness is the norm. I trust that in your local church family, you experience being God's family as you serve Him together.

No schism in the body

Sometimes young people can become very exclusive and form their own little groups. They look down on others their age, thinking that they are better because of how they dress or what they accomplish in school. In addition, such a group can become mean as the members make fun of others.

Sometimes, sad to say, such an exclusive group can be found in a local church. Certainly, a local church can have different groups whose members share specific interests or life experiences. But when a group starts thinking that it is better than another group, the local church family will be injured spiritually, for each person and each spiritual gift is needed in the local church. No cliques allowed!

—Paul R. Bawden.

Golden Text Illuminated

"Now ye are the body of Christ, and members in particular" (I Corinthians 12:27).

The truth expressed in our golden text was one the Corinthian believers desperately needed to understand. It is equally important for the church today to grasp this truth.

The Corinthian church was a church in conflict. There was division around various personalities—specifically, Paul, Peter, and Apollos. Various groups in the church elevated one of these godly men over the others (I Cor. 1:12-13). Likewise, certain spiritual gifts, particularly the more spectacular ones, were elevated over other gifts.

Paul condemned such attitudes, for they engendered pride and a false concept of the value of God's people. Pride is as much a temptation today as it was in Paul's day, and it is very subtle.

With his illustration of the church as a human body (I Cor. 12:12-27), Paul put everything in perspective. Every part of the body is essential to the proper functioning of the whole body. Thus, every part is to be properly honored and appreciated.

The same is true of the church. If all Christians possessed the same gift, the church could not function as it should. This is why the Spirit has given many different gifts to the church body. All are to be honored as essential.

Paul summed it up by saying, "Ye are the body of Christ." "Ye" is plural and refers to the entire Corinthian church. They were the one spiritual "body of Christ." The apostle then stated that they were "members in particular." Just as together they were the body of Christ, so individually they were members of the body.

Thus, no one is to be despised because of his or her gift, and no one is to be elevated above others as more important because of his or her gift. The church as a whole functions effectively when each member humbly employs the gift or gifts the Spirit has given and everyone recognizes that only Christ is the true Head of the body, the church (Col. 1:18).

As the Apostle Paul pointed out in his epistle to the Ephesians, "The whole body [the church] fitly joined together and compacted by that which every joint supplieth, according to the effectual working in the measure of every part, maketh increase of the body unto the edifying of itself in love" (4:16). Such spiritual growth and edification of the church cannot take place as they should if some members of the body are considered of no importance.

The church Christ established is designed to function effectively only when every member understands his or her role and is ministering to others within the church.

—*Jarl K. Waggoner.*

Heart of the Lesson

Our lesson this week speaks of the unity and diversity in the body of Christ, to which all those who put their faith in Him belong. We are all different, yet we are all one because the love of Jesus binds us together. There is truly no hierarchy in the church, for we are equal partners in ministry, using the gifts we have to serve the body of Christ in the very best way we can under His leadership.

1. Many members (I Cor. 12:14-17). Paul compared the local body of believers to the human body and showed how all the parts are very different. But each of the parts has a specific place in the local body of the church. One cannot claim superiority over the other. Every part has a specific task to do, having been given a special gift (or gifts) in order to bless and edify the local church. The local church could not fulfill its mission if everyone had the same gift.

Differing gifts in different people are crucial in order to do what Christ wants us to do. So every part is equally important in the service of the local church. If one person in the church does not use his or her gifts, then the local body suffers. All the areas of ministry are covered when every church member uses the gifts that God has given him or her. Their gifts are valuable in ministry, even though they may not consider them as important as the gifts another has. All are important in His work.

2. One purpose (I Cor. 12:18-26). It only takes us one close look to see how intricately our body has been woven together in its many parts. Every part has its special place and its special function. One part cannot do the work of another. Yet it is all these very different parts that make up one totally functioning unit. It is simply amazing to see how all this works, and God was the Divine Mastermind that put it all together. It is the same in the local church.

No part, no matter how insignificant, is

indispensable. God can use the most insignificant of us in ways we cannot imagine and bless the others we worship with. No gift is wasted in the economy of God when it is given to us. God has a definite purpose behind the gifts He has chosen for each of us in the body of Christ. What we think is not so important is really very important in the eyes of God. Some parts are more visible than others, and all are equally worthy for Him.

Some members are more vulnerable than others and may need extra care. Some parts are honored, and others have less dignity; and God has put us all together in the same place so that we may serve and build up one another. Mutual care is the mark of the body of Christ. Because of the integral unity between the members, it is important to see that when one suffers, the whole body suffers. When one rejoices, the other parts also rejoice because we are one body, woven together in love.

3. Many gifts (I Cor. 12:27-31). The abilities of apostles, prophets, teachers, miracle workers, helpers, healers, speakers of miraculous languages—these are only some of the special gifts that are given to the church (cf. Rom. 12:6-8; I Cor. 12:8-11). We all do not have the same gifts, and this is done deliberately by God. We should, however, earnestly desire the gifts that would be most helpful in the body of Christ.

—A. Koshy Muthalaly.

World Missions

The attack on Pearl Harbor in 1941 shocked the nation. Afterward, many were seething for revenge. One of those was a young bombardier named Jake DeShazer, who participated in the Doolittle raid on Japan.

After their successful bombing mission, Jake and his fellow crewmates were forced to bail out of their aircraft. They landed in Japanese-occupied territory in China. He was given a life sentence as a prisoner of war.

Already filled with hatred toward the Japanese, Jake's current situation only deepened those feelings. He was tortured and mistreated seemingly every minute of the day. The only thing that kept him alive was his desire for revenge.

However, things began to change when he received an opportunity to read the Bible. In the three weeks he was given to read it, he stayed awake day and night and could not put it down.

The Living Word captured his heart like nothing else. Before, he had had no comprehension why someone like Jesus would command someone to forgive his enemies, even as he was being tortured to death.

The day came when Jake prayed, "Lord, though I am far from home and though I am in prison, I ask for Your forgiveness." He knew he was a new man as his heart filled with the joy and presence of Jesus.

As his mistreatment continued, Jake understood that God was asking him to reach out to his tormentors with forgiveness and love.

Unknown to Jake, God was also working in the hearts of others. One was the leader of the attack on Pearl Harbor, Mitsuo Fuchida.

Even though Mitsuo's life had been miraculously spared many times during the war, he had no peace in his heart. He listened to the testimony of a young woman whose parents had been killed by the Japanese in the Philippines. Yet she showed great love and devotion to the Japanese.

He also read Jake's account of life as a POW and how he had found love and forgiveness through Jesus. Jake was now married, and he and his wife were missionaries in Japan. Thousands came to Christ through his witness, including two of Jake's former guards.

Mitsuo decided to study the Bible, and soon the gospel was planted deep in his heart. He spoke to his countrymen, sharing Jesus with them.

Jake and Mitsuo met and began ministering together. They shared their testimonies of God's grace all over Japan.

Only Jesus can heal the hurts and disappointments of our past and bring them all together for the good of others and for His glory.

—Christina Futrell.

The Jewish Aspect

"Now ye are the body of Christ, and members in particular" (I Cor. 12:27). The concept in this golden text has no counterpart in Jewish religious experience. At the same time, "peoplehood," or community, is what makes Jewish society tick.

When the synagogue is experienced up close and personal, we find it to be a gathering place where Jews express their heritage to other Jews. There is the lady who loves the hora and other Jewish dances, some that may date from the days of David. There is the man who is really nonreligious. He is, however, politically motivated. Arguing fine points by the hour, he joins a pro-Jewish faction.

Religious Jews do not agree on the kashruth (system of kosher foods and dietary rules). Nevertheless, there are plenty of pareve foods (that is, those that are not restricted by even the most observant Jews).

Rabbi Kertzer wrote, "Jewish community is positive, not negative; it is open, not closed; anyone who wishes to link his or her own personal destiny to that of the community . . . may join it." And yet the single, unifying factor for Jews the world over seems to be that they must stand together in resistance to anti-Semitism—hatred of the Jews.

It was once said that the degree of anti-Semitism depended on the number of Jews in a given district. At the time of the rise of the Nazis in the 1930s, anti-Semitism had already been deeply ingrained in the European psyche. And yet, not long before, German Jews were quite loyal to the Fatherland, calling themselves "Germans of the Mosaic persuasion."

One very damaging aspect of Jewish clannishness was their hatred of other Jews. German Jews dressed like other Germans, spoke German, and were content to be Jews one day a week. But many of them detested the Jews of Poland, who dressed in wide hats, side curls, and beards and spoke Yiddish. In 1944, when young Jews in the Warsaw ghetto sought to arm their people to resist the Germans, these long-standing divisions within Jewish life were exposed.

Anti-Semitism is satanically inspired. The wicked one has provoked many to strike out against the descendants of Abraham (cf. Ezra 4:4-7; Neh. 4:7, 11; Esther 3:8-15).

Sadly, many who are called Christians have been hostile toward the Jews. Jules Isaac, a secular Jew who lived through World War II, asked, "Did the Nazis spring from nothing or from the bosom of a Christian people?" (*The Teaching of Contempt,* Holt, Rinehart and Winston).

Jews remember that in the past, certain Christian institutions charged their whole race with deicide—killing God. The Bible, however, teaches that our sin was the reason Christ died. Scripture specifically indicts only Herod, Pilate, and the Gentiles and Jews in Jerusalem who worked with them (Acts 4:27). Their guilt remains; but ultimately, the wicked unwittingly did what God had "determined before to be done" (Acts 4:28; cf. 2:22-23).

—Lyle P. Murphy.

Guiding the Superintendent

The human body, having many parts that make up the one body, is often used as an analogy of the body of Christ.

DEVOTIONAL OUTLINE

1. God values every member (I Cor. 12:14-19). There is much that one can accomplish in the church, but the church's effectiveness is multiplied tremendously when all of its members harmoniously combine their gifts and talents, in the one Spirit, toward the fulfillment of God's desire "that all should come to repentance" (II Pet. 3:9). Whoever seeks to become a Christian must confess faith in the one true and living God. When the new convert trusts in Christ as Saviour and Lord, he receives the baptism of the Holy Spirit and is filled with that same Spirit. Every proselyte experiences this same filling, but all are not given the same assignment in the body. God in His sovereignty endued each member as it pleased Him.

2. God knows every member (I Cor. 12:20-27). One of the greatest challenges in church leadership is attending equally to each member of the one body. Some members are more confident than others and require less guidance. Their gifts are frequently used in carrying out the ministry of the church. It is not unrealistic to have members who feel inferior or inadequate; they need encouragement.

The truth is that every member wants to feel useful and appreciated. The highly gifted must not shun the dubious ones but embrace them and assure them that there is no division in the body of Christ. Each member, though different, is codependent on the others and shares in the others' joy and sorrow.

3. God loves His members (I Cor. 12:28-31). In God's church, there are no "Big I's" and "Little You's." He knows precisely what the church's needs are and has fitly joined together every area of church ministry (cf. Eph. 4:16). Looking around your church, you will notice that all members are not pastors and all are not teachers; rather, they are diverse, multigifted servants operating in their God-given grace. With God, no gift or office is more honorable than any other.

AGE-GROUP EMPHASES

Children: Assure the children that God has placed them in the church where they can best honor Him with their gifts.

Youths: Teach that there is no need to envy the spiritual gifts of other youths. God gave them their gift and values them all.

Adults: Love remains the ultimate gift. Remind the adults of God's great love for us. As members of His body, we must love and support all the other "parts" in glorious worship of the Gift-Giver.

—Jane E. Campbell.

LESSON 13   MAY 24, 2015

Scripture Lesson Text

ACTS 2:1 And when the day of Pen'te-cost was fully come, they were all with one accord in one place.

2 And suddenly there came a sound from heaven as of a rushing mighty wind, and it filled all the house where they were sitting.

3 And there appeared unto them cloven tongues like as of fire, and it sat upon each of them.

4 And they were all filled with the Ho'ly Ghost, and began to speak with other tongues, as the Spir'it gave them utterance.

5 And there were dwelling at Je-ru'sa-lem Jews, devout men, out of every nation under heaven.

6 Now when this was noised abroad, the multitude came together, and were confounded, because that every man heard them speak in his own language.

7 And they were all amazed and marvelled, saying one to another, Behold, are not all these which speak Gal-i-lae'ans?

12 And they were all amazed, and were in doubt, saying one to another, What meaneth this?

I COR. 14:13 Wherefore let him that speaketh in an *unknown* tongue pray that he may interpret.

14 For if I pray in an *unknown* tongue, my spirit prayeth, but my understanding is unfruitful.

15 What is it then? I will pray with the spirit, and I will pray with the understanding also: I will sing with the spirit, and I will sing with the understanding also.

16 Else when thou shalt bless with the spirit, how shall he that occupieth the room of the unlearned say Amen at thy giving of thanks, seeing he understandeth not what thou sayest?

17 For thou verily givest thanks well, but the other is not edified.

18 I thank my God, I speak with tongues more than ye all:

19 Yet in the church I had rather speak five words with my understanding, that *by my voice* I might teach others also, than ten thousand words in an *unknown* tongue.

NOTES

Gift of Languages

Lesson: Acts 2:1-7, 12; I Corinthians 14:13-19

Read: Acts 2:1-21; I Corinthians 14:1-25

TIMES: A.D. 30; A.D. 55

PLACES: Jerusalem; from Ephesus

GOLDEN TEXT—"They were all filled with the Holy Ghost, and began to speak with other tongues, as the Spirit gave them utterance" (Acts 2:4).

Introduction

At the beginning of human history, there was only one language, a condition that lasted until after the Flood (Gen. 11:1). But when mankind refused to obey God's command to replenish the population of the earth (9:1, 7) and instead settled down in Shinar to undertake great projects (11:2-4), God intervened. He confused mankind's languages, causing the people to scatter across the globe (vss. 5-9).

While diverse languages inhibited cooperation in evil schemes, it also hindered legitimate communication. Thus, when God wished to spread the gospel of Christ to the ends of the earth (Acts 1:8), He gave a special sign on the Day of Pentecost that He was reversing the curse of Babel and overriding language barriers. His gospel was to be for all nations, peoples, tribes, and languages.

LESSON OUTLINE

I. LANGUAGES ON THE DAY OF PENTECOST—Acts 2:1-7, 12

II. LANGUAGES IN THE CHURCH AT CORINTH—I Cor. 14:13-19

Exposition: Verse by Verse

LANGUAGES ON THE DAY OF PENTECOST

ACTS 2:1 And when the day of Pentecost was fully come, they were all with one accord in one place.

2 And suddenly there came a sound from heaven as of a rushing mighty wind, and it filled all the house where they were sitting.

3 And there appeared unto them cloven tongues like as of fire, and it sat upon each of them.

4 And they were all filled with the Holy Ghost, and began to speak with other tongues, as the Spirit gave them utterance.

5 And there were dwelling at Jerusalem Jews, devout men, out of every nation under heaven.

6 Now when this was noised abroad, the multitude came together, and were confounded, because that every man heard them speak in his own language.

7 And they were all amazed and marvelled, saying one to another, Behold, are not all these which speak Galilaeans?

12 And they were all amazed, and were in doubt, saying one to another, What meaneth this?

The circumstances (Acts 2:1). The remarkable events of this passage occurred "when the day of Pentecost was fully come." This festival in Israel marked the beginning of the grain harvest and occurred on the fiftieth day after Passover (Exod. 23:16; 34:22; Lev. 23:15-16). This particular Pentecost took place shortly after Jesus had ascended into heaven following His final instructions to the apostles (Acts 1:1-9).

At that time, Jesus' followers "were all with one accord in one place" (Acts 2:1). These included not only the apostles but also certain other disciples, so the total was about 120 (1:13-15). They had met regularly for prayer as they anticipated the coming of the Holy Spirit and were together on this special feast day.

They were together in a place that Acts does not specify. But since they were gathering in a house, it was probably the upper room they had been using regularly (cf. 1:13).

The Holy Spirit's coming (Acts 2:2-3). "Suddenly" marks the beginning of a dramatic scene, as the Spirit made His presence evident. The Spirit does not always reveal Himself in spectacular ways, but He has chosen to do so at certain crucial points in God's plan (cf. Num. 11:26-29; I Sam. 10:6; Matt. 3:16). Here He left no doubt of His presence with the early disciples.

First, "there came a sound from heaven as of a rushing mighty wind, and it filled all the house where they were sitting" (Acts 2:2). The disciples did not feel actual wind, but the sound was as if a strong wind were blowing through the house. This was an apt symbol for the Holy Spirit, for the Greek word is the same for "wind," "breath," and "spirit."

Next, "there appeared unto them cloven tongues like as of fire, and it sat upon each of them" (Acts 2:3). "Cloven" means "distributing." Tongue-like forms that looked like fire distributed themselves outward from one point and rested on each of the disciples present. These "tongues" were not actually fire but had its appearance to represent the Holy Spirit symbolically.

The symbolism was not new for these Jewish disciples, for fire had often signified God's presence in Israel's history. He had appeared to Moses in a burning bush (Exod. 3:2) and as a fire on the top of Mount Sinai (19:18; 24:17). A pillar of fire guided and guarded Israel in its journeys (13:21) and stood over the tabernacle (40:38). The fire of God consumed the sacrifices of both Moses and Elijah (Lev. 9:24; I Kings 18:38).

The evidence of the Spirit's endowment (Acts 2:4-6). The mention of tongues anticipates still another sign of the Spirit's presence—one that was evident not only to the believers but also to the crowds in Jerusalem. Under the Spirit's control, the disciples "began to speak with other tongues, as the Spirit gave them utterance."

It is evident that the "tongues" in Acts 2:4 were actual foreign languages current in that day. The word translated "language" in verse 6 and "tongue" in verse 8 is nearly identical to our word "dialect," and those who heard recognized the message being conveyed (vs. 11). Temporarily tearing aside the limitations imposed at Babel, God was symbolically revealing the universality of the gospel of Christ.

"Every nation under heaven" (Acts 2:5) should not be pressed to an extreme. It surely included the inhabited earth as Luke knew it at that time, and verses 9-11 give some idea of its scope. The entire Greco-Roman world, including parts of Asia and Africa, was represented, for Jews had migrated into all these areas.

The phrase in Acts 2:6, "when this was noised abroad," means something on the order of "when this sound occurred." It could refer to the sound of wind (vs. 2) or, more likely, the sound of the disciples' voices (vs. 4). The crowd came together to see what was happening. But as they did, they were bewildered, because each of them was hearing his own language being spoken.

The languages that would have been widely understood on this occasion were Aramaic, Greek, and Latin. But what happened on this day went far beyond these. The word used for "language" in Acts 2:6 includes the numerous dialects spoken throughout the Roman Empire. The breadth of languages spoken is also implied by the many regions mentioned (vss. 9-11).

Questions aroused by the witness (Acts 2:7, 12). Luke's description of the crowd's reaction is striking: "And they were all amazed and marvelled." "Amazed" translates a verb whose components literally mean "to stand outside (of oneself)." It describes a reaction of confusion mingled with fear in the face of the supernatural (cf. Mark 5:42; Acts 9:21; 10:45; 12:16). The crowd's marveling was a typical reaction to a wonder or an inexplicable phenomenon (cf. John 7:15; Acts 4:13; 13:41).

The crowd had good reason for amazement: all those who were speaking were recognized as being Galileans. All the apostles were from Galilee, and probably most of the other early believers were as well. In any case, the crowd correctly identified the tongues-speakers.

Since Galilee was the northernmost Jewish province, it was identified with neighboring Gentile ways. Though Galileans were generally pious, they lacked the Judaistic rigor of the Pharisees and were therefore despised by them (John 7:41, 52; cf. 1:46). They also were common people, noted for their openness and generosity but not for their learning.

Yet the Jews gathered in Jerusalem that day from the far reaches of the civilized world heard these Galileans speak "the wonderful works of God" (Acts 2:11)—each in his own language! Fifteen geographical regions from which they came are mentioned (vss. 9-11). Totally perplexed, they asked one another, "What meaneth this?" After some mocked the speakers as being drunk, it was left to Peter to explain the true meaning—that the Spirit was being poured out (vss. 13-33).

LANGUAGES IN THE CHURCH AT CORINTH

I COR. 14:13 Wherefore let him that speaketh in an unknown tongue pray that he may interpret.

14 For if I pray in an unknown tongue, my spirit prayeth, but my understanding is unfruitful.

15 What is it then? I will pray with the spirit, and I will pray with the understanding also: I will sing with the spirit, and I will sing with the understanding also.

16 Else when thou shalt bless with the spirit, how shall he that occupieth the room of the unlearned say Amen at thy giving of thanks, seeing he understandeth not what thou sayest?

17 For thou verily givest thanks well, but the other is not edified.

18 I thank my God, I speak with tongues more than ye all:

19 Yet in the church I had rather speak five words with my understanding, that by my voice I might

teach others also, than ten thousand words in an unknown tongue.

A spiritual gift that God had intended as a blessing had become a problem at Corinth. Those who possessed it fancied themselves to be more important to the church than others, even those who prophesied. It became necessary for the Apostle Paul to give special instruction on why prophecy was more important than tongues.

Opinions differ as to whether the "tongues" in Corinth were the same as the "languages" in Acts 2 (cf. Hawthorne, et al., eds., *Dictionary of Paul and His Letters,* InterVarsity). Some believe the Corinthian phenomena were unintelligible, ecstatic utterances.

The importance of interpretation (I Cor. 14:13-14). In their zeal to use their gift, those who spoke in other languages were doing so in the assembly without the benefit of an interpreter. So their gift was not edifying the body of Christ at all (cf. vss. 2, 4, 7-11). By contrast, prophecy was preferred because it brought God's message clearly to the hearers (cf. vss. 1, 3, 5-6).

Paul did not forbid the use of languages; in fact, he encouraged it (I Cor. 14:5). But he urged the person who did so to "pray that he may interpret" (vs. 13). Earlier he recognized interpretation of languages as a spiritual gift some possessed (12:10, 30), separate from the gift of languages. But if no such person was present in the meeting, the foreign-language speaker was to pray for this ability himself. If God did not grant it, he was to remain silent (14:13, 28).

Paul explained further the need for interpretation: "For if I pray in an unknown tongue, my spirit prayeth, but my understanding is unfruitful" (I Cor. 14:14). Not only does interpretation edify the hearers; it also enhances the blessing for the speaker.

The need for understanding (I Cor. 14:15). Is it important to benefit intellectually from worship? According to Paul, *all* aspects of worship should engage the mind as well as the spirit.

Thus Paul determined to pray not only with his spirit but also with his understanding, or mind. The same principle applies to singing. Any worship that bypasses the mind is incomplete and dangerous because it ignores the factual basis on which Christian truth is founded.

The danger of a useless exercise (I Cor. 14:16-17). One who blesses (gives thanks) in a foreign language is benefiting only himself. Paul asked, "How shall he that occupieth the room of the unlearned say Amen at thy giving of thanks, seeing he understandeth not what thou sayest?" Some in the congregation did not understand the language used.

There are differing views as to who is being described here. In Acts 4:13 the word "unlearned" is translated as "ignorant." In II Corinthians 11:6, Paul described himself as "rude (untrained) in speech." The basic idea is a lack of acquaintance with something. Some think the "unlearned" in I Corinthians 14:16 was a not-yet-saved inquirer into the faith. Others, noting the later juxtaposition with unbelievers (vss. 23-24), take the more likely view that they were fellow believers who were uninitiated in the language being used.

Whoever this person was, he could not intelligently join the speaker in saying "Amen" ("It is true") at the end of the blessing (I Cor. 14:16), for he had not understood a word of it. Paul mildly rebuked the foreign-language speaker: "For *thou* (emphasis added) verily givest thanks well, but the other is not edified" (vs. 17). The spiritual gift had been used competently, but in this setting it had not benefited the rest of the body of Christ.

The preference for clear communication (I Cor. 14:18-19). The apostle was not opposed to the use of languages in the service of Christ. He had already stated this, and now he again testified, "I thank my God, I speak with tongues more than ye all." Paul himself had this gift, and he no doubt used it often as a sign in his role as a pioneer missionary to the Gentiles. The gift had a valid place in ministry.

But a church assembly with no interpreter present was not the proper setting. Paul wrote, "Yet in the church I had rather speak five words with my understanding, that by my voice I might teach others also, than ten thousand words in an unknown tongue" (I Cor. 14:19). Here he exalted the two gifts of prophecy and teaching. The presentation and explanation of God's truth, which appeal to the understanding, are the gifts that will eventually strengthen believers in their faith (cf. vs. 6).

Paul had many gifts, but in the church he preferred to use those that would be most profitable. His is an example we ought to take to heart. All gifts the Spirit chooses to use can be profitable in the right setting, but we should pray for wisdom to discern how the church will best be edified.

—Robert E. Wenger.

QUESTIONS

1. What was the occasion God chose to send the Holy Spirit upon the early followers of Christ?
2. Why were the symbols of wind and fire appropriate for the Spirit's coming?
3. What was God symbolizing through the languages at Pentecost?
4. How diverse were the languages of those gathered at Pentecost?
5. Why did the fact that the speakers were Galileans add to the amazement of the hearers?
6. Why was the gift of languages a problem at Corinth?
7. What other gift was to accompany the use of the gift of languages?
8. Why is the mind as important as the spirit in Christian worship?
9. Why might the gift of languages become useless in the assembly?
10. What gifts did Paul prefer for use in worship services?

—Robert E. Wenger.

Preparing to Teach the Lesson

Any of us who studied a foreign language have probably wished that somehow it could just be poured into our brains. Unless you are extraordinarily capable, you had to exert much effort and spend many hours to learn another language. Such was not the case with the gift of tongues in the New Testament. God miraculously gave people the ability to speak a language they had never studied in order to be a testimony to His chosen people Israel, since "Jews require a sign" (I Cor. 1:22).

TODAY'S AIM

Facts: to discover that the gift of tongues entailed speaking in a language not known by the speaker.

Principle: to accept that God sometimes uses miraculous means to accomplish His purpose.

Application: to be a testimony for Christ in any language we speak.

INTRODUCING THE LESSON

English is sometimes a confusing language. Consider that there is no ham in hamburger, no egg in eggplant, and neither pine nor apple in pineapple. In spite of such difficulties, we manage to use it to communicate.

Our lesson this week also deals with language. God used language in a miraculous way to establish His church.

DEVELOPING THE LESSON

1. The gift of languages came from the Holy Spirit (Acts 2:1-7, 12). Jesus had promised that the Holy Spirit would come (Luke 24:49; Acts 1:8). The Day of Pentecost was the fulfilled time for that event. The Greek word "Pentecost" means "fiftieth." It refers to the fiftieth day after Passover, which introduced the Feast of Harvest, the ingathering of firstfruits. The firstfruits of the grain harvest stand as a figure for the spiritual harvest introduced by the foundation of the church on this day.

Two indications of the coming of the Spirit were sound and sight (Acts 2:2-3). The sound was "as of a rushing mighty wind"; there was no actual wind, but there was a sound like wind. The sight was of tongues like fire; there was no actual fire, but as each tongue settled on a person, it looked like a flame. The Holy Spirit then filled each disciple and gave the person the ability to "speak with other tongues" (vs. 4). The filling of the Spirit refers to His control. The disciples were filled again later in Acts (4:31).

The Greek word for "tongue" is used fifty times in the New Testament, frequently for the physical organ itself (Mark 7:33; Jas. 3:5) and often of languages (Rev. 5:9). The issue in Acts—and later at Corinth—is whether these were known languages or some unknown "ecstatic" speech.

The context in Acts makes it clear that these were known languages, since each person heard "in his own language" (2:6). The word for language is the Greek word *dialektos,* from which the word "dialect" comes from. It occurs elsewhere only with the sense of a known language (21:40; 22:2; 26:14). Jews from fifteen areas were present at Pentecost (2:9-11).

Another evidence that these were known languages is that no need for any interpreters is mentioned in Acts 2. Although people from so many lands were there, they all heard in their own language and did not need an interpreter. God worked the miracle of enabling the disciples to speak in languages they had never learned so that their Jewish listeners could hear in their native languages.

2. The gift of languages is incomplete (I Cor. 14:13-17). Paul knew that the gift of languages was limited in its value. He compared it to prophecy, as observed in verses 1-12. Prophecy is the gift second only to apostleship (12:28). Prophecy "speaketh unto men to edification, and exhortation, and comfort" (14:3). Languages do not edify the church to the same extent (vss. 5-12). Paul wanted the church to excel not in the gift of languages but in "the edifying of the church" (vs. 12).

Paul next observed a second weakness of the gift of languages: it is incomplete for three reasons (I Cor. 14:13-17). First, it is incomplete because it is insufficient by itself. It is a gift that must be interpreted to have value to the church. Second, it is incomplete because it is incomprehensible, for it does not come from the understanding. "Understanding" stresses that which is from the mind, the intellect. It is being able to comprehend what something means.

Third, the gift of languages is incomplete because it is not beneficial for others. Those in church who do not understand need to participate equally in the worship service. They need to be able to give assent, to say amen, to the ministry of the church. If they cannot understand the language, then they gain no spiritual benefit from the ministry.

3. The gift of languages is inadequate (I Cor. 14:18-19). Paul concluded this section by summarizing his emphasis. Paul himself exercised the gift of languages. It was a sign gift intended to confirm the message of the apostles (Mark 16:17), and Paul clearly exercised the sign gifts (II Cor. 12:11-12). At the same time, he knew that the mission of the church must be edification. To speak ten thousand words in a language you do not know is of little value. To speak five words with understanding can effectively teach others God's Word.

ILLUSTRATING THE LESSON

Use your gifts to edify one another in the church.

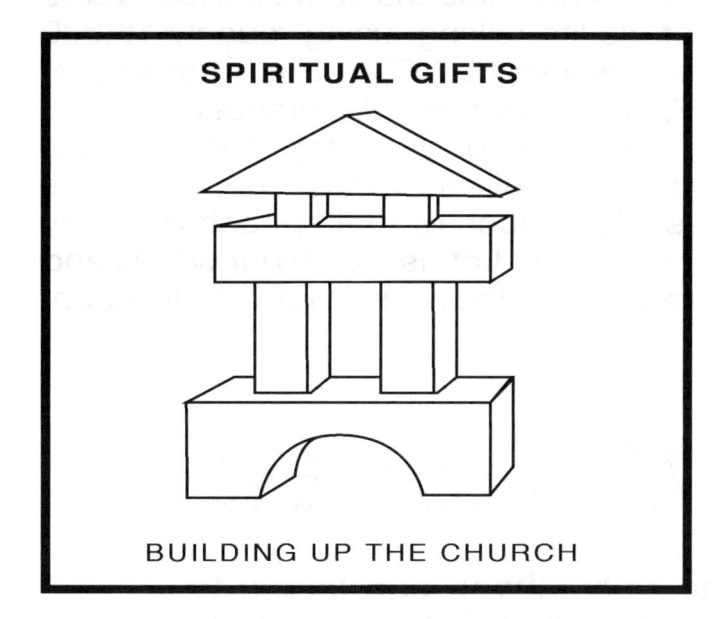

SPIRITUAL GIFTS

BUILDING UP THE CHURCH

CONCLUDING THE LESSON

In all denominations, there can be an emphasis on things that make us feel good to the exclusion of the clear ministry of Scripture. As individuals and as churches, we must be governed and directed by God's Word. This requires us to use our minds, our intellects, and to be deeply committed to understanding God's Word and ways.

ANTICIPATING THE NEXT LESSON

Our final lesson this quarter is next week. We will see that the greatest gift is love.

—*R. Larry Overstreet.*

PRACTICAL POINTS

1. God's work calls for unity among believers (Acts 2:1).
2. Believers must submit in prayer for the Holy Spirit to empower them for His work (vss. 2-4).
3. Some will be confused by the power of God, while others will be amazed (vss. 5-7, 12).
4. Spiritual gifts are used as intended when the entire body benefits (I Cor. 14:13-14).
5. A gift exercised merely for its own sake will edify few (vss. 15-17).
6. Christians must be mature enough to discern what is appropriate for corporate worship versus personal worship (vss. 18-19).

—*Cheryl Y. Powell.*

RESEARCH AND DISCUSSION

1. How was Pentecost significant to the Jews before the coming of Christ (cf. Lev. 23:15-22; Num. 28:26-31)?
2. Why did God pour out the Holy Spirit on the Day of Pentecost? Is it still necessary to be filled with the Holy Spirit to witness for Christ today? Explain.
3. When have you been empowered by God to witness about Christ?
4. How is speaking in tongues different from prophecy?
5. Is there a time and a place for the use of gifts that edify only the individual? Explain.
6. Why is it important to church members that our worship services be conducted in an orderly manner?

—*Cheryl Y. Powell.*

ILLUSTRATED HIGH POINTS

He may interpret

On a mission field where another language was spoken, I found that I was very limited in what I could say to people. But when I was accompanied by an interpreter and he translated for me, the people understood exactly what I was saying.

What happened at the Feast of Pentecost many years ago was entirely different. When the Holy Spirit came upon those assembled for the feast, believers were given the ability to speak in another person's language while still being able to understand one another. It was an evidence to the Jews that God was among them, authenticating His Son, the Lord Jesus, and His gospel. In this setting, no interpreter was necessary.

This was totally unlike my experience on the mission field, where I needed an interpreter. Perhaps this is what it will be like in heaven. We will not speak one language, but each of us will have the ability to speak and understand everyone else's language. How great that would be!

I had rather speak five words

Statisticians have estimated that the average person spends at least one-fifth of his life talking. Over a lifetime, the average man or woman speaks enough words to fill 132 books of 400 pages each. Calculated another way, the average person spends about thirteen years of his life talking, using roughly 18,000 words per day (Tan, *Encyclopedia of 7,700 Illustrations,* Assurance).

That is a lot of talking! The question that we believers must ask ourselves is, How much of that speech is of any real value? Let us weigh our words and make sure they count for the kingdom.

—Paul R. Bawden.

Golden Text Illuminated

"They were all filled with the Holy Ghost, and began to speak with other tongues, as the Spirit gave them utterance" (Acts 2:4).

In the upper room, before His crucifixion, Jesus had told the disciples that He and the Father would send them the Holy Spirit after His departure from the earth (cf. John 14:16; 15:26; 16:7). After His resurrection, Jesus had assured His followers that they would "be baptized with the Holy Ghost not many days hence" (Acts 1:5).

The baptism of the Spirit, which first occurred on the Day of Pentecost, marked the giving of the Spirit to permanently indwell Christ's followers and bring them into that one body we call the church (I Cor. 12:13). Today, every believer, from the moment of salvation, is a member of Christ's church. That church, however, had its beginning with the coming of the Spirit (Acts 2).

Ten days after Jesus' ascension into heaven (Acts 1:9-11), the disciples were still gathered together in Jerusalem, awaiting the fulfillment of the Lord's promise. The coming of the Spirit was accompanied by two physical evidences: a sound like a mighty wind and "tongues like as of fire," which "sat upon each of them" (2:3).

To the believers, these signs were clear evidence of the Spirit's coming. The result of the Spirit's arrival soon became evident to unbelievers as well, for the disciples were filled with the Spirit and "began to speak with other tongues." The following verses make it clear these "tongues" were languages known by the various peoples who had come to Jerusalem to celebrate the Festival of Pentecost. These languages had not been learned by the disciples, however; rather, the Holy Spirit "gave them utterance," that is, supernaturally enabled them to speak to the people present in their native languages.

Divine miracles are, by their very nature, rare, and they are not wasted. In this case, a great crowd gathered, and Peter was able to proclaim the gospel to them. As a result, about three thousand people came to know Christ that day (Acts 2:41).

On this unique day, it was important that God gave clear, undeniable, and supernatural testimony that the message of Christ delivered by the apostles and the newly formed church was approved by God and was, indeed, *from* God. Today, we carry the same gospel to the same needy world, and we are empowered to do so by the same Holy Spirit. We do not need miracles to proclaim the gospel; we simply need people who, like Peter, are committed to sharing the message of salvation through faith in Christ, the message that has changed their own lives.

—Jarl K. Waggoner.

Heart of the Lesson

This week we look deeper into one special gift that was given to the church that has often been a cause of misunderstanding and controversy. The Bible, however, speaks plainly and simply about this gift. It is evident that nowhere in Scripture are we given the impression that the gift of languages was of a higher order than the other gifts we saw last week. It is one of many gifts given to the church for the purpose of blessing the body of Christ.

1. Gift of languages (Acts 2:1-7, 12). It was an amazing event. It happened seven weeks after the resurrection of Jesus, on the Day of Pentecost, a special festival of the Jews. It fulfilled what Jesus had already told the disciples. There was the sound of a mighty, rushing wind, often a symbol for the Holy Spirit in the Bible, and tongues of fire rested on the heads of the gathered disciples. It was obvious that something special was happening.

After that, the disciples started speaking in many different languages that were represented in the crowd outside, even though these were languages that the disciples had never learned. It was the work of the Holy Spirit. The gifts of the Spirit were now evident. The people wondered what this could mean, for they had never seen anything like it before. We need to acknowledge the working of the Spirit in our midst. God works in mysterious ways even through different languages.

2. Gift of interpretation (I Cor. 14:13-17). Paul made it very clear here that the gift of speaking other languages is useless if God does not give someone else the gift of interpretation to make plain the message that the Spirit is giving to the church at that particular time. A language that is not understandable needs interpretation to make sense of what is said. One needs to pray for this so that what is spoken or prayed in the Spirit is made plain.

Prayer and praise are both equally important for us as Christians. The gift of praying and praising God in different languages helps in this, for God certainly understands all of them. Nothing is a mystery to Him. But for the sake of the congregation that worships and prays with us, it is important that everything we do together makes sense. Those who worship and pray with us need to understand what is going on. So for their sakes, it is important that our worship and thanksgiving are meaningful to them also.

3. Clarity must prevail (I Cor. 14:18-19). Paul did not deny the gift of different languages. In fact, he said that he too exercised that gift. But he did caution us in the church that it makes more sense to be discreet about how the gift of languages is used, especially in our congregational settings. Clarity and meaning must prevail in the church. If the church is not edified by the gift of languages, it is better if it is not used at the time.

Paul tells us that if the gift of languages does not bless someone when it is exercised, it is best that it is not used in a public church setting. Confusion must be avoided in the local church. Common sense must prevail, and we must use discretion in the exercise of our unique gifts. The presence of God's Spirit must bring clarity to the local church.

—A. Koshy Muthalaly.

World Missions

The Santal people live in a region north of Calcutta, India. In the nineteenth century, there were approximately 2.5 million Santal living among the many different people groups that call the Indian subcontinent home. In 1867, a Norwegian missionary named Lars Skrefsrud and his Danish associate Hans Børreson arrived among the Santal in order to share the gospel with this isolated group.

To the Santals' utter astonishment—and to his own—Lars was able to speak the Santal language fluently.

As soon as he was able, Lars began sharing the gospel with the Santal. He was very surprised to witness how ecstatic and excited his audience was to hear about God. One man said, "What this stranger is saying must mean that Thakur Jiu has not forgotten us after all this time!" (Boonstra, *Out of Thin Air,* Pacific Press).

In the Santal language, "Thakur" means "genuine," and "Jiu" means "God." An elder explained to Lars their knowledge of this "Genuine God" by retelling the oral history of the Santal people.

The Santals' ancestors, a man named "Haram" and a woman named "Ayo," were created by Thakur Jiu and lived in a beautiful land far to the west. An evil being named Lita deceived them into making a sacrifice to Satan.

Thakur Jiu called mankind to return to Him, but they refused. So Thakur Jiu caused a great flood to kill everyone but two righteous people, whom He hid in a cave on Mount Harata.

Descendants of the spared couple migrated further east, going from plain to plain and forest to forest. But when they came to great mountains, they could not find any way around them.

Desperate to go beyond the towering mountains, they lost faith in Thakur Jiu and did not believe He would help them. So they called out to the spirits of the mountains and made an oath to worship them if the spirits would help them pass.

Out of commitment to their oath, they began worshipping the spirits and engaging in sorcery. The memory of Thakur Jiu faded but was never completely gone.

Through the preaching of Lars and Hans, the Santal begged to learn how they could be reconciled to Thakur Jiu through His Son Jesus. During his time in India, Lars oversaw 15,000 baptisms and translated much of the Bible into their language.

The Santal Christians shared their new faith among their people, resulting in hundreds of thousands of people turning to Jesus.

—Christina Futrell.

The Jewish Aspect

The Holy Spirit effected an amazing miracle on the Day of Pentecost in the preaching of the gospel in foreign languages. People from at least fifteen nations were present to receive that important message.

A language is intricately interwoven in a people's culture. A person may be conversant with their customs, religion, and conduct, but if he does not speak their language, he has a significant deficiency in his understanding of that people.

Most American Jews have learned enough Hebrew from their prayer book and the liturgy to get along in the synagogue. Rabbis will speak in English with occasional lapses into some well-known story that employs a few words of Hebrew but more often Yiddish.

Hebrew is a West Semitic language that enjoyed its widest use around 1,000 B.C. It ceased to be an everyday language around A.D. 200 but was still used in Jewish liturgy and rabbinical literature. Jews of the Dispersion preferred the Greek tongue spoken all over the Mediterranean Basin.

Classical Hebrew continued to be the language of the synagogue, kept alive in the yeshivas (schools) for the training of the rabbis. Jews call Hebrew *Lashon Hakodesh,* "the Holy tongue."

Yiddish (literally, "Jewish") is a language based mainly on Middle High German. For the last century, few German Jews knew Yiddish. They viewed Yiddish as the language of the poor, Orthodox, oppressed Jews of Eastern Europe. At the beginning of World War II, there were more than five million Yiddish speakers there. Eighty-five percent of the Jews who perished in the Holocaust spoke Yiddish. Today, about 200,000 American Jews speak Yiddish. Many synagogues hold special conversational classes to keep Yiddish alive.

A modern reconstruction of Classical Hebrew began in the fertile mind of Eliezer Ben-Yehuda, who entered Israel in 1881. Searching for a way to get the Jews entering the Holy Land from Eastern Europe to use Hebrew, Ben-Yehuda looked for Classical Hebrew words that could be adapted to the changing times. For example, *ekdach* in Classical Hebrew refers to a carbuncle—a fiery red stone. Since the names for guns in other languages related to flint (that is, flintlock), Ben-Yehuda made *ekdach* the Modern Hebrew word for pistol.

Between 1904 and 1914, the Second Aliyah entered Israel. "Aliyah" literally means a "going up." It has come to mean emigration to Israel. The Second Aliyah involved Yiddish-speaking Socialists from Eastern Europe. Ben-Yehuda tried to convince these immigrants to learn to speak the "new" Hebrew language and drop Yiddish. Remarkably, this experiment was successful, and these new Israelis began to speak Hebrew.

Despite the unifying influence that having a common language has lent to the Jewish people, it has also been the basis for some discord. The Orthodox religious leaders in Jerusalem opposed using Hebrew as an everyday language because they felt it should be used only in Jewish religious settings.

—Lyle P. Murphy.

Guiding the Superintendent

The gift of tongues continues to be greatly debated and variously interpreted. In this week's text, the Apostle Paul focused on the giving of gifts and the benefits of properly operating in God's graces so as to edify and build up one another in the body of Christ.

DEVOTIONAL OUTLINE

1. The power of His presence (Acts 2:1-4). What an amazing power believers can experience when we are "all with one accord in one place"! In obedience to Christ's command to "wait for the promise of the Father" (1:4), the disciples tarried in an upper room, praying and seeking God (cf. vs. 14). This set the atmosphere for the miraculous. God may never again appear to man as He did at Pentecost. He may reveal Himself in other ways—if not in the wind or an earthquake or fire, then perhaps in a still, small voice (cf. I Kings 19:12).

2. Responding to His presence (Acts 2:5-7, 12). What is the proper response to such a phenomenal encounter? The disciples responded by speaking in "other tongues, as the Spirit gave them utterance" (vs. 4). They were filled with the Holy Spirit of God, and it was His Spirit who gave them the ability to speak in a foreign language as though it were their birth language. This response enabled them to be a testimony to His supernatural power. Through the Holy Spirit, God anoints with His grace those who yield themselves wholly to His divine will.

3. Using gifts to edify (I Cor. 14:13-15). What if every church leader were as conscientious about teaching and growing the church as the Apostle Paul? He was a true champion for the advancement of the church. He stressed the importance of using spiritual gifts to edify the church even if the one who possessed the gift received no recognition. We must never forget that ministry is not about us; it is all about lifting up Christ and leading the unsaved to Him.

4. Minister to edify (I Cor. 14:16-19). If the songs and prayers of the worship leaders are designed to minister only to them, it is of little value to the congregation. What benefit is it to the church body if the pastors and teachers are more concerned about being eloquent than about being understood?

AGE-GROUP EMPHASES

Children: Teach them not to fear the Holy Spirit but to welcome His presence.

Youths: Explore with the youths the gifts they believe they have and their understanding of how the gifts are to be used.

Adults: Teachers can use this lesson to restate their goals and allow the class to evaluate their effectiveness in terms of presenting the lesson in a manner that is clear.

—Jane E. Campbell.

Scripture Lesson Text

I COR. 13:1 Though I speak with the tongues of men and of angels, and have not charity, I am become *as* sounding brass, or a tinkling cymbal.

2 And though I have *the gift of* prophecy, and understand all mysteries, and all knowledge; and though I have all faith, so that I could remove mountains, and have not charity, I am nothing.

3 And though I bestow all my goods to feed *the poor,* and though I give my body to be burned, and have not charity, it profiteth me nothing.

4 Charity suffereth long, *and* is kind; charity envieth not; charity vaunteth not itself, is not puffed up,

5 Doth not behave itself unseemly, seeketh not her own, is not easily provoked, thinketh no evil;

6 Rejoiceth not in iniquity, but rejoiceth in the truth;

7 Beareth all things, believeth all things, hopeth all things, endureth all things.

8 Charity never faileth: but whether *there be* prophecies, they shall fail; whether *there be* tongues, they shall cease; whether *there be* knowledge, it shall vanish away.

9 For we know in part, and we prophesy in part.

10 But when that which is perfect is come, then that which is in part shall be done away.

11 When I was a child, I spake as a child, I understood as a child, I thought as a child: but when I became a man, I put away childish things.

12 For now we see through a glass, darkly; but then face to face: now I know in part; but then shall I know even as also I am known.

13 And now abideth faith, hope, charity, these three; but the greatest of these *is* charity.

NOTES

The Greatest Gift Is Love

Lesson: I Corinthians 13:1-13

Read: I Corinthians 13:1-13

TIME: A.D. 55   PLACE: from Ephesus

GOLDEN TEXT—"Now abideth faith, hope, charity, these three; but the greatest of these is charity" (I Corinthians 13:13).

Introduction

The era of the Christian church has been called "the age of the Holy Spirit"—and for good reason. The Holy Spirit is active in the church in ways He never before worked in redemptive history. He came in power on the Day of Pentecost and continued the work Jesus had begun to do.

The ministries of the Holy Spirit are marvelous. He convicts of sin and regenerates those who trust Christ.

If the gifts of the Spirit were the sole criterion for success in church life, the church at Corinth would have been effective. By Paul's testimony, these saints were enriched in Christ and not lacking in any gift (I Cor. 1:5-7). Yet they were wracked by doctrinal error.

Their case reminds us that being gifted by the Spirit is not the same as being filled with the Spirit. His gifts are not the same as His fruit, and we need to be reminded that all is in vain without love.

LESSON OUTLINE

I. **THE ABSENCE OF LOVE**—I Cor. 13:1-3

II. **THE CHARACTERISTICS OF LOVE**—I Cor. 13:4-7

III. **THE DURATION OF LOVE**—I Cor. 13:8-13

Exposition: Verse by Verse

THE ABSENCE OF LOVE

I COR. 13:1 Though I speak with the tongues of men and of angels, and have not charity, I am become as sounding brass, or a tinkling cymbal.

2 And though I have the gift of prophecy, and understand all mysteries, and all knowledge; and though I have all faith, so that I could remove mountains, and have not charity, I am nothing.

3 And though I bestow all my goods to feed the poor, and though I give my body to be burned, and have not charity, it profiteth me nothing.

May 31, 2015

Spiritual gifts without love (I Cor. 13:1-2). After giving a representative list of spiritual gifts, Paul urged the Corinthians to desire the ones most beneficial to the whole church (12:27-31). But he also told them he would show them "a more excellent way"—a way of living more important than even the best gifts. He now expounded this way to them—the way of love. "Charity" in the Authorized Version is *agapē*, which usually is translated "love."

Paul illustrated how useless spiritual gifts are without love. He began with the one his readers prized most—languages (I Cor. 13:1), citing himself as a hypothetical case—"Though I speak with the tongues of men and of angels, and have not charity." If anyone could claim this gift in abundance, it was Paul (cf. 14:18). Yet even if he spoke the languages of angels, it would have been useless without love.

An astounding supernatural linguistic ability not grounded in love would be no better than discordant noise; "I am become as sounding brass, or a tinkling cymbal" (I Cor. 13:1). "Sounding brass" refers to a noisy gong; "tinkling" is a loud clanging. Both are single-toned and can produce no melody. Such is language without love—useless.

Paul next applied the same principle to some of the greater gifts: prophecy, teaching, and faith. Even if he had prophetic insights into all the mysteries of God, knowledge to teach His truth, and even faith to remove mountains, these would be useless without love.

"I am nothing" (I Cor. 13:2) is a strong statement, but it expresses accurately what God thinks of a loveless person. Others may consider him important, but to God he is nobody.

Self-sacrifice without love (I Cor. 13:3). Paul now discussed self-sacrifice—giving away one's goods to feed the poor and yielding one's body to the fire in martyrdom. These would appear to be impossible apart from love. But such is not the case. And without love they are of no profit.

To bestow one's goods implies doling out items of food to many people. Giving up one's body for burning recalls the heroic act of Daniel's friends (Dan. 3), the willingness to make the ultimate sacrifice for the sake of a conviction.

But although these look like noble deeds, they must be judged by the motivation behind them. They may come from the selfish desire for praise and immortality in the eyes of men or to achieve merit before God. What is paraded as love for Christ and mankind may really be displays of pride.

THE CHARACTERISTICS OF LOVE

4 Charity suffereth long, and is kind; charity envieth not; charity vaunteth not itself, is not puffed up,

5 Doth not behave itself unseemly, seeketh not her own, is not easily provoked, thinketh no evil;

6 Rejoiceth not in iniquity, but rejoiceth in the truth;

7 Beareth all things, believeth all things, hopeth all things, endureth all things.

A basic description (I Cor. 13:4a). If love is essential to the success of the church, we need to know what it looks like. Therefore, Paul described it in terms of what it will and will not do. Paul began with a basic description: "Charity suffereth long, and is kind." "Suffereth long" means "is patient." Love puts up with wrongs suffered and resists the temptation to become resentful. To be "kind" means to put oneself at others' service to do them good. Love has no hint of self-centeredness.

What love does not do (I Cor. 13:4b-6a). This basic description manifests itself, in part, through the things love will not do. First, love does not envy; it does not promote itself or get puffed up with pride. It leaves no room for jealousy, boasting, or arrogance. It accepts God's appointed place without either desiring another's or taking credit for one's own accomplishments. The Corinthian believers had difficulty doing this. They envied others for their gifts or trumpeted their own.

Further, love does not act in an unseemly manner. It is not rude or dishonorable. The Corinthians needed this reminder because of their disorderly behavior at the Lord's Supper and their worship services. Love does not seek its own ends—that is, pursue self-interest at the expense of others. This fault was evident in the Corinthians' pursuit of Christian liberty in the face of those with weaker consciences.

Love is not easy to provoke. It is patient, not touchy or ready to sue, as were some of the Corinthians. It does not think evil of others; that is, it does not take into account the evil they do. It rules out keeping a mental record of wrongs one has suffered. Finally, love does not rejoice in iniquity.

What love does (I Cor. 13:6b-7). But love is more than what it refrains from doing. It reveals itself in the good it does. Rather than gloat over evil, it rejoices in the truth, or, one might say, *with* the truth. Love and truth are allies, so love will never seek to suppress truth.

Paul continued to portray love's positive fruits in four brief statements: "Beareth all things, believeth all things, hopeth all things, endureth all things" (I Cor. 13:7). "Beareth" in this context probably means to restrain oneself in the face of others' faults, not giving vent to frustration. "Believeth all things" does not imply gullibility but willingness to give another the benefit of the doubt. "Hopeth" looks for the future victory of God's purposes, and "endureth" sees the perseverance of love in the midst of adversity.

If we have difficulty understanding how to interpret and apply this portrait of love, we have only to look at the example of Jesus. He neither envied another nor pushed Himself forward ostentatiously. He was never rude, even to His enemies, and He always sought the good of others. He remained in control under provocation, held no grudges, and bore perfect witness to the truth. He patiently bore injustice and persecution, always holding out hope that even the worst sinner would repent.

THE DURATION OF LOVE

8 Charity never faileth: but whether there be prophecies, they shall fail; whether there be tongues, they shall cease; whether there be knowledge, it shall vanish away.

9 For we know in part, and we prophesy in part.

10 But when that which is perfect is come, then that which is in part shall be done away.

11 When I was a child, I spake as a child, I understood as a child, I thought as a child: but when I became a man, I put away childish things.

12 For now we see through a glass, darkly; but then face to face: now I know in part; but then shall I know even as also I am known.

13 And now abideth faith, hope, charity, these three; but the greatest of these is charity.

The temporary nature of gifts (I Cor. 13:8-10). The love of which Paul spoke "never faileth." It not only sustains an individual's life now but also endures into eternity. It will outlast all spiritual gifts. Paul chose three gifts prominent in the Corinthians' thinking and contrasted their transitory nature with the permanence of love. "Whether there be prophecies," wrote Paul, "they shall fail; whether there be tongues, they shall cease; whether there be knowledge, it shall vanish away." Spiritual gifts have been given to build up the Christian church, and their duration is thus limited to the time when the church needs them.

The words "fail" and "vanish away" in I Corinthians 13:8 are translations of the same word. It means "to be made idle" or "cease." The time will come when in God's sovereignty the gifts of prophecy and knowledge will cease to be needed. As for tongues (languages), they will come to an end. The use of a different verb for the cessation of tongues, combined with their total omission in the next verse, leads to the conclusion that Paul considered them more temporary than the other two.

The reason these gifts will cease to operate is that they are partial and imperfect. Paul explained, "For we know in part, and we prophesy in part. But when that which is perfect is come, then that which is in part shall be done away" (I Cor. 13:9-10). Expositors differ on when this point of perfection is reached (Walvoord and Zuck, eds., *Bible Knowledge Commentary,* Cook). But in light of verse 12, it seems best to take it as upon Christ's return for His church.

The gifts of knowledge and prophecy were given to aid the church in an imperfect state; thus, we know and prophesy in a fragmentary way. Each bit of knowledge of prophecy reveals a small portion of God's plan, so we are left with an incomplete picture. Even now, with the complete New Testament revelation, we cannot begin to comprehend the fullness of God's Person and plan (I Cor. 8:2; 13:12). We will not know that until the church itself is transformed into His image.

The idea of perfection here refers to what is complete, lacking nothing. Thus, when the gifts are no longer needed, the church will not suffer any loss, for the partial will be replaced by the complete. So the longest any gifts will be needed will be until the return of Christ. But since God sovereignly gave them, it is His prerogative to remove or modify them even before that time. Some believe this is what has happened to the gifts of prophecy and languages, being no longer needed.

We should be careful not to be distracted, however, by questions of whether this or that spiritual gift has been or will be discontinued. Paul's point is that *all* gifts, the greatest and the least, will someday reach the end of their usefulness and no longer be needed. But love is different; it is inherent in God's own nature and will therefore last forever. That is why it must take precedence over all gifts.

The expectation of perfection (I Cor. 13:11-12). To illustrate the transition from partial to complete spiritual development, Paul used two examples. The first is the change from childhood to maturity. He reflected, "When I was a child, I spake as a child, I understood as a child, I thought as a child." A child's speech is elementary and sometimes indistinct. His understanding is only partial. His reasoning lacks the depth that comes only through experience and education.

These three functions correspond to the three gifts Paul has been discussing. The gift of languages is suited to a condition of elementary communication, prophecy to a still incomplete revelation, and knowledge to a growing ability to apply doctrine to life. But when perfect maturity is reached, these gifts will no longer be appropriate.

Paul's second example is a change from looking at an object in a mirror and then seeing it directly. In his day a mirror was a highly polished piece of metal that reflected an image. The reflection was at best blurred and often dimmed.

This seems to describe the prophetic gift, which through revelations gave a partial image of God's character and will. But it was no substitute for a face-to-face encounter (cf. Num. 12:6-8; Deut. 34:10). This transforming sight will occur only when the church is perfected and glorified (I John 3:2).

The rest of I Corinthians 13:12 continues the contrast between indistinct and clear understanding. Paul seemed to have the gift of knowledge in mind as he wrote, "Now I know in part; but then shall I know even as also I am known." Our limited spiritual understanding will finally yield to complete comprehension.

The virtues that endure (I Cor. 13:13). A state of perfection will eliminate all need for the Spirit's gifts to the church. But three virtues the Spirit produces will remain eternally. These three are "faith, hope, charity."

But love is greater than either faith or hope. Faith and hope are human responses to God, but God is never said to believe or hope. But love is His very nature (I John 4:8, 16), motivating all He does. He implants His love in believers, and it becomes their permanent, distinguishing mark (John 13:34-35). We may vary in our expressions of love, but love itself never changes, for God never changes. Our churches should therefore value it more highly than any spiritual gift.

—Robert E. Wenger.

QUESTIONS

1. To what did Paul liken the gift of languages used without love?
2. What is God's estimate of a gifted person without love?
3. What, apart from love, might motivate a person to give up his goods or his life?
4. Why did Paul remind the Corinthians that love is not arrogant?
5. In what sense does a loving person not take evil into account?
6. How did Jesus set the example for all the characteristics of love?
7. What three gifts did Paul use to demonstrate that spiritual gifts are temporary?
8. Why will spiritual gifts eventually cease to operate?
9. How did Paul illustrate partial and complete spiritual development?
10. What virtues endure eternally? Why is love the greatest of them?

—Robert E. Wenger.

Preparing to Teach the Lesson

Antarctica was once touted as having no pollution, no dust, and no crowds. The air is clean. Since winds commonly start at the South Pole and move northward, many contaminants are kept away. All this makes it seem an idyllic place to live. However, the fact is that only 1,000 to 5,000 people live in 5,405,000 square miles. Why so few people? December is the warmest month, and the average high is -16° F. In the interior, the mean average temperature is -70°F. It is simply too cold for most people to want to stay there. Is it possible that our churches show a similar spiritual coldness?

TODAY'S AIM

Facts: to understand how the more excellent way is love.

Principle: to know that a spiritual gift benefits the church when it is used in love.

Application: to use our gifts in love is what makes them worthwhile.

INTRODUCING THE LESSON

People stop attending a church for many reasons. It might be because of poor leadership, preference for a different style of ministry, wanting a church of a different size, or some inner struggle a person is having. It could also be that behind many of these reasons is a deeper issue: feeling unloved by those in the church.

DEVELOPING THE LESSON

1. The priority of love (I Cor. 13:1-3). Paul began his discussion of the "more excellent way" (12:31) by focusing on the sign gift of languages (13:1). This was a logical starting place, since the Corinthians were exalting that gift so much. Using that gift to its highest degree, speaking the language of angels, is of little value without "charity," or love.

From the sign gift Paul moved to examples of some gifts that gave God's revelation in the early church. Paul again gave an example in the highest degree. Suppose that a prophet understood all God's mysteries and had all God's knowledge. Without love, even that person has no value in himself.

Suppose, however, that someone exercised the permanent gifts of faith and giving to their highest degree. A person's faith actually moved a mountain, and that same person gave his own life in ministry service. Even that, without love, is of no profit. Jesus said that even self-sacrifice (giving alms) can be done for self-centered glory (Matt. 6:2).

2. The perfection of love (I Cor. 13:4-7). The priority of love was introduced in a dramatic way. Love has immense value; but what *is* love? Paul answered by speaking of love in terms of specific qualities of perfection we are to cultivate. He began by describing two qualities of what love is. It is long-suffering—that is, patient with people. It is also kind—giving gracious, helpful service to others.

Next come eight qualities of what love is not. It does not envy, meaning it is not jealous of someone else's prosperity or success. It also does not boast ("vaunteth not itself" [I Cor. 13:4]); bragging belies an overestimation of one's own importance. It is also "not puffed up" with any trace of pride or arrogance toward others who might be considered inferior. Further, it does not act "unseemly" (vs. 5), or with rudeness. Nor is love selfish ("seeketh not her own") or "provoked" so that it becomes embittered by any wrong done to it. Love thinks "no evil"—that is, it never harbors a grudge. It also does not rejoice over "iniquity" (vs. 6).

The qualities of love conclude with five things it does (I Cor. 13:6-7). It rejoices in the truth, finding pleasure when truth prevails. Love bears up under all things, quietly enduring suffering. It believes all things, but is not eager to believe evil about anyone. Love hopes all things, desiring the best for others because of God's grace. Finally, love endureth all things; it is patient during difficult circumstances. This is the love Paul wanted all to have.

3. The permanence of love (I Cor. 13:8-13). In contrast to spiritual gifts, which are temporary in their use in the church, love "never faileth." This is a foundational truth. The fact is that God intended some gifts to be temporary. The gifts of prophecy, languages, and special knowledge all come to an end. The reason for their cessation is that they were only "in part"; they did not supply the whole of God's revelation at any time. God's purpose was for the partial to be done away "when that which is perfect is come."

What is this whole? Some interpreters believe this refers to Christ, but "perfect" in I Corinthians 13:10 is neuter, not masculine. Others refer it to Christ's second coming, but the Greek words referring to that event are uniformly feminine. The context seems to indicate that the "perfect" contrasts with the partial revelation given through the gifts. God's whole revelation is found in the completed Scriptures.

Paul next illustrated this. We act childishly when we are children, but when we become adults, we put those things away. The temporary spiritual gifts were childish things compared with God's completed Word. In a similar manner, in this earthly life, we see spiritual things unclearly; but when we are with the Lord, we shall see those things clearly.

An abiding principle remains true, regardless of the time. It was true for the early church; it is true for today. Faith, hope, and love make up the foundation for our Christian life. The greatest of these is love.

ILLUSTRATING THE LESSON

God gave gifts to use in building His church. They succeed only when they are used in the love of Christ.

```
GIFTS USED IN LOVE

       ♡        🎁

      GOD WILL USE
```

CONCLUDING THE LESSON

God gave gifts for the building of His church. We see many of those gifts in use today. As we use our gifts in God's service, we must exercise them in the love of God, demonstrating His love to everyone, both believers and nonbelievers, for the glory of Christ.

ANTICIPATING THE NEXT LESSON

Next week starts a new quarter of lessons on God's indictment against injustice.

—R. Larry Overstreet.

PRACTICAL POINTS

1. Our gifts and actions mean nothing without love (I Cor. 13:1-2).
2. Great sacrifice is worthless if it is not motivated by love (vs. 3).
3. Christian love is directed toward others (vss. 4-5).
4. Christian love looks for the best in others and gives the best it has (vss. 6-7).
5. Love will continue when all that we know has passed away (vss. 8-10).
6. Christians mature in their relationships with others as they mature in faith (vss. 11-12).
7. Love is the greatest gift we offer to others and to God (vs. 13).

—Cheryl Y. Powell.

RESEARCH AND DISCUSSION

1. How does love relate to the use of spiritual gifts described in I Corinthians 12?
2. How does love give meaning to our lives as Christians?
3. Is motive really important in our giving? Discuss.
4. As we consider what Paul says love is and is not, how does the love described in chapter 13 compare to the love seen today?
5. Why do you think love will remain when all other gifts have ceased?
6. What growth have you seen in your relationship with God and with others over the past five years?
7. What does it mean to be fully known by God (vs. 12)?

—Cheryl Y. Powell.

ILLUSTRATED HIGH POINTS

Charity

While counseling a Christian husband who was having an affair with another woman, I pointed out that his relationship with her was not love but lust. God's love residing in the believer is for better or worse, for richer or poorer, in sickness and in health, and until death parts the married couple. Lust comes from the old nature, which desires what it should not have. Lust leads down the path where the man loses his godly reputation. Read Proverbs 6:20-35. Only by constantly submitting to the lordship of Christ will the believer love as Christ loved and reject the temptation of lust.

Charity never faileth

A dear couple that my wife and I know dealt with cancer that the wife had for five years. We recently attended her memorial service. During those five years, she had been in for treatment at different times, including surgery as the cancer had spread. Through it all, her husband remained committed to his dear wife, serving her faithfully and giving God praise for His faithfulness and care. That is Christ's love in action!

Now abideth

We live in a fast-changing world in which absolutes have been thrown out the window. Marriage and any kind of right and wrong are turned completely upside down. Is anything lasting? "And now abideth faith, hope, charity, these three; but the greatest of these is charity" (I Cor. 13:13). Why is charity, or love, the greatest? Faith one day will be sight. Hope will be a reality. But love is the greatest because love is eternal.

God is eternal, and His love is eternal. The believer experiences God's eternal love now and for all eternity.

—Paul R. Bawden.

Golden Text Illuminated

"Now abideth faith, hope, charity, these three; but the greatest of these is charity" (I Corinthians 13:13).

Paul's great chapter on love, or "charity," as the Greek word *agapē* is translated here, comes in the midst of a lengthy discussion of spiritual gifts (I Cor. 12, 14). There was much confusion and much error about the gifts in the Corinthian church. Some gifts apparently were considered of much greater importance, and those who possessed such gifts were given preeminence in the church. Others were despised for having "lesser" gifts.

The apostle corrected this notion in I Corinthians 12, where he compared the church to the human body to show how all the various gifts work together to make the church function as it should.

In the midst of this discussion, Paul stepped aside to speak of love in I Corinthians 13. Why did he introduce the topic of love at this point? Love is the glue that brings unity to a church made up of various personalities and spiritual gifts. In fact, he said that the gifts themselves are of no value apart from Christlike love (vss. 1-3). He then described the attributes of love, making it clear that a loving person does not elevate himself above others. He elevates everyone else above himself.

Paul also stated that love "never faileth" (I Cor. 13:8). The gifts the Corinthians so valued, however, are partial and temporary and will be done away with. They will be set aside like the things of childhood, but love will endure.

Paul's whole argument brought perspective to the petty jealousies and pride of the Corinthian Christians. The things they most valued would disappear, but the truly important virtues of faith, hope, and love "abideth," or remain.

These three attributes are often mentioned together in Scripture (cf. Rom. 5:2-5; Col. 1:3-5; I Thess. 1:3; I Pet. 1:21-22). Faith is essential for salvation and for pleasing God (Eph. 2:8-9; Heb. 11:6). Faith in the sense of continuing trust in Jesus remains forever, as does hope (cf. I Cor. 15:19).

Paul declared that while faith, hope, and love all remain, love is the greatest of these three. In the immediate context, love was the answer to the Corinthian conflict.

Faith and hope likewise endure, but love is superior to both. Morris noted that it is probably a waste of time to inquire "into the precise manner in which love surpasses faith or hope (though it may not be without significance that in v. 7 those two are modes of love's outworking)" (*The First Epistle of Paul to the Corinthians,* Eerdmans). Paul was simply saying that the really important things are not spectacular gifts but rather faith, hope, and love. "And there is nothing greater than love."

—Jarl K. Waggoner.

Heart of the Lesson

The church that is marked by love exemplifies the life of Christ. This is the greatest of all gifts given by God to the church. When a congregation is marked by internal conflict, it does not reflect the life of Christ. This week we are encouraged to exercise the gift of love in our local churches. It is the gift of the highest order. In this whole unit, we have emphasized that every other gift must be used with love in order to be effective in the ministry in the church.

1. The primacy of love (I Cor. 13:1-3). Love is supreme for the Christian believer. If there is no love, it does not matter what else one can do in the way of ministry. Speaking in the languages of earth and even of heaven is useless if that gift is not wrapped in the spirit of love. One may have the gift of prophecy or even the gift of faith, but it is useless without the accompanying gift of love. Faith can move mountains but still needs love to make it effective in the church.

There are godly people everywhere, and some of them are even willing to sacrifice their lives for others; but without love, it would be meaningless. As a church, we need to show that love is the identifying mark of the faithful Christian believer. Love gives value to all the other gifts. As Christians, we must be marked by the gift of love, the highest gift of all.

2. The expression of love (I Cor. 13:4-10). If we asked ourselves what love is like, we all would give different answers. Paul taught us here that love is very patient, kind, not envious, and not proud. Love does not get irritated easily. Love is able to show grace to others by putting up with them. Love does not keep a logbook of all wrongs that others have done. Love feels sad when others get hurt and suffer injustice. Love is happy for others when they do well.

Love exults when right prevails.

Love rejoices when truth wins, for love is on the side of truth. Love never gives up on anyone. It never loses trust, it continues to hope, and it puts up with difficult circumstances. Love will flourish forever. Some of the other gifts are temporary, but this is not so for love. The gifts do not show us everything, and they are short-lived. Other gifts will not last forever as love does. As a church, we need to focus on what is eternal, like the gift of love.

3. The permanency of love (I Cor. 13:11-13). Maturity in the Christian life is marked by the gift of love. New believers in the faith are still learning how to love, taking baby steps in this direction. But as they grow older in the faith, they will learn to exercise the gift of love in a more mature manner. Mature Christians learn to abandon childish ways and grow out of them eventually.

As immature children, we often do not see things clearly; but as we grow older, we have a more mature perspective on life and the church. As new believers, we see things partially; but as God's Spirit fills us with the gift of love, we will be able to see things as God sees them. God Himself is love. He knows us well, and we cannot hide from Him. As believers in Jesus, we need to exercise the gift of love, God's greatest gift to the church, so that we show how we are woven together in love.

—A. Koshy Muthalaly.

World Missions

"There is no fear in love; but perfect love casteth out fear: because fear hath torment. He that feareth is not made perfect in love" (I John 4:18).

David Wilkerson was a small-town guy, busy with his family and the churches he pastored in the countryside of Pennsylvania.

One day David saw the photos of several teenagers on the front cover of a magazine. All had been charged with murder. Their crime was so horrifically brutal, so senseless that it shocked the nation. David later described what he saw in one of the teen's eyes—bewilderment, hatred, and despair.

The story revolted David, but it also filled him with an unexpected emotion—compassion. His soul cried out for these boys, who were victims themselves of the harshness and brutality they were raised in.

David was even more perplexed by the next thought that entered his mind: *Go to New York City and help those boys. What, Lord? What was that?*

David obeyed the call and began walking the gang-controlled streets of New York. Even battle-hardened police officers did not walk those streets.

Love is the greatest commandment God calls on us to fulfill, and it is also the most powerful. When all strivings cease, love remains. David was not fearful for his life because, as I John 4:18 says, love casts out all fear.

One day, David met a young man named Nicky. He was a member of a powerful and feared gang called the Mau Maus.

Nicky had been the victim of terrible abuse at the hands of his parents. He fled his home in Puerto Rico, came to New York, and found solace in the violence of the city streets. He adapted to gang life very well and became the leader of the Mau Maus.

On the day they met, David approached Nicky and told him about the hope that was in God and that God had the power to change his life. Nicky did not respond kindly to this. He cursed at David as he spit on him, beat him, and threatened to kill him.

David stood his ground. His reply was "You could cut me up into a thousand pieces and lay them in the street, and every piece will still love you" (Wilkerson, *The Cross and the Switchblade,* Jove).

That fateful encounter with Nicky did not end on the street that day. Nicky gave his life to Jesus and has had his own forceful ministry. The sweetest moment for Nicky was forgiving and loving his parents and leading them to their Redeemer, Jesus.

—Christina Futrell.

The Jewish Aspect

God is love (I John 4:8), and His love is evident in His dealings with individuals throughout the book of Genesis. Moses specifically revealed God's love for the people of Israel in Deuteronomy 7:6-8. Those who were grateful for God's kindness kept His covenant and commandments in return (vs. 9).

We have a remarkable example of love between friends in the lives of Jonathan and David. It was a genuine love born of their mutual love of God and His law (I Sam. 20:17, 41). Jonathan correctly saw that David would one day be king over Israel (23:17).

The very best of a mother's love is seen in the efforts of Jochebed to cheat Pharaoh and prevent the death of her son Moses. The love of God for His own was also on display in protecting Israel's future leader.

Jephthah, the son of a harlot, had a little girl he loved devotedly. Though exiled and a leader of worthless men (Judg. 11:1-3), he was used by God to deliver Israel (vs. 32). One evidence of his love is that his daughter loved him with the same devotion (vss. 34-40).

God picked a wife for the Prophet Hosea. He directed, "Take unto thee a wife of whoredoms . . . for the land hath committed great whoredom, departing from the Lord" (Hos. 1:2). What would people say about this man—his wife—his children—on Main Street today? Would they laugh at his plea, which is symbolic of the state of affairs in our country? "Then said the Lord unto me, Go yet, love a woman beloved of her friend, yet an adulteress, according to the love of the Lord toward the children of Israel, who look to other gods" (3:1).

The gift of love should be passed along. Eli the high priest fathered two sons, but they cheated the people and lived scandalously. They paid with their lives, and Eli died in shame (I Sam. 4:17-18).

Eli's contemporary, the priest and prophet Samuel, also had sons who did not follow their father's love of God. Samuel failed to pass God's love along, just as Eli had failed (I Sam. 8:1-3). How sad to read of those whose love for God could not be passed along to even one generation!

God's plan ordained that His people would be a praise in the earth (Jer. 33:7-9). Paul testified, "God hath not cast away his people which he foreknew" (Rom. 11:2). Christ's reign will confirm God's love for Israel in many ways. It will be the confirmation of His promise to the fathers of Israel. The promise to Abraham includes the dramatic extent of the land eastward to the Euphrates

River (Gen. 15:18). When true Jews obey the Lord, they "shall be a peculiar treasure unto [God] above all people: . . . and [they] shall be unto [God] a kingdom of priests" (Exod. 19:5-6).

The prophets kept the hopes of Israel alive. Hosea wrote, "I will love them freely: for mine anger is turned away from him" (Hos. 14:4).

The reign of the Messiah is the culmination of all the ages. "The kingdoms of this world are become the kingdoms of our Lord, and of his Christ; and he shall reign for ever and ever" (Rev. 11:15). We who have been washed in the blood of the Lamb will enjoy the fullness of blessing as we behold His glory.

—Lyle P. Murphy.

Guiding the Superintendent

Grateful Christians desire to be used by God to minister to others, but we cannot do a good work without God's spiritual graces. Perhaps some believers desire to teach, some to encourage, and others to heal. The Apostle Paul informed us that regardless of how gifted we may be or how eager we are to serve, if our souls are void of the love of the Almighty God, we can do nothing to profit ourselves or others.

DEVOTIONAL OUTLINE

1. What love does (I Cor. 13:1-3). Paul closed chapter 12 with the introduction of "a more excellent way" (vs. 31). This created a practical transition into chapter 13, in which he settled the question of what is the greatest gift. As an apostle, he was concerned about the continual misuse of spiritual gifts in the church at Corinth. In his letters, he addressed this matter at length. At the heart of his instruction to the church is the truth that without love, any gift is empty.

How do angels speak? How is knowledge measured? Can one truly interpret the mysteries of life? Even if these things were possible, if they are not based on the incomparable love that prompted God not to spare the life of His only Son, they are of no consequence.

2. The power of love (I Cor. 13:4-7). A closer look at this God-kind-of-love immediately reveals selflessness. Believers who possess true love will think more of others than they think of themselves; they will show kindness. There is no room for envy, haughtiness, or pride. They purpose to play fair and do not get angry when things do not go their way. Loving saints do not condone evil but look for the good in all people. They are hopeful and optimistic, having a faith that exceeds their own understanding—a faith that mystifies those who are ignorant of the influence of God's love.

3. Complete in God's love (I Cor. 13:8-12). Those gifts and abilities that we hold dear serve us only temporarily. A gift greater than these will complete us throughout eternity; then those graces we cherish will become nonessential. It is like playing with our favorite toys until we look in the mirror and see that suddenly we are no longer children but adults who have grown into the knowledge that life is more than carnal things. It is a call to love one another as God loved us.

4. The greatest gift is love (I Cor. 13:13). No longer should we wonder what the greatest gift is. It is love. This love is demonstrated by the substitutionary sacrifice of our Lord Jesus, who was made sin for us so that we might be made righteous before God (cf. II Cor. 5:21). Let us thank God for this precious gift!

AGE-GROUP EMPHASES

Children: The best way to teach love is to show love. Remind the children that Jesus loves them, but make it a point to show them how much you love them.

Youths: Survey the young people to determine what gifts they want from God. Guide them into understanding how love for God and others must be the motivating factor if they want to please God.

Adults: Some adults have grown up reading and studying the love chapter. Ask for volunteers to share how they have allowed this chapter to come alive in their daily lives.

—Jane E. Campbell.

TOPICS FOR NEXT QUARTER

June 7
> **Judgment on Israel and Judah**
> Amos 2:4-8

June 14
> **God Is Not Fooled**
> Amos 5:14-15, 18-27

June 21
> **Rebuked for Selfishness**
> Amos 6:4-8, 11-14

June 28
> **God Will Not Delay Justice**
> Amos 8:1-6, 9-10

July 5
> **No Rest for the Wicked**
> Micah 2:4-11

July 12
> **Condemnation of Corruption**
> Micah 3:5-12

July 19
> **Justice, Love, and Humility**
> Micah 6:3-8

July 26
> **God Shows Mercy**
> Micah 7:14-20

August 2
> **Our Redeemer Comes**
> Isaiah 59:15-21

August 9
> **Mend Your Ways!**
> Jeremiah 7:1-15

August 16
> **A Call for Repentance**
> Ezekiel 18:1-13, 31-32

August 23
> **God Demands Justice**
> Zechariah 7:8-14

August 30
> **Return to a Just God**
> Malachi 3:1-10

PARAGRAPHS ON PLACES AND PEOPLE

CAPPADOCIA

Cappadocia is the name given to a region in central Turkey. It is thought by some historians that the name "Cappadocia" was derived from an Old Persian word that meant "land of the beautiful horses." In ancient times, the region was famous for the wild horses there.

The unique landscape of Cappadocia is said to have been formed by ancient volcanic eruptions and eroding winds and rains, resulting in amazing rock formations. Ancient dwellers carved out homes and tunnels within the soft, volcanic deposits that cover the region. Its topography has been described as bizarre, otherworldly, and moon-like. Several underground cities were created long ago. Christians used the cities and tunnels to escape persecution during the Roman era. Today, the vast underground networks and cities, the astounding topography, and the history and culture of the area have made Cappadocia a popular tourist destination.

PONTUS

Pontus was a province in northern Asia Minor located along the southern shore of the Black Sea, from which its name is derived ("Black Sea" in Greek is *Pontus Euxenis*). Historians state that the earliest inhabitants may have migrated to the region by crossing the Sinai Peninsula from Africa. Traces of Assyrian culture have been found as well. The legendary Hittite warrior-priestesses, the Amazons, once inhabited the region. Supremacy was held by various tribes and conquering empires such as the Greeks, the Persians, the Romans, and the Turks (who have held dominion since A.D. 1461).

There is little historical information concerning the onset and growth of Christianity in the region, but it seems clear that it was when Rome controlled Pontus that Christianity spread into the area. On the Day of Pentecost, recorded in Acts 2, men from Pontus (vs. 9) were able to hear their language spoken by the apostles. First Peter was addressed to the believers in Pontus.

DIOTREPHES

Little is known about this man, who is mentioned in John's third epistle, but what is said about him speaks volumes as to his character. From what John reported, we can gather that he was ambitious, proud, disrespectful to John's apostolic authority, rebellious, and inhospitable. His official position in the church is not known, but he threw his weight around to prevent provision for some visiting missionaries. He also ignored John's letters.

We can infer from III John 1:11 that John wanted the recipient of the letter, Gaius, to reject Diotrephes's influence. His actions were threatening the fellowship of the church.

DEMETRIUS

Demetrius was a Christian disciple who was praised in III John 1:12. He was well spoken of by everyone, including the apostle himself. He was commended to the early church leader Gaius (vs. 1). He upheld the gospel, and he was worthy to be welcomed and provided for. Some believe he was the bearer of John's letters. It is possible he was a member of the same church as Diotrephes.

—*Don Ruff.*

Bible Expositor and Illuminator

Daily Bible Readings for Home Study and Worship

(Readings are for the week previous to the lesson topics.)

1. **March 1.   The Lamb of God**
   M.—The Spirit and Joseph. Gen. 41:38-43.
   T.—The Spirit and Bezaleel. Exod. 31:1-6.
   W.—The Spirit and the Elders. Num. 11:11-25.
   T.—Would That All Had the Spirit! Num. 11:26-30.
   F.—A Voice in the Wilderness. John 1:19-23.
   S.—One Greater Coming After. John 1:24-28.
   S.—One Who Will Baptize with the Spirit. John 1:29-34.

2. **March 8.   The Promise of a Comforter**
   M.—No Balm in Gilead. Jer. 8:18-22.
   T.—No One to Comfort Me. Lam. 1:17-21.
   W.—Behold Your God! Isa. 40:1-10.
   T.—This Is My Comfort. Ps. 119:49-64.
   F.—The Shepherd's Comfort. Ps. 23:1-6.
   S.—When the Comforter Comes. John 15:18-26.
   S.—The Comforter Will Abide Forever. John 14:15-26.

3. **March 15.   The Spirit of Truth**
   M.—Where There Is No Vision. Prov. 29:12-18.
   T.—The Vision of Prophecy Sealed. Isa. 29:8-14.
   W.—The Lord's Call to Samuel. I Sam. 3:1-10.
   T.—A Prophet of the Lord. I Sam. 3:11-21.
   F.—I Commit My Spirit. Ps. 31:1-8.
   S.—Worship in Spirit and Truth. John 4:21-26.
   S.—The Spirit of Truth Will Guide You. John 16:4-15.

4. **March 22.   Receive the Holy Spirit**
   M.—Testifying as the Spirit Leads. Mark 13:5-11.
   T.—The Spirit Given to Gentiles. Acts 10:39-48.
   W.—Full of the Spirit and Faith. Acts 11:19-26.
   T.—Joy in the Holy Spirit. Rom. 14:13-19.
   F.—Power from the Holy Spirit. Acts 1:4-8.
   S.—Be Filled with the Spirit. Eph. 5:15-21.
   S.—Receive the Holy Spirit. John 20:19-23.

5. **March 29.   Coming in the Name of the Lord**
   M.—Let the Nations Be Glad. Ps. 67:1-7.
   T.—A Just God and a Saviour. Isa. 45:20-25.
   W.—A Name Above Every Name. Phil. 2:9-16.
   T.—Keep Alert for His Coming. Mark 13:30-37.
   F.—Coming in the Clouds of Heaven. Mark 14:55-62.
   S.—Behold, Your King Comes! John 12:14-19.
   S.—Blessed Is the Coming Kingdom. Mark 11:1-11.

6. **April 5.   Resurrection Guaranteed (Easter)**
   M.—Jesus Has Died. Matt. 27:45-50.
   T.—Jesus Has Risen. Matt. 28:1-8.
   W.—Jesus Will Come Again. I Thess. 4:13-18.
   T.—The Resurrection and the Life. John 11:20-27.
   F.—The Hope of Eternal Life. Titus 3:1-7.
   S.—If Christ Had Not Been Raised. I Cor. 15:12-19.
   S.—Christ Indeed Has Been Raised. I Cor. 15:1-11, 20-22.

7. **April 12.   Love One Another**
   M.—God So Loved the World. John 3:16-21.
   T.—What Manner of Love. I John 3:1-5.
   W.—Loved to the End. John 13:1-15.
   T.—A Forgiven Sinner's Love. Luke 7:44-48.
   F.—The One Who Does Not Love. I John 3:6-10.
   S.—A New Commandment. John 13:31-35.
   S.—Love in Deed and in Truth. I John 3:11-24.

8. **April 19.   Believe God's Love**
   M.—Believing Without Seeing. I Pet. 1:8-12.
   T.—Be of One Mind. I Pet. 3:8-12.
   W.—Love Without Pretense. Rom. 12:9-18.
   T.—Nothing Can Separate Us. Rom. 8:31-39.
   F.—Test the Spirits. I John 4:1-6.
   S.—His Love Perfected in Us. I John 4:7-12.
   S.—Love God, Love Others. I John 4:13—5:5.

9. **April 26.   Watch Out for Deceivers!**
   M.—They Refuse to Know the Lord. Jer. 9:1-7.
   T.—The Things That Are Necessary. Acts 15:22-35.
   W.—False Prophets Will Deceive. Matt. 24:3-14.
   T.—Avoid Those Who Cause Dissensions. Rom. 16:16-20.
   F.—Our Confidence in Christ. I John 5:6-15.
   S.—God Protects His Own. I John 5:16-21.
   S.—Abide in Christ's Teaching. II John 1:1-13.

10. **May 3.   Coworkers with the Truth**
    M.—All God's Works Are Truth. Dan. 4:34-37.
    T.—Walk Before God in Truth. I Kings 2:1-4.
    W.—The Truth Is in Jesus. Eph. 4:17-25.
    T.—The Knowledge of the Truth. Heb. 10:23-27.
    F.—An Approved Workman. II Tim. 2:14-19.
    S.—A Teacher of the Gentiles. I Tim. 2:1-7.
    S.—Becoming Coworkers with the Truth. III John 1:1-14.

11. **May 10.   Gifts of the Spirit**
    M.—A Heart Not Lifted Up. Deut. 17:14-20.
    T.—The Gifts and Calling of God. Rom. 11:25-32.
    W.—Gifts of the Holy Spirit. Heb. 2:1-9.
    T.—Gifts Given in Grace. Rom. 12:1-8.
    F.—Understanding the Gifts God Bestows. I Cor. 2:11-16.
    S.—Gifts That Build Up the Church. I Cor. 14:1-5.
    S.—One Spirit, Many Gifts. I Cor. 12:1-11.

12. **May 17.   Members of One Body**
    M.—Speaking with One Voice. Exod. 19:1-8.
    T.—A Pledge of Obedience. Exod. 24:1-7.
    W.—A Pure Devotion to Christ. II Cor. 11:1-5.
    T.—Glorifying God in Unity. Rom. 15:1-7.
    F.—One Spirit, One Mind. Phil. 1:21-30.
    S.—One in Christ Jesus. Gal. 3:23-29.
    S.—Many Members, One Body. I Cor. 12:14-31.

13. **May 24.   Gift of Languages**
    M.—Hearing God's Instruction. Deut. 4:32-40.
    T.—Great Boasts from a Little Member. Jas. 3:1-5.
    W.—All Languages, One Loud Voice. Rev. 7:9-12.
    T.—Each Hearing in His Own Language. Acts 2:8-13.
    F.—They Shall Prophesy. Acts 2:14-21.
    S.—Excel in Edifying. I Cor. 14:6-12.
    S.—Speaking to Build Up Others. Acts 2:1-7, 12; I Cor. 14:13-19.

14. **May 31.   The Greatest Gift Is Love**
    M.—What God Desires. Hos. 6:1-6.
    T.—What God Is Like. Jonah 3:10—4:11.
    W.—What the Spirit Creates in Us. Gal. 5:19-26.
    T.—Abounding in Love for One Another. II Thess. 1:1-5.
    F.—Love and Steadfastness. II Thess. 3:1-5.
    S.—Filled with the Fullness of God. Eph. 3:14-21.
    S.—Love Never Ends. I Cor. 13:1-13.

REVIEW

What have you learned this quarter?
Can you answer these questions?

The Spirit Comes

UNIT I: The Pledge of God's Presence

March 1
The Lamb of God
1. What precedents from Israel's history, law, and prophecy gave rise to the term "Lamb of God"?
2. How did Jesus' self-sacrifice differ from other sacrifices?
3. On what basis did John say that Jesus was preferred before him?
4. For whose benefit did the Holy Spirit descend upon Jesus bodily?

March 8
The Promise of a Comforter
1. What is the idea behind the word "Comforter" (John 14:16)?
2. Why is the Holy Spirit referred to as the Spirit of truth?
3. How does the Spirit's indwelling in Christians differ from His ministry in Old Testament times?
4. What new insight would Jesus' resurrection give the disciples?

March 15
The Spirit of Truth
1. Why was Jesus' departure an advantage to His disciples?
2. What ministry does the Holy Spirit have to the unbelieving world?
3. What was the major sin of Jesus' generation in their relationship with Him?
4. What should be the purpose of any Spirit-directed ministry?

March 22
Receive the Holy Spirit
1. Why was Jesus' resurrection essential to the disciples' task?
2. How had Jesus fulfilled His mission? How was the disciples' mission similar?
3. How did Jesus impart the Holy Spirit to His disciples? Why?
4. Why was Jesus' appearance to the disciples a momentous occasion?

March 29
Coming in the Name of the Lord
1. Why was it important that the colt Jesus used be previously unbroken?
2. Why was it significant that Jesus rode a donkey, not a horse?
3. Why was Jesus' triumphal entry a crucial event for Israel?
4. What signs of royal homage did the crowds show to Jesus?

UNIT II: The Community of Beloved Disciples

April 5
Resurrection Guaranteed (Easter)
1. What is the first essential of the gospel?
2. Did Old Testament writers know the gospel message? Explain.
3. Why is the mere fact that Jesus died not the gospel?
4. How did Paul's conversion differ from those of other apostles?

April 12
Love One Another
1. What is the nature of the love that God commands?
2. How was Cain a prototype of the world Christians face?

3. In what sense is a hater a murderer? What does this prove about his spiritual condition?
4. What is the Holy Spirit's role in giving a believer confidence?

April 19
Believe God's Love
1. What truth did John draw from the fact that God is love?
2. Why is a person who claims to love God while hating his brother rightly called a liar?
3. Why should it be normal for children of God to love one another?
4. In what sense are God's commandments not burdensome?

April 26
Watch Out for Deceivers!
1. What dangers must we avoid in our balancing of truth and love?
2. How are walking in love and keeping God's commandments related?
3. Why is it important for Christians to be knit together in love in times of false teaching?
4. Can one worship God without worshipping Christ? Explain.

May 3
Coworkers with the Truth
1. John had heard that Gaius was walking in the truth. What does this mean?
2. Why was receiving God's messengers the same as receiving God?
3. What was Diotrephes's chief motive in rejecting John's authority?
4. What did John vow to do when he was able to visit the church?

UNIT III: Woven Together in Love

May 10
Gifts of the Spirit
1. What test did Paul propose to tell true from false teaching?
2. Where might the Corinthians have heard someone claim that Jesus was accursed?
3. What are the implications of the statement that Jesus is Lord?
4. Why is it logical that all spiritual gifts operate in harmony?

May 17
Members of One Body
1. What potential problem in the church did Paul illustrate through the foot and the ear?
2. How were self-important church members destroying the church?
3. Why should we welcome the diversity God has given the church?
4. How can a church of diverse elements present a unified witness?

May 24
Gift of Languages
1. Why are wind and fire apt symbols for the Spirit's coming?
2. What was God symbolizing through the languages at Pentecost?
3. Why was the gift of languages a problem at Corinth?
4. Why is the mind as important as the Spirit in Christian worship?

May 31
The Greatest Gift Is Love
1. What is God's estimate of a gifted person without love?
2. How did Jesus set the example for all the characteristics of love?
3. Why will spiritual gifts eventually cease to operate?